THE
EXECUTIVE
IN
CRISIS

THE EXECUTIVE

IN

CRISIS

EUGENE EMERSON JENNINGS

Professor of Management
Graduate School of Business Administration
Michigan State University

McGraw-Hill Book Company

New York · St. Louis · San Francisco · London · Düsseldorf
Kuala Lumpur · Mexico · Montreal · Panama · Rio de Janeiro
Sydney · Toronto · Johannesburg · New Delhi · Singapore

The Executive in Crisis

Library of Congress Catalog Card Number 65-64648

Reprinted by arrangement with MSU Business Studies.

First McGraw-Hill Paperback Edition, 1972

07-032446-8

2 3 4 5 6 7 8 9 MU MU 7 9 8 7 6 5 4 3

To my sons
Eugene, Mark, and Matthew

Preface

We are about to enter the private world of big business executives who, in this book, have one thing in common: they went to the top of the corporate ladder and stumbled. Each experienced a crisis that threatened his career and became a turning point in his life; none has been the same since.

What is an executive like who is caught up in the entanglements of big business life? What causes him to rise to the top, only to lose his emotional footing? And if mastery of his career crisis is delayed sufficiently, what kinds of problems are thereby created? How does an executive successfully resolve his crisis and restore harmony with his corporate environment? In short, why do executives crack up and how are they put back together again?

The intent of this book is to initiate discussion of the nature and causes of administrative anxiety. We attempt to show that although the typical executive is an autonomous type, he carries much anxiety and neurotic potential, but perhaps not much more than people in other occupational groups of the middle classes. On the other hand, these other people do not occupy high executive positions wherein the wrong decision can carry national consequences.

It is important to know that administrative anxiety has a lot to do with personal success and failure. What is equally important, however, is how this anxiety among a few powerful people might influence the direction and character of economic life. The acts of a few neurotic executives may directly or indirectly carry consequences for all society. So powerful are big business corporation executives that those who suffer the crippling effects of neurotic anxiety need to be better understood.

Advising executives in career crises has revealed a few insights that hitherto have not been reported, and which seem to crucially affect the manner in which our large economic concentrates are directed. The classical materials that a psychologist has available to him are his clients' impressions of their thoughts and feelings. The case histories of career crises reported throughout the book have been collected over a period of fifteen years of counseling. They uniformly reveal the anxiety potential inherent in the administrative task which stems from a feeling of impending danger to certain values held central to the executive's self.

The pressures of corporate existence are basically three. The first set of pressures comes from superiors who have the power to give and withhold rewards of many kinds. Next are the pressures that come from the goals and objectives of the organization as felt in the executive's particular role. Finally, there are the pressures that come from within the executive himself which represent basic definitions of who he is and what he wants to become.

These pressures combine to exert a formidable force in the executive's mind—a force that the counselor must reckon with and, in the author's opinion, actually use as a basic therapeutic device. From the time that this triad of notions of authority, organization, and self—what we call *the corporate triangle*—emerges in the counseling situation, the advisor must ascertain if these notions are responsible for the career crisis. Having attempted this, he must next strive to determine what notions of authority, organization, and self might be productive in devising a career strategy that will alleviate the crisis. This necessarily means helping the client perform more productively as an administrator in a particular executive group under a particular authority system and figure. Once again the authority, organization, self frame is involved. Realistic notions of authority, of organizational possibilities or opportunities, and of self-defined needs and drives have a major bearing upon the outcome.

The first chapter of the book contains the case history of a man called Mark Whiting, whose career crisis was precipitated by unproductive notions of authority. In most chapters, including the final one, Mark Whiting's case is recapitulated or elaborated upon. Although a number of case histories of big business executives are examined and discussed, Whiting's case, in addition to serving an illustrative purpose, gives unity to the book.

An administrative counselor has no particular tricks that will help to dissolve a career crisis. The typical tools associated with clinical psychology and psychiatry are useless if the client cannot perform more productively in the administrative role. In the final analysis the administrative counselor must be able to help the executive formulate a more productive solution of the administrative job than that which he has brought to the task.

Admittedly in a book that has had few, if any, predecessors, this attempt to examine the nature and consequences of administrative anxiety will be suggestive. Clinical evidence is suggestive for those who want more precise answers. However, such evidence may be usefully presented to point the direction toward more systematic research. It is hoped that it will help also those counselors who frequently or occasionally counsel big business executives.

Acknowledgment must be accorded the numerous executives whose case histories have been instrumental in formulating the orientation and content of this book. Every attempt has been made to keep their anonymity.

To Dr. Alfred L. Seelye, Dean of the Graduate School of Business Administration, Michigan State University, and Dr. Dalton McFarland, Chairman of the Department of Management, are accorded thanks for providing time to do the research and writing of this manuscript. The cooperation and encouragement of Dr. Leo G. Erickson, Director of the Bureau of Business and Economic Research, Graduate School of Business Administration, Michigan State University, is appreciated. Thanks are given to Dr. Anne C. Garrison, Bureau Editor, and Mrs. June Beeson, Associate Editor, who read and commented on the manuscript. Special indebtedness must be accorded to Mrs. Esther Waite, Associate Editor, who aided greatly in preparing the manuscript for production.

My wife, Marilynne, has graciously provided through the years the secretarial help to record the many case histories, to type and proofread the manuscript, and give the necessary emotional support for the carrying out of this latest venture.

The book is dedicated to my three sons, Eugene (Chip), Mark, and Matthew. While this manuscript was in preparation, they showed the usual jealousy and discomfort normally associated with the appearance of a new member of the family.

Eugene Emerson Jennings
East Lansing

Contents

I

Man in a Crisis

A career crisis involves a decisive moment that will alter, reverse, or sustain progress toward a goal of administrative effectiveness. Such a crisis implies a high degree of stress. A response to such stress may be anxiety: a feeling of inadequacy and helplessness. The individual does not know what to do and may or may not turn to another for help and guidance.

At such a critical time, a man must make a judgment upon which his future will largely depend. Quite literally, he is in *crisis*—the Greek term for "the decisive moment." His career is at stake. For the executive, the stakes are large; his *career* (the Latin original suggests progress along a difficult road) involves the achievement of considerable competence in problems of administration and organization.

This book is about those men who have moved into arrival stages at the top of big business corporations only to reach a point at which the central values of their lives are threatened. At the moment when they would seem to be best prepared to lead, some of them crack under the stresses of corporate life. They have achieved greatly, they have much more to give of themselves; now they are unable, for one reason or another, to remain intensely and meaningfully engaged in

1

their roles. These men are undergoing a painful experience. They are men in career crises. The case histories included in this book reveal problems of executives who have come to an administrative counselor for help in resolving such crises.

THE CASE OF MARK WHITING

Mark Whiting's own crisis began when word came to him that he had been passed over in favor of an outsider for the corporation presidency. During the course of several counseling sessions, his interpretation of that crucial day was revealed.

It was a day when he would achieve, he thought, the highest point in his career. The board of directors was meeting, and he felt certain that before they were through, he would be named president of Universal Chemical Corporation. All those years he had spent as a manager in almost every department in marketing and sales, and the last four years as vice-president of marketing, seemed to be coming to a logical conclusion. He went over in his mind, as he had done countless times, the sequence of events and achievements, the careful planning, the long hours of work that had brought him to this point. Who else knew the corporation well enough to energize its sprawling resources to accommodate a swelling competitive market? Few men knew marketing and sales as well as he.

He was commonly credited with many firsts in the chemical industry. For his achievements, he had been elected to numerous important committees in the various chemical industry associations and to the presidency of the American Chemical Manufacturers Association. He traveled extensively, giving lectures and speeches before university and non-academic audiences. He was a familiar figure in Washington, testifying before the Federal Trade Commission, the Pure Food and Drug Administration, and various other agencies concerned with chemical manufacturing. His home life, church, and community associations were exactly as they should be for an executive who conscientiously attempted to be a man on top of his work and career.

Recent events seemed to assure his promotion to the presidency. A rumor had been circulating that his long-range program had been adopted by the board of directors. Only this morning an old friend and long-time associate had reported a rumor that the board had definitely rejected the manufacturing vice-president's program. Such a report from a creditable source increased his confidence that his program was to become the master strategy for the future growth and development of the corporation. After all, there were only two really good reports before the board, and the elimination of one automatically spelled successful adoption of the other.

On an impulse he called his wife, Helen. As he listened to her congratulations, a vague feeling of apprehension moved over him. This feeling of being threatened from no particular direction and yet from all directions was not new to him. But why should he be experiencing it now? His mind turned to previous attacks of anxiousness, and he tried to recall the situations in which he had felt them. Helen's voice brought him back to the present. She wanted to know if he was still there. But his affirmative reply was more to assure himself than his wife.

He rang off and buzzed his secretary to ask if the president had returned to his office from the floor above, which housed the board room. He found that the conference was still in progress. Unable to control his mounting tension, he decided to take a walk to bridge the waiting period. For Mark Whiting, the streets below his office had a special significance. In the course of his spectacular rise to the near top of his corporation, he had walked them many times. He sometimes walked to think over his problems and search for decisions that seemed to elude him in his elaborate office many floors above. The anonymity of the crowded streets often seemed preferable to his office where the noise and lack of privacy seemed to increase with responsibility.

Today he went into the streets hoping to be overwhelmed by the excessive stimuli of the heavily congested business district. Anything to occupy his mind until he was certain that the board had made its decision. Then he would return to be summoned by them and given the mandate of carrying out as president the program he had authored as senior executive of marketing.

But the clamor, the variety shops, and the masses of people did not work their spell this afternoon. He could not rid himself of the growing feeling that something was not quite right with his appraisal of his career possibilities. As this feeling increased, he quickened his steps, and by the time he reached his favorite restaurant he was almost out of breath. Finding his lunch unsatisfactory, Mark went outside again, stopping occasionally to look at this or that item in the display windows but seeing nothing.

It was no particular impulse that caused him to awaken from his self-chosen anonymity. An overwhelming urge forced him to turn abruptly and run back to his office. It suddenly occurred to him why he could not relieve his tension and apprehension. He needed to be in his office in case the board had need of clarification of any kind. Yes, that was it. He should be there to rectify any minor mistakes that had escaped his attention.

But such was not the reception awaiting Mark Whiting. A telephone in his private office was ringing. He almost crashed through the door to see if it was the phone that was used only for conversation with the president and chairman. That phone was silent. He leisurely hung up his hat and coat and walked to his desk, sat down and picked up the other phone which was still ringing.

It was the same friend who had reported the favorable rumor earlier in the day; a long-time associate who had been director of public relations for the firm for over thirteen years. He apologized and expressed his sympathy to Mark—without the latter knowing why. Mark finally learned that the board of directors had arranged a press conference to announce that a new president had been appointed, a man from the outside with whom the board had been in contact for several months. By calling him, his friend had stumbled into a situation in which the prime heir to the presidency had not been informed of the board's rejection of him. In utter disbelief, Mark muttered a few incoherent words, not knowing what possibly could have gone wrong. He sat there crouched over in his chair looking down at his faint image in the top of his well polished mahogany desk.

Mark remained for several hours in a state of shock, moving about in an almost complete daze. The sympathetic remarks of his friends and subordinates, the formal announcement that he was to remain as vice-president for marketing, and the attempt of the retiring president to assure him that his future career was indeed secure in the corporation, failed to draw him out.

Mark Whiting, fifty-three years of age, at last staggered out of his office toward the now darkened streets below to catch the next commuter train home.

These events had occurred some five years earlier. As Whiting recalled the day that had been relived so many times before, he gradually opened up to register his indictment of the man who had taken the place he felt should have been his. When he first came for professional counseling he wanted to know what an administrative counselor did. He was told that the counselor helps executives who are apprehensive about performing their assignment. His immediate response was that the counselor should get the new president of Universal Chemical on his couch before the man ruined the firm. He emphasized that he, personally, had no problems that wouldn't evaporate if only the president was "straightened out."

When Mr. Gray agreed to become president and chief executive officer, he reserved the right to select his own team. This reservation is quite customary in corporate affairs. If the new executive is to be held responsible for executing a program, he must be free to draw upon the managerial personnel as he sees fit. Usually each executive offers his services, even though he knows that others more familiar to the new executive officer may be entrusted with the critical offices and responsibilities. Whiting did not offer his services. He could not even bring himself to congratulate the new president, a man ten years his junior.

Gray had developed a team of highly trusted and skilled executives in his former firm. He brought three members of this team to Universal Chemical. One was made vice-president in charge of marketing, another executive vice-president, and the third, vice-president in charge of scientific and engineering research. The latter was a formally trained scientist with a Ph.D. It was the first time a man with such training had ever moved as high as vice-president in this corporation. Gray had developed a reputation in the industry for organizing and coordinating scientific research for the purpose of developing future markets.

Whiting's program for the future of the corporation did not take basic research into account. He proposed a more vigorous marketing approach with somewhat more emphasis on applied research. But the corporation had already pioneered a marketing orientation, and Mark Whiting had perfected the approach to the point that the whole corporation pivoted around marketing. The board, however, had decided that the long-range direction and future of the corporation should now come from basic research.

It was not long before Gray and Whiting clashed. Whiting did not "like an outsider coming in and tinkering with my corporation. How could he possibly know what we need and do not need?" He felt that the board had made a terrible mistake, and everything had to be done to protect the corporation from this alien. With this in mind, he attended the first executive committee meeting only to be told that he had been made general manager of all sales under the direction of the vice-president of marketing. He could keep his title of vice-president, however.

There were no punches returned when Whiting jabbed away at the president's scheme of separating marketing from sales. Gray belonged to the new school of management that believed in a subtle form of contest and resistance. Mark Whiting was given the whole floor, was encouraged to fully develop his view, and was thus allowed to hang himself by showing how incapable he was of working with the new team.

Gray encouraged Whiting, recognizing his many fine achievements in the chemical industry and emphasizing how important he was to the new team. That was it, and the clash never really occurred. This engagement set the tone for the years to come. Whiting always struggled to assert himself but could never find the fighting front. The new executive team did not fire any of the old members; it was merely broadened to include them. Yet the old members were kept from the sensitive areas.

In his career development, Whiting had strengthened already strong needs to know exactly who was boss, what was right and wrong, and to aggressively determine for himself what should or should not be done if a question was not settled by superior authority. What was wrong with Mr. Gray? Whiting did not believe he was a boss who could win the respect of his subordinates by knowing the job better than anyone else.

Mark Whiting's counseling involved another critical day in his developing career crisis. During this day, Whiting discovered that he no longer counted for anything. This attack of anxiousness was cued off when he discovered that the executive committee had been meeting regularly twice a week without him. This fact he could not assimilate. He was now separated completely from the heart of the corporation.

During the many years that he climbed the corporate ladder, Whiting wanted to get closer and closer to the center of the corporation. The center to him was the decision-making process that spanned the affairs of the whole corporation and was symbolized by that small group of men who met regularly to help the president with these crucial decisions. His new assignment as general manager of sales, however, took him out into the field again.

It was during one of these trips that a division sales manager let it be known that one of his subordinates had recently been picked to become a staff assistant to the new vice-president of marketing. One of his jobs was to take notes in all formal executive committee meetings, which were held twice weekly by the new president.

Upon hearing this, Whiting sped back to the corporate head-quarters. His old friend confirmed that he was no longer a member of the executive group. Whiting had now lost more than the antici-pated presidency. He had lost his position on the executive com-mittee, which during the last three years had given him much of his self-respect and self-confidence.

Mark Whiting had been no mere employee of a huge, complex, and progressive corporation. He had been a vital member of a small group of powerful men who prided themselves on their exclusive con-cern for the overall welfare of the Universal Chemical Corporation. This executive group jealously guarded their prerogatives. In the past, Whiting had considered himself the central figure in the corporate drama that continually unfolded within the human relationships of the group. He had never really thought of what it might be like if he did not have this secure membership.

But now he began to realize that he had lost his emotional anchor-age and was adrift in a sea of indifference and loneliness. The humilia-tion and shame bordered on ignominy. This exclusion from "his" executive group amounted to a personal rejection of himself. This hurt, deep inside, far more than having lost something he really had not yet possessed. He had gone from a secure administrative position in an executive group to a boundary position that was partly administrative but largely managerial. Sales policies were being made by the executive committee under the tutelage of the vice-president of marketing. Whiting's job was managing sales policy, and this became excruciatingly painful, self-humiliating, and disgraceful.

Whiting rebelled by not leaving his office for the field. To him, staying on top of the job meant not leaving the office. If the president was trying to keep him from exerting an influence by sending him out to pasture, he simply would not go into the sales field again. And he did not.

Eight months after the arrival of the new president, Whiting was appointed vice-president of special projects. No one ever criticized him for failures that occurred in the sales field due to his lack of attention. In fact, he was congratulated by old and new members of the executive committee for his promotion. Once again, he could find no fighting front. He seemed to be fighting phantoms.

He was assigned a bigger and better office with a higher classified secretary. He now had a private toilet, shower, and liquor cabinet—all of the trimmings of a corporate president. But he was powerless. He was given problems, every one of which seemed so fuzzy and vague that he could not come to grips with them. When he appealed to Gray for clarification, he was sent on this or that trip, first to Europe and then to Japan as a special emissary of the president. An inspection trip, an investigating assignment, a good will mission, whatever it was, he never did much of anything that really tied into the administrative decision-making process. He was never invited to attend executive committee meetings.

Gray, however, always made a point of talking to him at least twice a week over cocktails and lunch. This he did for no one else apparently. Whiting came to enjoy these special occasions with Gray and to look forward to them. One day Gray did not keep his usual "social" engagement. Whiting had another attack of anxiousness. He wanted to know what had happened. "Now what had he done that was so wrong." The president kept his next appointment for lunch and apologized for being busy earlier. Everything was all right after all.

An alternating pattern of contempt and affection for the authority figure, Gray, eventually caused Whiting to make a crucial decision. He would think of himself as being as big as the office he occupied. This rationalization allowed him to believe that he was so important that Gray needed the luncheon sessions with him. He idealized his importance on the basis of this presumed friendship and the status symbols of his finely appointed executive suite. His image of himself became idealized to enhance his own feelings of self-worth.

However, these same factors that buoyed up his spirits also caused him to become depressed. The presence of Gray symbolized his failure. Because he could not attend executive committee meetings, Whiting could not gain respect for Gray's administrative skills and organizational dedication. Gray came chiefly to stand for his separation from the central administrative process of the firm. The unearned status trappings of his private office reinforced the feeling that he was nothing. He alternated between moods of elation and depression, feeling one day big and the next day small. When he felt weak, inadequate, and helpless, he would search for signs to assure himself of his power and support. A favorable nod by a member of the executive team, an invitation to any conference or meeting, an attentive ear here and there became crucial to his state of well being. But of all the sources that could affirm his importance and status, none was as crucial as the president. Failure on the part of Gray to take him into consideration as a special person set him into an acute state of anxiety, and he would once again feel terribly weak and puny.

The Universal Chemical Company grew considerably throughout the five years after Mark Whiting was rejected for the presidency. New faces began to appear in high-level positions. Scientists and engineers began to fan out to occupy many positions in the upper managerial functions. The new general manager of sales was an engineer by training; the new manager of the organic chemical products division was a chemical scientist. Several men directly assisting the vice-president of marketing were scientists or engineers.

The corporation acquired a new direction and character. And with each passing day, Mark Whiting's corporation faded into history. What emerged was an entirely different corporation with many different kinds of people and competences. Many on the old team had retired, some earlier than expected. Occupying an isolated role and position, Whiting lacked information about what was going on around him. As he was a stranger to the new breed of managers, so was the corporation a stranger to him.

Whiting came gradually to disbelieve in the corporation as an object or activity which could justify his continued affection and loyalty. In a final effort to salvage a respectable role for himself, he attempted to find employment elsewhere. For eight months he pursued this goal, only to be rejected because of his age, or because he was too high salaried for the jobs for which they thought he was fitted.

He had one very fine offer. To accept would mean that he would have to forego pension rights and other privileges with this new firm because of his age. If he left his present firm he would sacrifice the same benefits. The several weeks during which he tussled with this decision were the most agonizing in his life. It was during this critical period that he came to the administrative counselor for help.

Mark Whiting's career crisis centered around his problem of authority. He thought that his problem started with Mr. Gray. Furthermore, he thought that Gray was the only one who could solve his problem. Mark Whiting believed his problem was Gray, and that Gray alone could relieve him of it.

What is salient about Mark Whiting's career crisis is that he had a long history of difficulty with figures who carried superior authority and with his own acquisition and exercise of authority. In some of the later counseling sessions, he revealed several of these previous difficulties. They had to do with a particular kind of boss. In each case, the superior was very autocratic in his approach to supervision, usually better educated, and of larger physical stature and build. Mark Whiting had finished only high school. Because he was smaller and shorter than his classmates, he attributed many of his difficulties to his size.

In a very real sense his aggression tapped experiences that occurred as far back as when he sensed that his small stature embarrassed his father, who always wanted a son as strong and powerful as he was. He never really forgot the many times that his father shoved him away from manly activities, such as chopping wood, because he was too small. His father once remarked that the ax weighed more than he did. The weight of the ax was infinitesimally small in proportion to the weight of this remark upon the development of Mark's self-esteem and self-confidence.

Mark never resolved the question of who he was because the one person who could help him, his father, never allowed him to feel important and worthy. Eventually he was forced to come to grips with this question of self-identity.

Upon further analysis of his past, and with the aid of tests, a pattern of distrust toward authority figures became very evident. These figures symbolized restriction of his aims and deprivation of his needs. Authority figures such as teachers, principals, policemen, or ministers were unconsciously perceived as threats to his security and self-esteem.

During his early career in business he was a salesman, and as such could be relatively free to express himself in the field away from the sales manager. Because he was one of the best, he was subsequently given a territory to both manage and work. This called for a close relationship to the sales manager of his division and the responsibility for organizing and controlling twenty salesmen. Whiting was fired from this job within six months, after which he took a sales position with another firm.

A brief description of this encounter is necessary to show that he could not maintain satisfactory relationships with the division sales manager, nor could he supervise his salesmen. He was an autocratic superior who never allowed his salesmen any opportunity to exert choice, recommend changes, initiate grievances, or communicate in any way except formally. His upward relations consisted of offering a constant supply of grievances, gripes, recommendations, suggestions, and sometimes even edicts.

In his next job as a salesman, he regained the vigor of his previous sales style and once again was picked to be a district sales manager. He was fired about a year and a half later for the same reasons.

He found another sales job, this time with Universal Chemical. A friend encouraged him to enter a Dale Carnegie course. Successful completion of this program seemed to give Whiting more self-confidence in handling people, including his district sales manager. For the first time in his still young career, Mark Whiting decided to aim for the top of the corporation. He won an early promotion to district sales manager and then to division sales manager.

At this point he again ran into a thorny relationship with his boss. With his drive intensely engaged in making a success of himself, he resolved his problem for the first time by not leaving the scene. He decided to defer completely to the superior in every minute way and to insist upon such deference from those below him. However, he still distrusted superiors. He kept free and clear of them when possible, drawing mostly from himself the reasons for his managerial decisions. In addition, he threw himself into his work, setting high goals and efficiently achieving them for his organization. In a matter of ten years he moved to the position of general manager of sales with a bright future ahead. He was now in the arrival stage. Here he began to entertain the expectation of becoming the next president. Because such ambition was logical, given his spectacular rise, he allowed a close identification to occur between himself and the corporation. The corporation, its goals, values, people, and rules became a part of his personality. To conceive of himself without reference to the corporation had become an impossibility.

Whereas few superiors trusted him explicitly, everyone had come to admire his steadfast loyalty and his dedication to the goals and values of the corporation. In his private and community life he imparted the meaning of the corporation. Everyone who knew Mark Whiting knew of his great love for Universal Chemical. He had become a fine speaker, an active member of some of the more prestigious groups, a dependable family man, but most of all, a Universal Chemical man.

When he was promoted to vice-president in charge of both sales and marketing, he enlisted the active support and competence of a marketing man who had some years earlier tangled with the president. When news of this appointment reached the president, he called Whiting in to inform him of the new appointee's inadequate skill and disloyalty. Whiting took this suggestion as an intrusion into his administrative responsibility, a reflection upon his own competency. He scoffed at the whole affair. He pointed out that few were more loyal than he, and he thus was in a position to see loyalty in others. This remark brought the president to his feet. "Are you, sir, suggesting that I am less loyal than you are?" Whiting retaliated with the point that loyalty to the corporation meant to him that petty past grievances with a subordinate should not stand in the way of seeing and utilizing the latter's competency. Whereupon the president moved out from behind his desk to confront the accuser directly. "Are you, sir, suggesting that I don't know incompetency when I see it?" Whiting replied, "You don't if you can't see competency in this new appointee."

After an intensive hour of this mangling of egos, Whiting was ordered to leave the president's office. He left with his mind made up that he would never let any "knuckle-headed German tell him what to do." During the six months that followed, his relations with the president were strained to say the least. Each seemed to be obstructing the other. Neither one was able to defer to the other for this reason or that.

Whiting's sustained hostility and aggressiveness appeared to be fed by something more than the incident with the president. His attitude was largely energized by the unresolved conflicts with the several superiors who had fired him early in his career. Whiting was getting even with them by attempting to destroy the president. The subordinate over whom the clash occurred turned out to be totally incompetent, a fool, and a knave. This fact only made Whiting more hostile toward the president.

The executive committee was soon split, with some members privately favoring Whiting and others the president. But all were publicly deferential to the president—except Whiting. The storm continued unabated for a year. By the middle of the second year, Whiting's indictment of the president included a list of mistakes, miscalculations, and improprieties. The only reason why he was not removed was because everyone, including the board, felt that Whiting was irreplaceable as senior executive of marketing. While everyone below Whiting deferred to him in the strictest sense of the word, Whiting deferred to no one.

Mark Whiting did not thoroughly understand that the president had more to say about the choice of his successor than any three of the twelve board members. He had made up his mind that Whiting would never become president. He set about on a mission to inform his several close friends on the board of Whiting's limitations as a potential candidate for the presidency. He began to look around both inside and out of the corporation for a trustworthy replacement. He had vowed that he would retire only when he found someone who could square around Mark Whiting.

Whiting sensed that the president was considering retirement. He also had heard that he was not the most popular candidate with the board. He felt accurately that the president had influenced the board members. He must somehow change them in his favor.

He devised a scheme that included submitting to the president and executive committee a long-range program for the future growth and development of Universal Chemical. Since two members of the executive committee besides the president had formal access to board meetings, Whiting was sure the plan would get a hearing with the board of directors. He would be so thorough, clear, and precise in his description of the problems that faced the corporation and how they might be attacked, of the future goals of the corporation and how they would be achieved, that the board would see through the smoke screen laid down by the president.

To soften his aggressive effort, he encouraged the manufacturing vice-president to submit a plan for consideration too. This tactic was aimed at two objectives. One, to show that he was really interested in the corporation and in getting the best ideas to the board. Two, he knew the board would reject the manufacturing vice-president's program. Whiting had sized up his colleague's plan accurately. It was less thorough, clear, and precise than Whiting's. It was rejected, as was Whiting's, but for reasons that Whiting did not understand until halfway through his counseling sessions. Both plans were rejected because the president had made up his mind about his successor.

Gray had already been given a contract with the corporation to become its next president. In one of the interviews, Gray sold the board on his belief that the future of the chemical industry depended upon long-range basic research. The two programs submitted by the manufacturing and marketing vice-presidents were given to Gray for his opinion. He showed how these two men would be useful to him, but could not remain in their present roles. Whiting's program had the effect of giving Gray sufficient information about what men to take along with him when his transfer was made complete.

However, he made a gratuitous commitment. He promised that no senior executive would be fired. Whiting's several remaining friends on the board were disarmed by this suggestion and gratefully requested that his offer be read into the minutes of the meeting. Mark Whiting would never be fired.

Actually, Gray was not giving up anything. He really believed before he entered the corporation presidency that Whiting could serve as a liaison officer between scientific research and marketing. He had hoped to appoint him to this position, but such plans were dropped when he discovered that Whiting could not work in such a fluid situation as coordinator. Whiting was so organized emotionally that he had to have firm lines of authority and responsibility. Very early in his relationship with Whiting, Gray decided to shift Whiting to general manager of sales rather than coordinator of research and marketing activities.

The fact that his judgment was accurate was a tribute to Gray's capacity to judge people. But it spelled an ominous future for Mark Whiting. The more Whiting showed anxiety, the more Gray relieved him of important work. The more Whiting fed off of his kindnesses, the more Gray was concerned that Whiting was "sick." Then Gray made an even greater effort to hold his hand and sooth his ruffled feathers. Soon Gray was privately devoted to Whiting as his special charity. He stood up for Whiting, defended him, encouraged others to go out of their way to be kind to him. Gray strained the resources of the corporation to relieve Whiting's growing anxiety. He was more of a corporate patient than a subordinate. When Whiting became extremely anxious, he would go to Gray, hating himself for it later.

Mark Whiting has never fully recovered from his career crisis. Few do who delay too long the mastery of anxiety. Counseling helped him to see that the problem was as much a part of Mark Whiting as the situation which he faced; that he could not appreciably change the situation confronting him until he changed his notions of who he is and what he wants to become. His career crisis caused him to examine what things in life were worthwhile to him. Such an examination helped him to give up his tenacious hold on the presidency as the highest and only form of self-validation. As this hold relaxed, he looked elsewhere for sources of self-realization, satisfaction, and respect. He now wants to become a useful person in his corporation, community, and society. Consequently, the presidency no longer represents his only form of self-justification.

At first he clung to the roles outside the corporation, much as a drowning man clings to a rescuer. He worked hard in community and national organizations to become useful and constructive. With each little success, Mark Whiting grew more confident and ranged further and wider into his community and society in search of meaningful roles.

One day he discovered that he was actually enjoying these positions. He found himself reordering his whole life around actively advising or directing organizations that ranged from charity to education, religion, and politics. His frequent public appearances and speeches brought much favorable publicity to the corporation. Various members of the board of directors asked him to make speeches for them in their home towns before their business and charitable organizations. Mr. Gray came to believe that Mark Whiting was the best "soft seller" of the social responsibility theme of the business corporation that the chemical industry had. He remarked many times that there were not enough Mark Whitings in America who could effectively get the message across to the people that the large business corporation is not just some economic machine turning out profits to the exclusion of moral and social responsibility.

When Whiting presented a proposal to him that Universal Chemical Corporation contribute to a fund that advanced the educational resources of a consortium of three private colleges, Gray sponsored it before the board of directors. The board ratified an annual contribution of three quarters of a million dollars. Whiting was selected by the consortium to be on its executive committee. He was later elected the chairman and executive officer of the consortium.

It is apparent that Mark Whiting is achieving his goal of finding useful, meaningful roles in his corporation, community, and society. However, periodically he catches himself moving aggressively against some authority figure who makes him feel that he is trespassing or his efforts are unworthy. To this day, Whiting has as an occasional recurrence of anxiety, but now has the ability to bounce back and prove his usefulness through positive administrative achievements.

As a man approaching sixty, Whiting is carving out a useful role for himself. He has lowered his estimate of self, obtained insight into his authority problems, and found other roles outside the corporation to which he may become dedicated. His level of anxiety has become reduced and stabilized, but not completely mastered.

Unfortunately, not all career crises are as favorably resolved as Mark Whiting's. The cases to be reported in this book may seem somewhat disturbing because of the damage often inflicted upon the executive's personality and the destructive forces often directed toward the corporation and other people, including family members and friends.

It is interesting to note that anxiety was believed by the early Greeks to be the disease of their gods. The rulers who today live at the corporate zenith are no less vulnerable to feelings of failure than subordinates below who tend to regard them as more successful.

The Mark Whitings have come to profoundly understand how each successful step forward may increase the threat of failure.

II

The Success Ethic

An anatomy of a career crisis must necessarily include the basic drives or needs that compel individuals to want to move to the top of the corporation. The counseling of executives in career crises reveals uniformly a high level of need to succeed. This drive has many idiosyncratic aspects, depending upon the particular executive. The common factor is the close relationship between corporate success and self-affirmation, respect, and confidence.

The executive's notions of self become affirmed by his corporate roles and achievements. Corporate failure tends to threaten his feelings of self-importance. To understand this connection between self and corporate success, we must examine carefully the value our society attaches to success in general and success in big business in particular.

The American public generally identifies positively with the big business executive. He has the ability to evoke deep feelings of sentiment and emulation. While his power in this regard has not been precisely assessed, it has emerged from a set of values basic to the American culture. The big business executive is a dominant social model in our society. His achievements and his values are emotionally upheld by the middle-class strata in which he has deep roots. Carl Kaysen writes:

There is the familiar proposition that we are a business society, and that the giant corporation is the "characteristic," if not statistically typical, institution of our society, and, in turn, the social role of high executives is that appropriate to leading men in the leading institution.[1]

This proposition is right in some ways, but wrong in others. The significance of the executive does not lie in the fact that the corporation is the statistically typical institution of our time. There are currently some 4.5 million business enterprises, more than half of which are small and unincorporated. In fact, corporations form only 13 percent of the total number. Clearly the corporate form of enterprise is not the statistically dominant institution. The magic and glory of the executive image is not related to the form of enterprise. Nor is it related to the knowledge of a "free enterprise" system.

In a nationwide survey, adults were asked to define free enterprise. Less than one-third had an adequate answer, while many told the interviewer that it meant something given away free.[2] The average American really does not understand the workings of the economy, and particularly the big business corporation.[3].

However, the public has attitudes of faith where they lack fact. Studies by Katona, Gallop, and Roper all seem to agree that the public rather likes bigness. Said Roper:

We've done surveys on big business, and we find that an overwhelming majority of the public expects that large corporations, rather than small, will make the best inventions, will give the best merchandise for your money, will give the best values, will pay the labor the best wages, will give a man greater job security if he works for them.[4]

In studies of this kind, labor is more often blamed for inflation than management and is more often singled out as being the greatest threat to our economy. The public in general is inclined to advise taking jobs with business rather than government.[5] Many of the above beliefs are not in fact real, but big business carries positive symbolic values.

THE PROTESTANT SUCCESS ETHIC

It would be more correct to consider the executive halo as arising from the influence of big business on tastes, which range from the direct effects of the design of material goods to the subtle effects of persuasion conveyed through advertising, publicity, and public relations. However, the true psychological basis of identity with the big business corporation and the big business executive lies in their representation of vast achievements. They represent success through growth, competition, power, and influence. They symbolize a dream whose origins are both sacred and secular. Max Weber referred to this dream by the term *Protestant Ethic.* He coined this term in an attempt to explain why the Protestant Reformation gave rise to the spirit of capitalism.[6]

According to Weber, the Protestant Reformation represented a shift toward self-reliance. He noted that Protestant working girls seemed to work harder and longer, saving their money for long-range goals; that Protestants rose to the top more often in the business world despite the initial advantages enjoyed by the many wealthy Catholic families on the Continent; that the early Calvinist businessman was prevented by his faith from spending money and indulging in luxury. Why, then, did he work so terribly hard and achieve prodigious feats of business enterprise? Weber felt that the answer was found in the Calvinist's belief that he should get nothing out of wealth for himself but the emotional and spiritual satisfaction of having done a job well. The Protestant Reformation produced an intense determination to achieve; success was found in the doing, not in the receiving.

Close examination suggests that the so-called Protestant Ethic is at base a success ethic. For example, the Protestant insistence on the importance of an individual's "calling" meant that he was primarily responsible to do his best with whatever task God had assigned him in life. The self-assumed pursuit of one's calling was in direct contrast to the Catholic Church's counsel of perfection through withdrawal from the world and devotion to God. The Protestant's calling was backstopped by his conviction that he could achieve his own salvation, or the conviction of it, through systematic self-control and self-realization.* The rebellion against excessive reliance on the institutional church became a pervasive feature of home life. Early in life,

---

*The Calvinistic doctrine of predestination may have caused a psychological vacuum which was partially filled by the need to see some indication of being among the chosen few. The sign that many Protestants settled for in America was perhaps the degree of success in one's calling.

Protestant children were encouraged to be self-reliant, to leave home early, and to achieve higher goals than their parents had themselves accomplished. The internalization of the leaving-home ethic produced in the adult a vigorous quest for achievement of success. Primary satisfaction came from achievement and secondary satisfaction from the extrinsic rewards of money, status, and power.

The basic values of the Protestant Ethic were found in the rearing of work-oriented children performing economic functions in the family, in early separation from parental and family attachments, and in setting out to achieve success in a self-chosen calling. The Protestant success ethic is preserved today in many essential ways. The big business executive has a high need to achieve, but gains only secondary satisfaction from such results of his achievement as money, status, or power. These latter rewards are not goals, but bench marks showing degrees of achievement. Research also shows that the successful executive has become emotionally separated from his parental figures, but retains positive regarding feelings, which he transfers to his authority set and corporation.

The Protestant success ethic led to a systematic justification of the expenditure of time and energy. Wasted utilization of time and energy essentially constituted labor lost for the glory of God. Wasted time is the first and, in principle, the deadliest of sins. Loss of time through sociability, idle talk, luxury, even more sleep than is necessary for health are upheld as moral wrongs. In *Poor Richard's Almanac,* Benjamin Franklin set forth a version of the success ethic aimed at the rising strata of the industrial middle classes. To him time was money. "He that can earn ten shillings a day by his labor, and goes abroad, or sits idle, one-half of the day, though he spends but sixpence during his diversion of idleness, ought not to reckon that the only expense; he has really spent, or rather thrown away, five shillings besides." He wrote, "credit is money"; "the good paymaster is lord of another's purse"; "keep an exact account for some time back of your expenses and your income." Franklin's moral attitude may seem grossly utilitarian: honesty is useful because it assures credit; punctuality, industry, and frugality are virtues for the same reason.

However, the mere acquiring of money and credit for purely egocentric motives was not the objective of Franklin's version of the Protestant success ethic. In his *Autobiography,* he clearly showed that the earning of money within the modern economic order is, so long as it is done legally, the result and the expression of virtue and proficiency in a calling. Max Weber interpreted Franklin as believing that the real ethic of success is an obligation which the individual is supposed to feel toward his calling, no matter whether it appears on the surface as a utilization of his personal powers, or only as his internal possession—money, etc.[7] The desire to achieve one's self-chosen calling was the basis for making time count as money and credit as money.

This Americanized version of the Protestant success ethic became the dream of opportunity to seek self-chosen goals and achieve them by the efficient utilization of one's own resources. Success came by the affirmation of one's self. It was a personal affair emanating from character qualities of the individual. The heroes of the American dream of success are manifold. Among them is Benjamin Franklin himself, the son of a candle maker. In 1730, he became the first successful newspaper editor in Philadelphia. He was a hustler who not only worked hard, but made sure that as a tradesman he maintained his credit and character. He had no time for leisure, and no interest in pomp and scarlet. Although he attained great wealth, and was a devoted representative of the nation's developing success ethic, he could not himself benefit from his own wisdom. He lent money carelessly and relied upon his wife's thrift to balance his imprudence.

Nevertheless, he became the symbol of Yankee practicality, courage, and achievement. He is emulated by more groups than almost any other person in our history. Prohibition, labor, business, religion, education, all have used Franklinian symbols and sayings in their slogans and spiritual commitments. As Dixon Wecter shows, "He is invoked by printers, merchants, masons, sons of the revolution, publicists, diplomats, engineers, efficiency experts, scientists, advertisers, newspapermen, purveyors of correspondence courses, inspirational preachers, Christians, deists, and atheists."[8] As colonial emissary to England, he became accepted as the symbol of true British courage and, later, as American Minister to France he became accepted as the symbol of the true Gallic spirit. In America he became the epitome of the success ethic.

HORATIO ALGER'S HEROES

High achievers who gain secondary satisfactions from the kudos of money, status, security, and power have always been central to the American dream. Of all the heroes, none have caught the imagination as irresistibly as those in the rags-to-riches stories of Horatio Alger. Each of these hundred-odd stories, written in the latter part of the nineteenth century, uniformly preached the same Franklinian moral in language so simple that few could fail to grasp the meaning. "Opportunities are all around you; success is material and is the fruit of hard work and virtue." This trite formula, overworked in a host of clumsily written novels, has been picked out many times by skilled observers as characterizing a fundamental and crucial aspect of American culture.[9] In analyzing American democracy, Harold Laski found this country's workers "living in a state of psychological coma embodied in Horatio Alger." In 1951, David McCord Wright selected the Horatio Alger rags-to-riches story as one of the small bundles of belief which he felt formed the underlying faith of American capitalism.[10] Alger found 50 million readers for his books and created a legend of his own.

The Horatio Alger dream emerged from the backdrop of frenzied economic activity marking the half-century after the Civil War. During this period a vast railway system, investment banking, large capital formations, huge technological production systems, and massive corporate empires began to emerge. In 1870, more than twice as many people were involved in farm work as in business and industry. By the turn of the twentieth century there were very nearly as many in business and industry as in agriculture. During this period the population almost doubled.

The movement to the cities in search of success was the central theme in the Horatio Alger dream. The ethic of success reinfused a spiritual vitality into the building of a business and industrial society. DeTocqueville saw Americans carrying with a religious passion their ethic of success into all pursuits. "The business of America," said Calvin Coolidge later, "is business." The ultimate Horatio Algers were those who emerged from this frenzied, passionate pursuit of success as serene, indomitable victors.

The Titans

Theodore Dreiser called them the "titans," and *Fortune* called them "tycoons." But whatever the name, they served as models of the success ethic for the ordinary man. They started their own businesses, and through fierce, intensive single-mindedness they brought forth their corporate empires. Rockefeller, Mellon, Morgan, Vanderbilt, and Carnegie were only a few of the culture heroes of the nineteenth century. Sigmund Diamond observed that their successes were attributed to personal qualities. Character determines destiny; so long as one has the requisite qualities, success will be his at any time, in any place, under any circumstances.[11] Few of the titans' many successes were attributed to the upward arc of an expanding economy. The doctrine of the calling, the gospel of work and thrift, the disbelief in sentiment, and the obsession with accumulation were values open to anyone who might avail himself of their magical leverage. The vast economic enterprise became merely the length and shadow of the "captain of industry," and, in turn, society seemed to emerge from the length and shadow of the corporate empires.

The nineteenth century entrepreneurs assumed that they were a naturally superior lot. Workers were inferior, to be distrusted and coerced into being productive members of society. These titans accepted the notions prevalent at that time that society is organized chiefly for the survival of the fittest. They applauded the assertion of the railroad executive Chauncey Depew that the guests at the great dinners and public banquets of New York City represented the survival of the fittest of the thousands who came there in search of fame, fortune, or power, and that it was "superior ability, foresight and adaptability that brought them successfully through the fierce competitive jungle of the metropolis."

Carnegie, Rockefeller, Hill, Vanderbilt, and others believed that the industrious, temperate, and frugal man of the Protestant idea was the equivalent of the "strong" or the "fittest" in the struggle for existence. Not only were they the best developed of the human species, but they believed they were the heroes of civilization. As heroes their personalities weighed heavily upon their environments. They so dominated that businesses were identified with their single owners. The right to ownership meant the right to be vigorous, aggressive, domineering, and arbitrary up to, and sometimes beyond, the point of personal and corporate hazard.

American popularizers of the success ethic typically paid homage to these cultural heroes. A journalist writing in 1892 about the financier, Jay Gould, declared his life to be a "thrilling task, full of romance and fraught with importance for generations."[12] The Reverend M. D. Babcock declared that "business is religion, and religion is business. The man who does not make a business of his religion has a business life of no character." As did many clergymen, Babcock put a religious stamp of approval upon the success ethic. "What is the true conception of life but divine ownership and human administration?"[13]

Academic support was affirmatively provided when a distinguished professor of Yale University wrote, "The lowest passions of mankind, ostentation and ambition, petty rivalry, the love of saving and the love of gain, while they bring their own penalty upon the individual who unduly indulges in them are still overruled for good in their operation upon the interests of society."[14] A sociologist writing in 1896 reported that in this country great prizes are not found in government, literature, law, or medicine, but in industry. The rewards of success in business are so great as to entice men of the greatest intellectual faculties. "In this fierce, though voiceless, contest, a peculiar type of mankind is developed, characterized by the vitality, energy, concentration, skill in combining numerous forces for an end, and great foresight into the consequences of social events."[15]

Max Lerner in *America As a Civilization* points out that even the novelists who attacked the titan were covert admirers of his greatness and sharers of his values.[16] Dreiser's titan was a hero cast in a Nietzschean image of superior character who roamed far above the groundlings and held himself superior to human law. Dreiser and many others saw the titan as half man, half child. The restless search for novelty, and grief and remorse at failure were the lot of a child. The man was illustrated by his quick sense of grasping at opportunity and finding the right talent and resources to close the grasp.[17]

Horatio Alger stories are no longer popular. Many libraries do not include them because they are uninteresting to the present-day reader. Yet in American elementary history and social studies classes, Horatio Alger has become a national byword. In the text books, the Horatio Alger dream describes a boy born in the slums of a great city with a very low social position, who works hard, saves his money, and rises through Herculean skill to a high position in economic and social affairs.[18] A definite lower-class beginning is today associated with Horatio Alger's heroes.

Yet a careful study of Alger's novels reveals a decidedly different pattern. "With few exceptions the children are not slum children at all, but rather well brought-up, comfortably nourished middle-class boys, the sons of property owners with substantial social standing."[19] They did not come from great cities, but from farms; they did not conform to the niceties of common good manners but, as Henry Steele Commager reports, they were almost vulgar.[20]

The appeals in the Alger stories and the titans' lives were to people who essentially identified with the emerging middle class and its central values. Lerner remarks that to the middle-class mind the appeal of business success as a way of life is to the Puritan values of austerity and acquisitiveness, and to the Faustian spirit of movers and shakers and empire builders. The Puritan spirit stressed efficacy in the sight of God, the Faustian spirit, power in the sight of man. "One moves step by step, the other by big, bold leaps. One is the accumulative spirit, the other the gambling spirit. One operates best in the realm of production and managerial organization, the other in the realm of promotion and finance."

Lerner considered the ultimate Alger, the titan, to have both Puritan and Faustian spirits. "Their combined appeal has been powerful since the groundlings, who could not live the life of the titan, could identify themselves with his economic efficacy and share vicariously in his magnitude."[21] In the Alger stories, both Puritan and Faustian spirits are represented in the heroes and are distinguished from the real live titan only by their lower level of achievements. The titans are Alger's heroes writ large.

THE EXECUTIVE AS HERO

The middle-class hero of today is no longer the self-made man whose firm is founded on the psychic interplay of Puritan and Faustian values. The middle-class hero is the big business executive who epitomizes the middle-class values of achievement and the extrinsic values of money, security, power, and status. His implementation of the success ethic is radically different from that of the entrepreneur of the nineteenth century. In the first place, the success ascribed to the entrepreneur came by virtue of his personal qualities and his ability to take advantage of a rising economic curve. By the turn of the twentieth century, the businessman is discussed in newspapers, biographies, funeral eulogies, and death obituaries, not in terms of individual uniqueness, but in terms of all that he has in common with the rest of his countrymen.

Diamond reports that the businessman occupies his esteemed position "as much by virtue of qualities attributed to American society as by his own."[22] Whereas before, criticism was directed against a particular individual, by the close of the century it was directed more often than not against the very position of businessmen and business. "More disquieting was the development of opinions which held out alternatives to the existent structures of society."

These indictments of a business-dominated society revealed a growing disbelief in the disciplines required by the success ethic and epitomized by the entrepreneur. The entrepreneur was becoming a focus of dissatisfaction rather than emulation, and the particular social structure that supported him was becoming threatening.

In a positive sense, in the struggle for success, "failure was a function of individual incapacity, success a function of a system which served the interests of all and which, therefore, deserved the support of all."[23] An increased awareness by all of what really gave rise to the titan provided a basis for merging the interests of society with the interests of business. In Diamond's study of obituaries, it was found that at the end of the entrepreneurial era, signaled by the death of Henry Ford, "The economic system is presented as synonymous with the nation itself, and nation and economic system are interchangeable parts of the same mechanism."[24] The men at the top of business are no longer seen as charismatic figures who lead by "divine grace," but products of an economic system that gives them the opportunity to succeed and that devolves their status, power, and wealth.

The success ethic was expanded to account for the interplay of the individual and the economic social system. But awareness of the role of the economic system was only one factor that transferred the halo of success from the entrepreneur to the executive. It became apparent to all that the age of building had come to an end. The success of the corporation as an instrument of production, power, and social leverage grew to the point that by the middle of this century, about 50 percent of our gross national product came from the well-established, large corporations. The executive, the product of this system of a few large corporations that overshadow the many, many small, is an individual who merely guides an already-constructed, well-equipped ship through the sea of economic disturbance.

In this role as executive he symbolizes the middle-class notion of success through competition. Life in the corporation is an emotional experience that cannot be approximated by any other institution in our society. Few who arrive at the top have not at one time been pulled away, or nearly pulled away, from their emotional anchorages. Instead of achieving success by building an empire, success comes via mobility through the many and intricate layers of a modern corporation. The titan did not need to be maze bright because it was he who created the system of rewards and punishments, positions and roles necessary for the kind of economic activity of the preceding century.

The modern large-scale corporation is saturated with the symbols of success, power, status, and wealth, as well as the symbols of failure, devotion, early retirement, alienation, and corruption. Maze brightness for the modern executive constitutes knowing how to get cheese and avoid shocks. His organizational savvy is far greater than that of the titan.

But while the corporate executive has displaced the titan as the central figure in our economic system, he has not displaced entrepreneurship. Although the economic system has produced some big corporations, there were as many or more new business firms started in the decade of the fifties as in any decade during the last hundred years. Ours is both a big-corporation system and small-firm system. The dominance of the former is incontestable. Few will deny that it is big business that has largely brought about unprecedented and unanticipated affluence. Many will question the costs, social and psychological. Nevertheless, the big business spirit has penetrated the heart of our national being.

The Middle-Class Success Ethic

The Protestant success ethic today is basically set in a work orientation. To succeed one must serve an economic function. An

American male who is not performing useful work is not considered a man. Robert S. and Helen M. Lynd, in their study of a typical American community fictitiously called Middletown, report that the Middletown man believes in being successful, and owes it to himself, family, and society to succeed. "One should be enterprising, one should try to get ahead of one's fellows."[25] Numerous other observers report the same emphasis upon success. In a study of middle-class college students, Morris Rosenberg found that 88 percent considered it either very important (45 percent) or fairly important (43 percent) to get ahead.[26]

Great weight has been given to the observations of Margaret Mead. She reports that the American measures his own worth by the distance he has progressed from the point of departure, rather than by the position which he occupies. Success, thus, is related to mobility: economic, and social. In projecting this success ethic to his children, the American expects them to have a different future and an achievement greater than his own.[27]

Many investigators believe that the success ethic represents a predominantly middle-class set of values. Robert Cohen studied the middle-class values and found them to basically involve ambition, individual responsibility, skills, achievement, worldly asceticism (postponing immediate satisfaction for long-term goals), rationality, social skills, manners, inhibition of physical aggression, and respect for property. Numerous other studies have reported how middle-class children are subjected earlier than lower-class children to achievement opportunities, conscientiousness, personal responsibility, and taming of the physical aggressive drives.[28] In a well-recognized personality test (TAT), the middle-class values are used to assess personality characteristics. These values include believing that the experiences of adulthood are more powerful than those of childhood, children should honor their parents, will is superior to physical skills, self-aggrandizement is wrong, carelessness is evil, and work and achievement are superior values.

It is obvious that these middle-class values in practice serve to maximize self-control, achievement, obedience to authority, and personal responsibility, and to generally embrace the Protestant success ethic. One is what one does, and the tangible evidence of what one does becomes what one has. Work and the tangible rewards of achievement have become so central to our society that those who are not working or who have difficulty in their work are considered "mentally disturbed." In studying work and neuroses, Stanley A. Leavy and L. Z. Freedman concluded, "The psychiatrist in accord with the convention of his era, which sanctions work and condemns idleness, assumes as a rule that this person who does not work is ill and that the ability to work once more is evidence of the recovery of mental health."[29]

Work is considered to be therapeutic, and those who suffer incipient neuroses may actually allay or avert them by the pursuit of economic gain. In contrast, those who strive for economic security are often viewed as developing a neurotic defense mechanism, called displacement, as a symptom of a deeper emotional insecurity. It follows that denial of the immediate pleasure drives in favor of long-term occupational goals is assumed to be both an ultimate social value and an indicator of mental maturity. Upward mobility and achievement are assumed to be "natural" to man.

Thus, everyone must work usefully in order to maintain his mental health. When a man moves upward, he may incur neuroses, but if he moves downward he may pay the heavier penalty of psychosis. For this reason, the men who have achieved greatly, such as executives, are viewed by many today as superior psychological specimens.

In a recent study, Leonard Reissman observes that striving for success is strongest among the middle class, is less strong among the upper class, and is weakest among the lower class.[30] Thomas S. Langner and Stanley T. Michael's study of midtown Manhattan reveals that people of higher economic status tend to worry more about their work than do those in the lower classes. Among males, 40.9 percent of the lower classes and 65.5 percent of the middle and lower upper class worried about work. With regard to social economic status, one-fourth of the population studied had status anxiety that incurred mental health risks. There is some indication that lower-class people tend to lower their expectation of success and to resign themselves to a limited future.[31] Russell Lynes refers to this reaction to status anxiety as "dreaming in second gear."[32] The way the lower classes characteristically look at the American dream is wrapped up in a phrase, "It's all a racket." To them the success pattern depends not upon their skill and stick-to-itiveness, but rather on some freak and irrational accident. This attitude is evident in the midtown Manhattan data, which show that a greater proportion of persons of lower socioeconomic status worry about the cost of living, feel that life is futile, and are more concerned with security than persons of middle-class status. For them the American dream is more apparent than real.

The middle and upper classes have more successfully internalized the whole success ethic. They have created the social system for the perpetuation of success values and for the protection of their achievements (property, power, status). The American dream for them is more of a reality.

In another study, lower-class persons and their children were seen to anticipate lower incomes for themselves than do the upper classes.[33] When asked to choose between a secure job with a low income and a risk job with chances of a higher income, a far greater percentage of students with business and professional parents were willing to go for the risk and higher income than the secure, lower salaried position.[34] W. Lloyd Warner and James Abegglen's studies of achievement levels confirm the same fact.[35] In studies of auto workers, several point out that the lower classes are less actively ambitious.[36] In cases where the lower-class people set lower success standards, they probably transfer their success aspiration to their offspring, as Mead has pointed out. Morris Rosenberg's study shows that middle-class students more often choose business than do lower-class students, who tend to choose such areas as engineering, teaching, social work, and science.[37]

Although the lower classes have learned to "dream in second gear," many have initially internalized the goals of the success ethic just as firmly as have the upper classes. The observers of midtown Manhattan suggest that they want to get ahead so badly that they will use means unacceptable to the middle class in order to obtain success. They have internalized the goals of success but not the means to achieve them. "Thus, we find many lower-class persons with a strongly internalized success drive becoming gangsters or going into ward politics."[38]

The success ethic is a central force in American culture and predominantly anchored in the attitudes of the middle and upper lower classes. For the believer, the success ethic holds out the reward of achievement, money, and security. The big business corporation emerged largely because of the powerful influence of the success ethic. Today it offers the dream of success through mobility, power, achievement, and status within the organization. The success ethic continues to be kept alive and real both by cynics and patriots. Horatio Alger awards are still being presented to those who personify heroism, twentieth-century style.

SUCCESS AND MOBILITY

The success ethic is kept alive by many activities, among them being the fact of mobility itself. If the strength of the success ethic is largely dependent upon movement up the social and economic scale, and such mobility is not probable for many, it stands to reason that the success drive, as we know it, would not be very strong. Taking the most agreed-upon results from four studies made in 1910, 1933, 1940, and 1947, it is apparent that mobility patterns into and out of occupations have not decreased greatly in this century. The greatest amount of immobility occurs at the top and at the bottom on the occupational structure. That is to say, the professions and unskilled labor acquire more than their share of people from their respective levels. Reissman reports:

The unskilled are immobile because they have no monopoly of skills and usually remain committed to the same occupational level as their fathers. The professional occupations, on the other hand, are closed to many, except to sons of professionals. There is considerable opportunity between these two extremes. Lower white-collar jobs, salesmen, and self-employed proprietors symbolize the channels for upward occupational mobility for those coming from manual occupational backgrounds.[39]

For those who are members of the middle class, a major channel of success is via the big business corporation.

Warner and Abegglen report that over half of all the major executives of contemporary corporations are the sons of men who have been executives, major or minor, or owners of small or large enterprises. The other 48 percent is constituted as follows: 15 percent are sons of laborers, 8 percent come from white-collar families, 14 percent are sons of fathers in the professions, and another 9 percent had fathers who were farmers.

Warner and Abegglen show that no other occupational category draws as many sons of middle-class parents. "But among the American executives with executive fathers, for every 100 that might be expected by their proportion in the general population, there are 473 or nearly five times more than would be expected by chance."[40] The evidence seems also to point out that mobility into and up through business is as open or great as it was at the turn of the century.[41] A fair to high rate of general mobility upward and downward seems to still exist today. In the midtown Manhattan study, of 1,660 in the sample studied, 375 persons had moved down from their parent's socio-economic status, 371 had moved up, and 914 had stayed the same. While in the country as a whole, the numbers whose educational and occupational levels rose above the father's level increased, about equal numbers moved up and down, and a majority stayed the same.

Although he is the cultural epitome of success, the big business executive is largely a middle-class product. He symbolizes the success ethic for many in the middle classes. There is some evidence that for the man who goes into business for himself, the entrepreneurial role has become by and large a working man's preoccupation. According to Reinhard Bendix and Seymour Lipset, "Though it may have animated both working class and middle class in the past, it is no longer a middle class ideal today. Middle class people aspire to the professions and to upper white collar occupations foremost among which are the managerial kinds."[42] The success ethic is kept alive for a number of reasons, but largely because of the reality of success itself. Warner concludes that mobility is not diminishing, and we may be assured that the success ethic is not either.

THE SUCCESS ETHIC OF THE EXECUTIVE

The success ethic is a dominant value in the character of the successful executive. Numerous studies seem to confirm the high level of the success drive. But this drive takes on a different form in the executive than in lower occupational groups. The middle-class person values achievement and utilizing and developing his innate capacity more than the lower-class or upper-class individual. The middle classes out of which the majority of big business executives emerge value achievement highly, followed by money, security, and status, in that order.

William Henry found that successful executives have a strong drive and achievement desire. They conceive of themselves as hard working and achieving people who must accomplish in order to be happy. They get satisfaction from doing rather than contemplating. The dreamers seldom make it to the top. In addition to achievement, successful executives have a high mobility drive. "They feel the necessity to move continually upward and to accumulate the rewards of successful accomplishment."[43] Some gain a sense of accomplishment in the struggle for increased responsibility. Others rely upon the prestige of increased status in the corporation, home, and community. "The energy and zeal put into the job is the same in both instances."

Warner,[44] Gardner,[45] and Rosen,[46] among others, confirm the high level of achievement and mobility drive in successful executives. The success ethic found in the middle classes is a salient and forceful feature of the executive personality. It would seem entirely proper to add that the success ethic provides a large supply of the zeal and energy consumed in the administrative routines of the corporation. In this sense, the success ethic is what ties the middle classes and the big business corporation together.

In summary, today the executive displays the success ethic in a form different from the titans, the Horatio Alger heroes, or the Franklinian great men. He is every bit the high achiever. Contrary to Packard's stereotype of him as a pyramid climber who climbs the slippery slopes of the corporate hierarchy for the sheer gain of power, the big businessman seeks first the satisfaction of work well done. Contrary to Whyte's notion that he has substituted the social ethic for the Protestant ethic, he has merely sought for achievement through the guides and values framed by the corporate structure. The executive is, at root, no less the high achiever than the titans of the past.

The success ethic may be a functional and constructive force in the affairs of society. It may also have some seemingly negative characteristics. The success ethic holds out the possibility of a life of anxiety. The anxiety of the middle-class life and of those who aspire to middle-class values, is today becoming apparent. Middle-class people bear in their family matrixes the future leaders of our society. Business in particular depends largely upon the middle-class family for an abundant supply of managerial talent. Whereas some anxiety is good, too much anxiety over success may have ruinous effects upon the corporate system and the national economy. We turn, therefore, to observe the potential terror of the success ethic.

III

Success Anxiety

Mark Whiting had an overwhelming urge to achieve his ambitions at all costs. To him success was the measure of the man. Early in his career, as an extraordinarily effective salesman, he expressed this compelling urge to make things happen his way. Gradually his success drive became enmeshed with the corporate hierarchy. He set out with a realistic awareness that he must succeed within the framework prescribed by the corporation's goals, policies, and procedures, and by the special expectations of each authority figure.

Mark Whiting had a pervasive fear of failure. With each step upward, this fear gathered strength. In his more private moments or in the middle of major administrative decisions, his mind would become flooded with a feeling that he might not really succeed and be able to do the things he wanted. Such thoughts mobilized his energy more efficiently to perform his tasks.

He arrived at the post of vice-president almost out of breath because of the pell-mell rush up the corporate ladder. He privately congratulated himself on his ability to succeed, and reassured himself that failure was not in the cards after all. His fantastic success pattern somewhat anesthetized his lurking fears of failure. He had left behind many superiors and subordinates and was not prepared to let anyone block his final bid for success. In this last step upward he placed the total resources of his self.

Mark Whiting's career plans illustrate the central importance of the big business corporation in the minds of executives. Their corporations are experienced as giant mothers who provide the necessary resources for their personal growth and development. Mark Whiting believed that men at the top had to be big and powerful figures in order to master their giant organizations. To him, movement up signaled growing and becoming an important and influential person not only in his corporation but in his community and society. The American dream was real to him until his career crisis activated the terror of failure.

For the executive, the American dream holds out both triumph and terror. Success has a strong kinship to anxiety. Successful executives are more than high achievers. They are chronically anxious. It is common to regard the big business corporation as heir to the vigorous assertion of the success ethic. However, the big business corporation is both a product and a process of human anxiety. It affirms the central values of success through achievement and satisfaction gained from the secondary rewards of money, status, power, and security. It also tends to reject those individuals who cannot achieve in their work the goals and values of the corporation and the blessings of their superiors.

Success breeds anxiety partly because it is so precariously based upon the expectations and demands of others equally human as one's self. Often these expectations and demands do not rationally fit the corporation's goals and purposes. Many hurts and inconveniences have been inflicted upon subordinates in the name of corporate efficiency and welfare. The irrational needs, whims, and fancies of superiors may be as crucial to career success and failure as the requirements of corporate efficiency and welfare.

The executive knows that successful achievement of the goals and values of the corporation as represented in his job situation may spell failure without the blessings and support of superiors. He also knows that successful achievement of the superior's peculiar expectations and demands may spell failure, owing to the possibility that an even higher superior may indict both subordinates for disregarding the objective necessities of organizational efficiency and success. Of course, the individual who acts without regard to either the objectives of the corporation or the expectations of superiors is headed for self-defeat. The successful executive knows that success presents opportunities for failure. In his inner world, success is closely linked to anxiety. We must now examine more carefully the meaning of success anxiety.

ANXIETY AND HYSTERIA

Anxiety is exerting an increasingly painful effect in our society. In a 1948 study of 1,000 patients examined and tested in a psychiatric clinic, it was found that one-third had chronic, benign nervousness.[1] If this number who were courageous enough to seek professional help had anxiety, how many in the general population have anxiety for which they do not receive treatment? The midtown Manhattan study made fifteen years later investigated the incidence of anxiety among an urban population. This study of a compact residential area in New York City found anxiety in 75.5 percent of the study population. The authors state: "We find that the average respondent has mild or moderate symptoms which do not particularly interfere in his life adjustment. The symptoms are not frequently of a neurotic type. When questioned about it, the average individual recognizes in himself significant worries, tension, and nervousness."[2]

It is generally agreed that anxiety is to this generation what hysteria was to Freud's. Man in the nineteenth century lived in a society of stable values. Through the family and other mediating agencies, the child internalized these values into his conscience to become a permanent force for decision-making. As long as the social order remained fixed and integrated, the inner-directed decisions received positive affirmation and support through the rewards of work and success. A drive that conflicted with his basic values was repressed and driven into the unconscious. If the drive was sufficiently strong, it would emerge in the form of bodily changes or personality disturbances. Significant among these changes was a class of symptoms called hysteria, which included irrational fears (phobias) and afflictions of the body (conversions). The symptoms of hysteria were oftentimes quite dramatic. The patient could not walk, see, or hear (conversions), or he would become dizzy in high places, terrified at the sight of an animal, or afraid to go to sleep (phobias).

Hysteria was felt to be so common that therapists were formerly trained intensively in its diagnosis and therapy. Today clear-cut instances of hysteria have become relatively rare.[3] In a study of the incidence of neuroses among people in a New England city who reported for psychiatric treatment, hysterical reactions were relatively rare compared with other forms of neuroses.[4] The common hysterical pattern observed today includes a variety of minor phobias and conversion phenomena occasioned by mild attacks of more or less temporary anxiety.

The decline of hysteria seems largely accountable to the decline of inhibition. Many drives, such as sex and parent-directed hostility, which were commonly inhibited in the nineteenth century, are now less inhibited. Emotional suffering today tends to derive from inadequate ego functioning. These minor forms of emotional disturbances make people jittery, miserable, and on edge, but do not disqualify them from the daily business of making a living. They may work with mild to severe handicaps and strain. The total number today who suffer unreasonable fears and anxieties defies reliable estimate. However, a recent study suggests that there are no basic differences in anxiety from lower classes to upper classes of our society.[5] Rather, anxiety is a pervasive phenomenon that few people escape today. In many cases, anxiety may develop feelings of impending danger of breakdown. In a national study, 19 percent of the people in the sample population answered "yes" to the question, "Have you ever felt that you were going to have a breakdown?" And 23 percent indicated that at some time they had a personal problem for which some professional help might have been useful.[6]

Almost all authorities on anxiety agree that the cause basically stems from value conflict. Few, if any, societies offer a well-integrated, generally-accepted pattern of life values. This seems particularly true today. The individual who emotionally commits himself to a traditional or prevailing set of values risks the chance in a changing society that he will become at some future time obsolete or unacceptable. If he does not commit himself and waits to find a steady stream of universally acceptable values, he risks the loss of or delayed sense of self. Either in commitment or in withdrawal, there is the risk of not knowing what to stand for or to become. It seems that the penalty for over-commitment may be neurosis, and for withdrawal, psychosis.

The uncertainty of the future and the unending array of choices in the present produces anxiousness and anxiety. Clear-cut symptoms of neurososis may emerge, but more often vague feelings of aimlessness, futility, despair, and inadequacy become the standard pattern. Complexity, value disunity, instability, rapid change, and weak group identification, including those of family and community, create an atmosphere of hostile tension. A condition of pervasive, anxious concern may be considered normal for our time, leading to transitory episodes of acute or debilitating anxiety.[7]

The Nature of Anxiety

Freud believed that anxiety is something unpleasurable felt by the individual. It arises as a response to a situation of danger. It involves various intensities of unpleasant feelings and effects, including apprehension, timidity, dread, anguish, panic, and terror. Or it can be felt simply as a trace of abashment, clumsiness, embarrassment, or confusion. Common to all of these is a vague, uncomfortable sense of something impending. Anxiety is intimately associated with things to come and is a future tense episode.

It may be registered in the organism by an increase in excitation. Physical manifestations include hyperactive bowels, perspiration, tremors, sinking abdominal sensations, vomiting, and changes in muscular reactions, heart beat, pulse rate, and respiration. If anxiety becomes too severe, mental symptoms and illness may evolve.

The function of anxiety is to signal the organism of an impending danger so that it may act or react in relation to that danger. The signal function of anxiety serves as an alarm clock.[8] If the alarm goes off and the person hears it, then he can mobilize his resources. By fight, flight, and adaptation he is able, upon heeding the alarm, to restore himself to normalcy. Thus, anxiety performs the normative function of protecting and enhancing the individual's welfare. By analogy, the person hearing the clock gets out of bed, clothes himself, eats his breakfast, and moves on to the day's routine. By triggering the appropriate response to the particular danger situation, anxiety is a necessary and positive state of the human being.

Man is perhaps bound to be always anxious. He acquires idealized views of what he can or cannot do. Through the ideals fostered by civilization, he acquires the distinct belief that he is the center of the universe and the essential means of its control and his perfection. The ideals of progress, destiny, and the great society carry inflated notions of man's extraordinary capacities. Man can also be afraid. But fear is a direct, unmediated response to an objective danger. All animals can be afraid, but Freud thought that only humans could be anxious. Fear is an automaton-like reaction to danger. Because man has the capacity to imagine and anticipate, he "futurizes" the present, which makes anxiety rather than fear his unique quality. Anxious anticipation of impending danger is viewed by many as the basis of human civilization. In general, anxiety is constructive and preservative, and if it always functioned normatively there would probably be no need to discuss it as a disabling force today in human growth and response.

The root words of anxiety in many families of language refer to narrow passages or to being besieged. Anxiety restricts individual behavior to a limited set of choices. This restriction is partly based upon previous experiences in which anxiety was evoked. The specific danger awakens the unpleasant association with the previous danger. An illustration contrived by Seward Hiltner is especially relevant here. He used the analogy of driving a car at high speed on a good highway when suddenly a narrow and dangerous bridge looms dead ahead. The perception of this narrowness is like the alarm signal itself. "The sense of narrowing, of constriction, of tightening of the breath that occurs at once, as one tries to guide his car through the narrow place is not pleasant."[9] The signal arouses the individual to a state of readiness instead of paralyzing him or leading him to crash by too much wheel or too heavy brakes. It has given him an accurate perception of his need to "narrow," to guide his car within a fraction of an inch rather than by a couple of feet as will suffice in much driving. Even though the effect is painful, the driver is really too busy to feel it. If he is smart, he will stop and attempt to calm down a bit. Then he will be more aware of the excessive excitation and unpleasantness of the experience.

Whereas the immediate result of anxiety may be to adapt to the danger, the after effect may be to "master" the situation by explaining to himself what went wrong and how close a call he had with death.

Anxiety may be felt intensely after crossing the bridge rather than during the crossing. This after effect may be stored in the memory to make the individual apprehensive of narrow bridges. When sometime later he encounters another similar restriction, the affective residue may allow for heeding of the signal even more quickly and accurately than before.

Or quite the reverse may happen. The anxiety occasioned by the first experience may be so traumatic that the affective residue may paralyze the individual upon the sight of a similar constriction. To avoid any future anxiety of this kind, symptoms may develop. To Freud, symptoms are created to avoid the outer or inner danger situations of which anxiety sounds the alarm.[10]

Thus, anxiety is a state of reproduction of an early experience. When the anxiety cannot be transferred into adaptive responses, symptoms emerge, among which may be phobias. The driver may come to fear narrow roads and passages and to avoid them. As long as he does, he has partially allayed the anxiety that is associated with his traumatic experience of crossing the bridge.

Mark Whiting's Anxiety Pattern

Mark Whiting was anxious about authority figures. He perceived them to be threatening to his feelings of self-esteem, confidence and security. To allay this anxiety, he developed a number of symptoms, one of which was work addiction. Whiting devoted his whole day and much of the evening to the corporation. Whenever he felt anxious he delivered the goods in the form of specific, meritorious achievements. This pattern of behavior was to allay the anxiety that came from failure to resolve his conflict with authority figures and their threatening nature. He came to avoid such threatening figures much as the driver above came to avoid narrow roads and passages.

His avoidance pattern took several forms in his rise up the corporate ladder. He tended not to become emotionally involved with authority figures. He never sought them out for informal, leisurely activities of any kind. He tended to be very official with them, deferring completely to them—until he ran into the president and Mr. Gray. By these techniques he avoided feeling anxious. But because he failed to come to grips with his problem, he eventually was forced to resolve it in something less than ideal circumstances, namely, a career crisis.

THE NEUROTIC PERSONALITY OF OUR TIME

The question that must next be tackled is why anxiety is often closely associated with success and failure. Failure may arouse anxiety because it is a threat to self-values, status, power, or achievement, that is, success of some kind. The more dominant the success drive the more substantial the amount of anxiety. Numerous observers, scientists, and therapists refer to this correspondence between strength of the success drive and anxiety.

Karen Horney prefers the term, *the neurotic personality of our time,* by which she indicts anxiety as the dynamic center of common neuroses.[11] The principle of individual success through competition generates hostilities and fears by collision with the antithetical values of brotherly love, cooperation, and humility. We are told that we should feel free, strong, and independent, but our organized society seemingly calls for vast amounts of deference, dependence, and compliance. To dissolve the anxiety brought on by these normative contradictions, the individual enters the first or basic stage of incipient neurosis. He prefers to become compliant, aggressive, or detached. This initial neurotic attempt only brings more disturbances in his human relationships. He needs a more comprehensive solution. He imagines that he can be master of these contradictions by ascribing to himself tremendous powers and skills. Self-idealization in fantasy leads to attempts to actualize the idealized self in the real world. Horney calls this more advanced stage of neurosis the "search for glory."

The neurotic's needs are then attached to prevalent values and become claims. He claims security, position, money, status, leisure, material gadgetry, and all the other values and services available in an affluent society. The idealized image is one of perfection and carries tyrannical shoulds, rights, musts, and must nots. Nothing should be, or is, impossible for one's self. A style of life evolves aimed at making the person into what he would actually be were the claims fulfilled. Horney believes that these claims basically lack the support of genuine ideals, since they do not aim at hard effort and real change—achievement—but at making it appear as if the perfection has been attained. The tyranny of the claims is manifest by the constant state of strain which impairs human relationships and spontaneity.

In the search for glory, the neurotic becomes estranged from his real self. As he becomes alienated from his real self he becomes impersonal to others. Occasionally he sees himself as the person he really is and hates himself for being what he is. Disparity between his idealized self and his real self involves intense intrapsychic conflict that produces advanced stages of anxiety. To Horney, neurosis is a disturbance in one's relations to self and to others.

The mechanism of neurotic aggression, detachment, and compliance may be briefly described because of their relevance to subsequent material. The aggressive individual tends to demand power, status, and prestige for coping with a hostile world. His picture of the world as a jungle provides exploitation with moral relief, ruthlessness in business as sanctioned capitalism, and sexual prowess as masculinity. Outsmarting others becomes his central cognitive facility. He may appear as loyal, lovable, and honest as the compliant type who is docile, passive, and companionable. The compliant type tends to move with the life streams and the institutional patterns. Whereas the aggressive type demands mastery, and the compliant type demands affection, the detached type demands freedom. Typically, it is freedom that in practice cripples the productive activities of others.

The cultural backdrop out of which these neurotic solutions emerge is an ever persistent feeling of normlessness and uncertainty. A high level of chronic anxiety created by conflicting values of success, competition, cooperation, and humility makes possible the neurotic appeals to mastery, love, and freedom.

In this vogue, Erich Fromm also would refer to our age as that of anxiety founded upon the success ethic. The ideals of the market place prescribe that in human affairs the highest value is given to the most salable personality. Notions of self are derived and validated by their exchange value in the commerce of human relationship. What one becomes is what others want and will pay for. Contemporary economic processes have not only encouraged treating others as objects or instruments but the self as well. Man becomes alienated from both man and self. Feelings of anxiety consequently develop out of intense competition for the highest exchange values.

Fromm regards basic human experience today as having seller and buyer characteristics. In the market place of competition, notions of self are beyond personal validation. The individual enters a region beyond his personal control. The degree of uncertainty and insecurity can hardly be overestimated. "If one feels that one's own value is not constituted primarily by the human qualities one possesses, but by one's success in a competition market with ever changing conditions, one's self-esteem is bound to be shaky and in constant need of confirmation by others."[12] The urge for constant confirmation creates a restless drive for success, which only brings on a need for a still higher validation.

The success and confirmation spiral and the need to alleviate anxiety brings neurotic mechanisms of escape. Fromm submits that the most frequently employed mechanism is automaton conformity. The individual adopts entirely the kind of personality offered to him by society. He becomes exactly like all others and as they expect him to be. He thereby attempts to overcome isolation and anxiety. The automaton conformist is basically receptive, believing that all that is good is external to him. He is dependent on authority for knowledge and direction and upon the goals of the group for cues as to his work contribution and value.

A second mechanism of escape is found in the sado-masochistic personality. In the sadistic phase, the emphasis is on inflicting hurt upon others by control and mastery of them; in the masochistic phase the hostility is directed toward self. The individual of sado-masochistic tendencies enjoys the advantages of controlling weak and inferior people and deferring to the orders and values of strong, superior individuals. In short, Fromm believes that the methods of conformity (automaton conformity) and aggression are highly prevalent as mechanisms of escape from competition and anxiety.

David Riesman also sees a growing anxiety potential in American culture. As he sees it, values have radically changed in the course of three periods of human adjustment.[13] In the Middle Ages, society was more static than today, and social patterns, norms, and expectations were highly persistent. For most of the situations that were apt to arise, specific responses were easily transmitted through stable family and community ties. Because these responses were transmitted as tradition, the model of that period is referred to by Riesman as *tradition-directed.* The individual's penalty for deviation from prescribed norms and rules was shame.

As the business society emerged, innovations in the basis of employment, technological changes, and larger than local markets brought eruptions in the tradition. It was no longer possible to have specific responses to any given situation. A set of fixed directives that had general application for any situation were internalized in the children at early periods in the socialization process. Such directives became the fabric of the implacable success ethic that dominated the nineteenth century. They served as a stabilizer or gyroscope to keep the individual upright in the pursuit of success goals. Riesman called this model type *inner-directed*. The psychic penalty for transgressing from one's inner directive was guilt.

The early entrepreneur was probably much inner-directed. By the mid-twentieth century social change became rampant. The movement from self-employment to organized work in large factories increased drastically the necessity of gaining the favor of individuals, winning friends, and influencing people. Disdain for the group, the public-be-damned attitude, and justification by moral principles became liabilities rather than assets. What emerged was an *other-directed* individual whose radar antenna scanned the social scene for cues about what to do and become. The penalty for not being sensitive to the group was anxiety.

Notice must be given to the underlying competitive struggle in the inner- and other-directed societies. Only the means of obtaining success—inner-directions and values versus social norms and values—have changed. To succeed, the traits of popularity, persuasiveness, and attractiveness have become essential competitive resources. Obviously, the need to be other-directed is not idly conceived. Behind this other-directedness is the implacable success motive.

Success without the group is impossible. Success within is difficult because everyone else is doing the same scanning. Wanting to become somebody, but not knowing what others will value for any durable period, prescribes anxiety as a concomitant of other-directedness.

The group becomes not an end but a means to the achievement of success. Conformity waxes high as a central value. But as Margaret Mead suggests, the excessive American concern for conformity need not be inconsistent with the drive for success. Conformity basically implies embracing the goals of the competitive system, its behavior, codes, the belief systems. The incidence of anxiety lies in the difficulty of succeeding and achieving membership character in the group

Not everyone has the cognitive adequacy (antenna) nor the psychic energy to productively meld these potentially polar positions. Outwardly the anxiety may stem from ineffectual group relationships, but the more dynamic center lies within the individual and his strong drive for success. Americans are learning that success within the group is not easy.

A mixture of Riesman's two more recent types seems descriptive for many. Such a mixture would show the mid-twentieth century individual to have internalized the success ethic. This is what largely remains of his gyroscope. With an antenna to scan the scene for opportunities and means to achieve in the group, the mixture would seem to be ideal. Perhaps few have attained this ideal capacity. In any case, basic to all three views (Horney, Fromm, and Riesman) is the element of the intense need to compete for success that undergirds our society.

THE CAUSES OF SUCCESS ANXIETY

The question is how do success and anxiety actually become interrelated. Abram Kardiner studied a midwestern rural village, Plainville, and found much anxiety and intrasocial hostility. Social prestige goals are dominant, and in the competition for these goals the individual finds his notions of identity and their validation. Failure brings loss of self-esteem and feelings of inferiority. As we might expect, Kardiner observed a high level of success anxiety.

Why this compulsive competitiveness, however? His answer related to three basic growth patterns in Plainville. In this community the maternal care, emotional satisfaction, and protection given the child lays the groundwork for a high self-valuation. A second pattern is the introduction of taboos via parental discipline. The enforcement of sex and toilet training norms distorts the psychological growth, raising doubt in the child's mind concerning the continuity and permanence of parental care and protection. The pleasure seeking pattern becomes partially blocked, giving rise to hostility toward parents and rivaling siblings. Hostility creates anxiety, which may lead to increased dependence upon the parents. Parents may come to occupy an inflated position in the mind of the child as relaxers of anxiety.

The third phase in the growth pattern of the Plainville child is the enlargement of the notion of obedience. Great significance becomes attached to allaying anxiety by obedience, and, conversely, disobedience brings heightened feelings of anxiety. Thus Kardiner saw blocked expression of emotions. Success anxiety arises out of this growth pattern by utilizing socially approved goals of success as compensation for all other shortcomings in the blocked pleasure drives. "As long as the individual can pretend to some goal of success, or security, he can claim some self-esteem."[14] In other words, in Plainville the struggle for success is a relaxer of anxiety, an equivalent of self-preservation and self-esteem.

Success is both frustrating and self-validating. Whenever anxiety arises, the individual's tendency is to allay the anxiety and recoup self-esteem by striving for new levels of success. An added motive for competition is the intrasocial hostility arising from blocked pleasure drives. Kardiner observes that this hostility tends to be self-increasing because the individual, blocked from pleasure seeking activities, joins with the group in restricting others. However, the outlets for intrasocial hostility are common, since there are many occupations that demand competitive work. Such competitive hostility deprives the individual of spontaneous, warm human relationships. He feels alone and isolated.

Competition for social prestige arises out of the parent-child struggle. The apparent inconsistency between affection giving and suppression of aggression drives the child into competitive social channels. This is borne out in Kardiner's analysis of the Alorese society in which parental behavior is marked by irregularity, undependability, and deceit. The child grows up feeling mistrustful, anxious, and isolated.

Kardiner maintains that competitive social prestige has been the dominant goal for Western man since the Middle Ages. For that matter, there has been a uniformly strong system of parental obedience, with rewards and punishments to keep under control the system of taboos against hostile aggression. In the Middle Ages, control was maintained by the established family, power and protection of the feudal lord, and by the religious system of confession and expulsion. Obedience could be obtained by family, lord, and church, and these same figures could allay anxiety. When these figures lost their essential power of control during the Renaissance, the concern for social success and prestige was substituted. This drive was greatly facilitated by the development of science and capitalism. These institutions could demand obedience and allay anxiety as well. The self found validation in competitive striving. In modern times, success has tended to replace the salvation of the Middle Ages.

Evidence of the anxieties that beset a society upon emerging from a well-ordered social arrangement to a dynamic, unstable order is found in the Lynd's "Middletown" study.[15] The advantage of this study is that it includes three phases. Through diaries, newspapers, letters, and memoirs of the still living, Middletown was studied as it appeared in 1890. In 1923-24, it was studied at first hand, and revisited in 1935. These dates approximate the emergence from a frontier society, the rise of the industrial revolution, and the rearrangements following the depression. This analysis gives support to the relationship of the success drive and anxiety.

In the 1890's, Middletown people possessed a highly standardized pattern of attitudes. Mother uniformly taught practicality, honesty, hard work, obedience, self-control, persistence, and will power. With the men, the Horatio Alger dream of struggling to the top was strong, but a spirit of equality of opportunity prevented the evolving of exclusive segmental social groups. The prosperous spoke to the poorest without condescension. There was spontaneous intermingling within the spirit of free enterprise. Essentially, Middletown was a home-grown, rugged, individualistic, democratic community: a one class town.

After 1890, the growth of industrialism and finance capital began to change the economic structure of Middletown. A wave of feeling against capitalism and big industry was spawned by Greenbackism, the Sherman Act of 1890, and the technological revolution in the making of glass preserving jars, the town's major industry. Some men got richer and others got poorer. For the first time men became rich by inheritance of wealth rather than by working their way up through the ranks.

By 1923, the population was split into two definable classes in about the proportion of one member of the business class to about three of the working class. The businessmen directed the companies by means of symbol manipulation: marks on paper, and command through subordinate staff. The workers manipulated physical objects: glass blowing machines, cylinderheads, and drill presses. The organic relationship between the bosses and workers had been destroyed by the symbol-physical skill dichotomy.

While the mothers in the working class of 1890 represented a traditional outlook and family practice, the business mothers were endeavoring to inculcate originality, independence, and flexibility. Working-class mothers continued to emphasize hard work, thrift, and obedience. The educational system continued to emphasize this old pattern of success, while new factories called for the different qualities. By now there were definite inconsistencies about getting ahead.

The Horatio Alger dream had more affinity with the business class. The occasional individual who did struggle upward lent renewed hope and authenticity to the traditionally good behavior. The unsuccessful experienced success vicariously.

The depression exerted a somewhat leveling effect. The wealthiest men were becoming salaried executives, having to give up their entrepreneurship or wishing to avoid the constant risk. They were beginning to feel insecurity and anxiety about their failures and their chance of future success. Workers were suffering the stresses of unemployment. Their helplessness affected their faith in the possibility of success by aggressive personal achievement. Both business and working classes, conditioned to accept success, found that success was no longer assured. Believing that success came by personal virtue, failure arrived via conditions beyond their control.

The growing disparity between what they believed constituted success and the reality of it provided the dynamics of insecurity and anxiety. No doubt the inner-directed values, internalized early in childhood, proved a liability in the new society beset with change. Industrialization, urbanization, and large-scale corporate collectivism made the other-directed skills functional assets. Traditional values of success as inhering in the qualities of the individual gave way to the social notions of success as based upon interpersonal relationship.

After the depression an upper-class set arrived. One particular family bought up business after business as they went under during the depression years. The major banking firm, the leading department store, the YMCA, and a substantial part of the residential section were all directly or indirectly under the control of one family. The Lynds remark that the modest, reserved sense of power and leadership that marked this family in 1923 had changed to almost a sense of eminent domain. The remainder of the former business class consisted of insecure, deferential people, beholden to those above and insecurely pushing down those below.

In short, Middletown anxiety consisted of deferential behavior upward and dominating behavior downward. But all three classes showed in 1935 the clear marks of the themes of terror and triumph of the success ethic. The upper-class family experienced security on the one hand, and anxiety on the other because of the growing restraints of governmental regulation and the gradual appearance of a democratic political majority.

MIDDLE-CLASS ANXIETY

Success anxiety is no respecter of classes. All classes more or less share the prevailing state of anxiousness and anxiety. However, anxiety seemingly occurs in certain occupational strata more than in others. There is some evidence that the middle class is the dominant carrier of success anxiety. Rollo May states: "The individual competitive ambition, a trait in our culture intimately associated with contemporaneous anxiety, is a middle-class trait."[16] Willoughby makes the suggestion that the anxiety is heaviest with the middle class because it is bound by difficult standards without important material support.[17] Seward remarks that striving toward higher status tends to be more powerful in the middle-class environment, and, hence, the forces of anxiety are more commonly present.

In the studies of the communities of Plainville, Elmtown, Brasstown, Yankee City, and Middletown, status striving was largely equated with economic success. The image that emerges from these studies is that the middle classes' compulsive competing and striving elicit highly disturbed and perpetually dissatisfied states of mind. The lower-class image on the other hand, stereotypically composed of non-strivers, non-competitors, or small strivers, makes that class appear calmer. The upper classes appear to show symptoms of boredom, snobbery, alcoholism, and stress from having to perform traditional social duties.

Robert E. L. Faris and Henry W. Dunham report that the middle and upper classes were relatively free of severe mental illness.[18] In studying admittance rates to public and private hospitals, Robert E. Clark concluded that psychoses were more frequent among the lower classes.[19] Neuroses seemed more characteristic of those among the middle and upper classes.

The New Haven study by August B. Hollingshead and Fred R. Redlich found that neuroses were more common with the middle class and psychoses with the lower classes. The suggestion was made that middle-class persons are able to make productive use of their anxieties by the more accessible channels of prestigeful work and social entertainment. The lower-class individual has little opportunity and fewer supportive values that would present adequate escape mechanisms. Apparently, the middle classes are able to lose themselves in their work enough to prevent psychoses.[20]

In the midtown Manhattan study, it was found that people in the middle class and lower upper class tended to worry the most about their work. Although the lower classes may worry about work, they seem more susceptible to risk of radical mental health impairment. The reason the middle classes worry more but have fewer psychoses is probably due to the fact that they have more mental health assets to begin with. It is a sign of mental health among people of higher status to worry about work, getting ahead, and pursuing long-range goals.

It is in a way normative behavior for a professional or executive to complain about the burden of work and responsibility. The job, however, may be the very thing that is preserving these individuals. In a way they derive their identity from their jobs; they are their jobs. The concept of the job as a "social corset" holding the personality together is quite apt here.[21]

This means that the middle and lower upper classes tend to channel their anxiety to work and succeed into their career goals. "Their worrying has practically become a way of life."

To get at the economic factor, Leavy and Freedman analyzed 500 case studies of patients in a psychiatric dispensary and in private psychiatric hospitals. They wanted to know what were the possible psychological effects of economic life upon individuals. They studied case records to gauge economic insecurity, and relationship to work and competition. Although it was hard to clearly separate these factors, it seemed to them that economic insecurity could provide the necessary environmental conditions that made anxiety almost certain to occur. When work becomes interfered with, another set of anxieties develops, owing to the importance of work and the condemnation of idleness in the success ethic. Patients reported that when their work was interfered with because of their neurotic symptoms, their self-respect and self-esteem were shaken. In some cases work turned out to be a neurotic escape.[22]

The organized imperatives of work tended to contain the neurotic tendencies. Managers and executives could relieve their aggressions through the various administrative mechanisms of authority, control, competition, and high corporate goal-setting and achieving. Leavy and Freedman found that competition and struggle were central forces in many neurotic individuals. Feelings of hostility were liberated by either success or failure. In still others the neurotic drive for success was an extension of unresolved conflicts dating back to childhood.

One of the most precise explanations of why middle-class people are more susceptible to neuroses is provided by Arnold W. Green.[23] In the study of lower-class Polish groups, parents used physical punishment for control and discipline, but the children could escape total parental tyranny by judging their parents in cold, harsh tones, and picking models other than their own parents. The core of the self was not injured as much as the posterior end of the body. The advantage to the lower classes was the opportunity to identify with the pervasive middle-class culture.

The middle classes became absorbed by their own values. Hence there was no escape outlet. Middle-class parents controlled and disciplined by a physical and emotional blanketing of the child, bringing about slavish dependence upon parents. The child was encouraged to accept as supremely important the need for love. The withdrawal of love, in contrast to physical punishment used by the lower classes, was a continued threat to the child who failed to live up to parental norms. Green saw that love was at once the goal of the family and the means of disciplining the child.

Green observed that middle-class parents were usually ambivalent toward their own families as indicated by their planned fertility rates. The achievement of success goals interfered with responsibilities to children. As part of the child's heritage this ambivalence was passed on to the child. His lowered estimates of self-importance encouraged dependency toward parents and counter dependency toward peer groups. These conflicting pressures and counter claims prescribed the necessary ingredients of anxiety, and the development of neurotic symptoms.

Regardless of the validity of Green's interpretation, there are few studies that do not fail to offer it support. Fromm and May contend that neuroses of the anxiety type are predominantly middle-class property. After studying the available data, Leonard Reissman concluded that neuroses and neurotic conflict are still the hallmark of the middle class and perhaps the upper class as well. "What the studies of mental illness have substantially proven was that neurotic conflict does not usually become intense enough to lead to severe psychotic disturbances, that the middle and upper class person has learned to live with his neurosis and to mobilize it for his own purposes toward socially legitimate goals."[24]

We have seen that the intensity of the success ethic seems strongest among the middle classes. The search for success through achievement, and the acquisition of status, prestige, money, and power necessarily pits the individual against others, owing to the relative difficulty of acquiring these highly sought-after values. Whether one fails or succeeds, the condition of mild anxiety is alway present. One of the most complete psychiatric examinations of a community found that "climbers" who appeared to move upward rather steadily exhibited reactions of severe anxiety, depression, anti-sociability, and sometimes suicidal tendencies when their careers were seemingly blocked. The "strivers" with high ambition but slow upward mobility were "defensive" and tended to be dreamers or schemers, or resorted to job-hopping, each time hoping to get a better deal elsewhere.[25]

Mobility upward brings anxiety in its own right. As Reissman shows, for some period of time an upwardly mobile person is in a marginal social position. "The individual's former friends and associates may find him threatening; his success is a mark of their failure. His newly created friends and associates produced by his successful achievements may find him too 'different,' too 'raw,' and too recent to be accepted as a bona fide member."[26] The individual, suspended in a success limbo, and momentarily meaningfully unattached, may feel a deep hostility and anxiety every bit as intense as his counterpart, the failure.

In the midtown Manhattan study it was found that the upwardly mobile are more likely to be neurotic than those who remain in the same class as their fathers, and the downwardly mobile are more likely to incur various forms of psychoses. The upwardly mobile are more apt to be incipiently neurotic: they cannot sit, always feel restless, are troubled with sleep, their hands feel damp or tremble often, etc. Anxiousness and expectation without direction or objective is their predominant emotional pattern. The downwardly mobile are more prone to probable psychosis, alcoholism, depression, rigidity, and suspiciousness.

These data show the possibilities of impaired mental health as a consequence of mobility downward, and increased anxiety levels tending toward neuroticism as a consequence of upward mobility. Or the reverse might be true. Psychotic trends may produce downward mobility, and neurotic trends upward mobility.[27] Whatever is the case, success and failure and mental disturbances are closely interrelated.

THE ANXIOUS EXECUTIVE

The risks of success and failure are inescapable, particularly for the middle classes. We have seen the importance of mobility opportunity. The reality of mobility and the concomitants of glory, power, status, and prestige sustain the success ethic which, in turn, largely sustains the mobility rates. The strong motivations of advancing and securing the values of the success ethic relate directly to the corporate system. Sizable numbers of those who tower over our national economy are sons of businessmen, and many are sons of upper lower-class workers.

As W. Lloyd Warner remarks, "When men from the bottom are able to prepare themselves for advancement, the more competent among all men are most likely to be selected."[28] He suggests that "the increase in the number and importance of the giant corporations is directly related to the advance of men from the lower levels to top positions in management." However, the mobility rate of the extreme lower class is not so great as to make this much of a contribution to enlarging the manpower base from which future executives are selected. His point has some relevance to the upper lower classes and lower middle classes, however.

For the most part, the middle classes and the upper lower classes are the spawning bed of big business executives. Yet these classes have the highest incidence of anxiety and neurosis. The question is whether the executive carries high levels of anxiety. The evidence so far presented would logically support the conclusion.

As a group, executives are good representatives of the middle-class hallmark of success anxiety. In an extensive study of over 200 managers, Ephraim Rosen found that executives show marked defensiveness, strong control, relative lack of insight into themselves and their emotions, and considerable use of denial and repression mechanisms. These traits hang together in the following way: First, the typical executive is very ambitious for personal growth and achievement. He values competition very highly. He gives a moral equivalent to being ruthless with colleagues by equating the results he achieves with corporate goal achievement. This belief in competition serves to justify any acts the executive might regard as unfair or immoral. In reality, the function of competition as a spur to corporate growth is really a facade behind which lies his guilt-bearing competitive drive. He is ruthless in his striving to get ahead, but to avoid the middle-class stigma of ruthlessness, he keeps himself in tight rein. He tends to deny his ruthless tendencies by repressing them under the rubric of strength of character, or of company loyalty. "While insisting that he does not wish to hurt any one, he will at the same time point with a certain satisfaction to other people who are 'really tough.' "[29]

Control of his aggressions shows up in the tendency to inhibit because to do otherwise would hurt his chances of advancement or violate the norm of emotional stability. Control may be seen in his work patterns. He likes his work, values it for its own sake, and controls any tendency to let go and really enjoy himself. Rosen's picture of the executive makes him out to be well-fitted to compulsively strive for achievement, status, advancement, and popularity in his organization.

There are three classifications of executives in Rosen's study: sales managers, production managers, and scientific research personnel. Rosen reports that sales managers are the most free of neurotic trends, production managers less free, while the research group is even less so. In a classification of these findings the executives with greater increases in status over a fixed period of time seemed to have more drive, enthusiasm, and action-oriented qualities. In other words, they had more aggressions but not of the personal kind. Rather, their aggressiveness was effectively channeled and controlled by acceptance of the prevailing standards of business conduct. The less successful executives seemed to have either less control of their aggressive tendencies or stronger amounts of them.[30]

The success ethic is a major factor in executive personality. It is well-controlled and put in service of rational corporate pursuits. Any anxiety that erupts from occasional conflict between what the executive must do to get ahead and his moral dictates of conscience is repressed, driven back into the unconscious. But anxiety is not the less operative simply because it is repressed. This is where the executive is emotionally fragile, and why he is vulnerable to certain neurotic symptoms as are many others in the middle classes. Rosen reports, "There is something shallow or brittle in his adjustment to life—a lack of solidarity that may lead to breakdown."[31]

His anxieties may erupt to give him momentary loss of control—just enough at the right time to harm his opportunities and advantages. Furthermore, the executive's emphasis on conformity and on how he is evaluated by others (other-directedness) seems to suggest more fragility than appears on the surface. An unexpected crisis may produce loss of control patterns resulting in alcoholism, extreme irritability, or delusionary feelings of persecution. Rosen suggests that when the individual's crisis involves loss of emotional ties to corporations or family or both, "it may become apparent that he has no real self to fall back upon, with the result that he is left floundering in a state of turmoil."

Rosen continues with the interpretation that underneath the optimism, confidence, and willingness to sacrifice for the sake of corporation and self, typically there is a deep fear of failure. "The executive strives for success to assure himself and others that he is not a failure."[32] Like everyone else, the executive strongly seeks success and equally fears failure.

This matrix of emotional opposites supplies vast amounts of neurotic energy. He is driven to achieve both for the inherent sake of it and to avoid failure. The rationalization that competition is organizationally functional in order to control and absorb aggressive tendencies is not a sufficiently dependable basis for an enduring way of life. "A real failure, a strong threat or series of threats of failure, or disappointments with such success as has been achieved, may expose the executive's negative motivation and bring home to him the inadequacy of his roles and values."[33] When this happens a neurosis is well along the way toward precipitating a crisis.

Burleigh Gardner studied 473 executives from fourteen firms in several different industries. He found similar results. He gave particular emphasis to the strong drive to succeed via achievement, mobility, and status. With this drive there is a strong need to overcome a sense of frustration. "Successful executives have a pervasive fear of failure. . . . In spite of their strength of character and their drive to activity, they also show a rather pervasive feeling that they may not really succeed and be able to do the things they want."[34]

What happens when these successful executives face an arrestment of opportunity to achieve and move up? Gardner reports that the most common ailment among unsuccessful executives is a deep and abiding depression, common because many of these men believe that they are not as productive, or admirable, or worthwhile as they should be. "The unsuccessful executives are to a large extent so sensitive to their real or imaginary shortcomings that their sensitiveness approaches a paranoidal conclusion that they can not possibly succeed."[35]

Much the same pattern of a strong drive to achieve, compete, and move upward comes out of the findings by both Henry and Warner. The big business executive has a deep push-pull within his personality. In describing the personality profile of the executive, Warner and Abegglen report these seemingly incompatible reactions: The successful executive has a positive feeling toward other men. He likes them, does not feel personally competitive toward them, and makes solid efforts to cooperate. "However, and this counter-current seems strong (he) does not really trust other men, for he believes that if he places reliance upon them they will or at least are likely to let him down." While having to share work at times, he "does not believe basically that this cooperative arrangement will work out, for he sees other men as unreliable. Therefore, he believes he must fall back on his own resources and make his own way unaided."[36]

This description suggests that when held in constraint these external incompatibilities could provide for a high degree of autonomy. Committed to the general goals and patterns of the organization, the executive would in their name cooperate sufficiently and still utilize his resources of self to remain a dynamic center of independence. However, what all this seems to say is that most executives have this affirmation-distrust pattern. If most substantially do, the problems of cooperation may be as severe as those of competition.

What is to prevent an eruption of latent distrust toward or by a few strategically located power figures? What will the executive do who has more than ideal amounts of distrust? It is clear that the success ethic holds no fewer terrors for executives than for the middle classes in general from which executives often come. Henry pointedly refers to the stress and strain of executive life. "The large percentage of failures among fancy-titled, high paid corporation executives is not due to breakdown of skill, it is due to breakdown of personality."[37]

Lower-Class Anxiety Potential

Failure may also be due to inadequate personality. Men from the lower classes who seek to become executives incur certain difficulties that are largely related to their class and family structures. Although anxiety is related to all classes, the particular form of symptoms varies with the class structure. The typical individual coming from the lower classes seems to lack sufficient impulse control that the middle classes insist upon.

The middle-class person tends to repress overtly aggressive drives. This gives rise to obsessional behavior and repetition compulsion. This classical middle-class reaction to anxiety manifests itself in undue need for punctuality, orderliness, and perfectionism. These reactions have high payoff values in the large, organized business system. These anxiety reactions stem from a civilizing or taming of the aggressive tendencies.

The middle-class child is first trained to oral combat with and against parents. The lower-class child is prohibited from combating with parents and thus has learned to release the aggressive drives in more primitive ways, usually physically against others outside the home. He has acquired the goals of success but has not learned to so sublimate the aggressions as to allow early and rapid achievement of the success goals. He is often quite obnoxious, authority resistant, and quick to lash out at restraining objects. He is more apt to act out his aggression and to blame the "system" than to accept the reality and deprivations of moving ahead. In contrast, the middle-class person seems more capable of "acting in" his destructive aggressions.

When lower-class individuals set goals too high without sufficient control of the aggression impulses, they incur the risk of acute failure, frustration, and self-rejection. When, by luck or otherwise, they move up much faster than they had anticipated, they incur the risk of conflict over values—problems of acting in conformity to alien beliefs and practices. Lower-class individuals who move up incur substantially more risk of mental health impairment than if they had stayed contented at their father's level.

Several studies show that this lower-class individual is more apt to have unsuccessfully internalized the rules of the game of the middle-class success ethic (weak conscience), to have a weak capacity to control or tolerate frustration, to bear a distrustful and suspicious orientation toward poor interpersonal relationships, to have strong feelings of inferiority, low self-esteem, and to have a tendency to act out problems with violent expressions of hostility and extrapunitive tendencies.[38]

The study of New Haven shows that the lower-class individual tends to have a deep-seated distrust of authority figures. "Suspicion is directed toward police, clergymen, teachers, doctors, public officials, public health nurses, and social workers."[39] Hostility against authority figures is linked to the feeling that he is being exploited. He also shows a similar hostility toward organizations.

Relatively few people in the lower classes who suffer anxiety belong to organized groups outside of work and the home. They have a conviction that people will not work together, and that the benefits of organization accrue to those who "have." In contrast, the studies of successful executives show conclusively the necessity of believing in the usefulness and necessity of authority and organization.

The anti-authority and organization tendencies force the lower-class individual to fall back completely upon self. The widespread belief among the lower classes is that every man has to "rely upon number one" and "trust to luck and your common sense." No doubt this rebelliousness toward authority and organization causes some to build their own little kingdoms. In a study of 100 entrepreneurs who went into business for themselves, massive quantities of anti-authority organization drives were found.[40]

It was found that the vast majority of these entrepreneurs came from lower-class families, which prepared them for low social and hierarchical drives. Believing authority to be essentially exploitative and organization to be essentially restrictive and inhibiting, these lower-class individuals found within themselves the necessary courage to set up their own businesses and become their own bosses and contrivers of organizational claims and purposes. Needless to say, not all in the lower classes have the necessary inner resources to successfully defy authority and organization by entrepreneurial activities. Many eventually become passively dependent or act out their aggressions in less productive forms.

Success anxiety for the individual coming from the lower classes is different from that of the individual coming from the middle classes. The latter has more completely embraced both the goals and means of the success ethic and mobility does not incur as much risk of mental disturbances.

We may speculate that without a firm sense of identity, sufficient amounts of self-esteem, adequate control of the aggressions, and a strong conscience the opportunities to move upward into the refined activities of top administration are fewer and carry greater amounts of anxiety potential. This set of factors may largely account for why more and more of the top executives come from middle-class backgrounds. They have more properly integrated the values of the success ethic and received the achievement payoffs for which the success ethic was originally devised and accepted in our culture.

One point seems clear. The middle-class success ethic has been sufficiently internalized in the personalities of most big business executives to auger a life filled with potential triumph and terror. The big business executive is near the top of the success ladder. He has accomplished more than many, if not most. His salary is in the highest income bracket. His prestige, status, and role are well-respected and highly sought after. Many would believe that he has been well blessed when measured by the success values of contemporary society. But to him, he may be still a failure or without the entire trappings of success. Each new round of success may only bring additional fears of failure. The energy from these emotional states, redirected back into his career pattern, may assure continued successes and mobility. He may vigorously drive on, submerging self in work without play.

This description of the executive suggests that achievement, properly conditioned by the realistic requirements of authority and organization, promotes the basis of self-development. The self can become a dynamic center of influence and change only when it is committed to the necessary minimal identifications to the responsibilities of the administrative role. The urge of the executive to become a dynamic center of influence and change stems from his drive to achieve.

However, his level of success anxiety today is quite high. Anxiety may be a force as constructive to his career as the success drive itself. Signals of impending danger to his administrative career may serve to sharpen his awareness, prepare for application of effective skills and solutions, and generally enlist the necessary reserves of the self to eliminate the causes of difficulty and restore the executive to the relaxed state of successful accomplishment.

When the executive feels an abnormally high level of chronic success anxiety, a signal of impending danger may cue off unproductive attempts to resolve difficulties. These ineffective solutions in turn become anxiety-producing. The danger to self from the anxiety created by unproductive solutions may be far greater than the potential danger of the original administrative situation.

A high level of chronic perpetual success anxiety may indirectly become a destructive force increasing the career crisis rather than lessening it. The executive may cease to be a dynamic center of influence and change; the administrative function may cease to be the creative innovative force for shaping and reshaping the goals and strategy of the overall corporation. The function of authority may cease to be the rational ratification and legitimization of realistic corporate goals and strategy and become directly the means for the allaying of anxiety and resolution of intrapsychic conflict. (See the cases of Neal and Norman in Chapter VIII.)

When authority and goal-setting achievement activities serve the need of neurotic success anxiety, the corporation's integrity and welfare may become gravely jeopardized. In this way we may see how the inability to tolerate or master success anxiety may have drastic repercussions to the firm, the economy, and society in general.

Mark Whiting: A Recapitulation

In conclusion, the executive today is regarded by many as the success ethic personified. To the members of his community, his trade association, and his family, Mark Whiting was a splendid example of success. He made a six-figure salary and had access to an impressive variety of privileges and advantages. Although he appeared big and powerful to others, inwardly he felt dismally small and weak.

For many years he had felt apprehensive, as though there was an impending threat to his central concern, career success. He developed a high level of chronic anxiety that broke out occasionally in the form of specific fears. These fears included fear of being wrong, of not being thorough enough, of not having all the facts, or not being efficient. The most disturbing fear was that of having his work invalidated by his superiors. Of course, he pretended not to fear his superiors' rejection of his achievements, much as a child will pretend to be brave about something he fears.

As marketing vice-president he set goals for the firm that were the direct result of his need to be powerful and important. The program he submitted to the board of directors on the long-range direction and character of the Universal Chemical Company did not come from his vital concern for the corporation. It came from his own self-defined needs for success at all costs.

His attack on the president was not relevant to the situation. The whole force of his previous difficulties with superiors came to bear upon the argument. He was oblivious to the president's right to determine who was to operate in all the vital areas of his administration. Whiting's hostility and aggression increased rather than lessened his developing career crisis. His vindictiveness and fear of reprisal from the president brought the unproductive solution of attempting to overthrow the president and capture the office through a "palace revolt." The attempt failed, and his problems were multiplied. The president countered by the selection of Mr. Gray, thus putting Mark Whiting "in his place." With Gray ensconced in the corporation, Whiting thought he could bull his way onto the new executive team by demanding recognition as a very important person. He privately believed that he was indispensable.

Out of this conviction he unleashed a verbal onslaught on the new president. His treatise on the inseparability of marketing and sales was a case in point. This indiscriminate onslaught, which eventually encroached upon the role of the new members of the executive team, caused Gray to feel that Whiting was "sick" and could not be trusted in a sensitive area.

Whiting next made another unproductive solution that increased rather than allayed his anxiety. After a while, Whiting attempted to make peace with Gray by becoming his friend and supporter. He seemed to operate on the maxim, "If you can't beat him, join him." Gray saw the intent of this maneuver but allowed the relationship to develop. Although they went to cocktails and lunch twice a week, Gray never gave Whiting a sensitive administrative post on his team. Feeling all the more frustrated, Whiting's hatred of the old president was transferred to Gray to vie with his need for Gray's affection and emotional support.

In Mark Whiting's career crisis we can note how one unproductive solution led to another. Whiting got in deeper and deeper, seemingly without corrective measures to first stabilize and then reverse his career crisis. Anxiety has the capacity to narrow one's set of alternative solutions to problems. Decisions become faulty, which in turn increases anxiety, which in turn may force upon the executive an even narrower base of alternatives. If he does not get professional help he may be responding to problems without regard to any of their objective characteristics. Men in career crisis experience anxiety that may tyrannize the thought processes and put them under the total domination of the emotions. At such times, anxiety and administrative success may become antithetical.

IV

Administrative Anxiety

For Mark Whiting, the dynamic basis of success anxiety was the threat of becoming separated from the central administrative process of his firm. The executive group at the top that administers the overall long-range goals of the corporation is an exclusive group. It is composed of a relatively few individuals representing in their collective backgrounds the basic functions of the corporation: finance, personnel, production, marketing, research, and planning.

Because most of them have come up through these lower operating divisions, they have some difficulty in abstracting themselves from their prior operating activities and responsibilities. Entrance into the arrival stage and later into the executive committee always involves some degree of stress. This stress may activate anxiety that inhibits and precludes effective performance. How administrative anxiety may escalate into a career crisis will be carefully studied.

SEPARATION ANXIETY

To understand the psychological pressures of the executive we must explore fully the conditions of *separation anxiety*. The anxieties appearing in adulthood repeat the symptoms that appeared in adolescence. The latter reactivates the pattern of anxiety of approximately the first five years of life. The anxiety which serves as the prototype to the administrative variety is caused by threats to values held central to the self. The earliest and most enduring value internalized by the child is that of being attached to the sources and objects of nourishment and love.

Otto Rank believed that birth is the foremost event in this process, with the separation of the child from the mother.[1] This experience of separation occurs again in greater or lesser degrees when the child is weaned, toilet trained, enters school; and when, as an adult, he gets married, finds a job, or gets a promotion. It occurs at all steps in personality development.

The counterpart to separation is *attachment*. At each of these stages of separation the problem of attachment is more or less present. The child leaves for school and becomes attached to a wider circle of acquaintances and friends. The youth enters adolescence and becomes attached to the all powerful peer-group. The adolescent enters college and becomes attached to social entities, such as fraternities and dormitory groups, classes, and informal groups of all kinds. The college graduate beginning a career becomes attached to various work groups and their objectives and values. Life is a constant process of leaving and arriving.

The executive life is essentially one of going and coming. As Warner puts it, "Going to is away from." The movement upward in the corporation is a continual process of arriving, departing, and arriving. At each level the developing executive must disengage from a previous role, acquire a new role, and disengage again. In this going toward and moving away, the engineering of role validation and commitment involves a capacity to contain the anxiety that emerges in the transitional phases. Warner and Abegglen write, "The mobile man is that person who is able successfully to initiate and sustain this complex interwoven series of changes." Because he must learn, rapidly and thoroughly, the new behavior in each new situation, he must be able "to tolerate uprooting himself and to make use of or create the opportunities to move to a new position."[2] He must be able to leave the past, move into the present, and prepare for the future.

Warner and Abegglen feel that the process of separating and

attaching pivots on the figure of the mother. Among mobile executives, the mother is the person "who has trained them, who provides them with a sense of a larger and different world from the one in which they live, and who is the close and stable figure in the family." However, the mobile executive has emotionally left home. The most common element that shows up in successful executives is that their deep emotional identifications with family have been dissolved. "They are people who have literally and spiritually left home."[3]

But the executive's separation from past family identifications does not involve hostility and apathy. Henry feels particularly strong on this point. "It seems to be most crucial that he has not retained resentment of his parents, but has rather simply broken their emotional hold on him and been left psychologically free to make his own decisions."[4] Those who have retained this tie are resentful of authority and fail to engineer role validation, that is, they fail to relate properly to established authority and organizational values and requirements. Others who have retained family ties fail to engineer role commitment, that is, they fail to exert independent notions of self and achieve validation by the group. The one is overly independent, the other overly dependent.

The tie to the father should remain positive in the sense that the individual views the father as a helpful, but not restraining figure. This positive tie allows for self notions of masculinity and strength, without which success seems difficult. The tie that is most often broken, according to Henry, is the relationship to the mother. The reason is that the dependency upon the mother image seems contradictory to the necessary attitude of activity, progress, and channelized aggression. However, a moderate mother attachment may allow for the utilization of the energy and the emotions in the service of group and company objectives and goals. Both ties to mother and father figures, however, must to some extent be broken and a positive, affective residue must remain.

The *leaving home* process sets a pattern of relations with authority figures and organizations that is necessary for success. The mobile executives can become attached to authority figures and clearly disengage when this is prescribed by their career demands. With peers they are able to make close emotional ties while keeping sufficiently aloof. They can break these ties and move on to establish new ties without feelings of anxiety. We know clinically the problems of executives who cannot separate and attach, or who feel abnormal anxiety when they are forced to move against their private wishes and fears. The studies of executive personality clearly place the process of separation from parent and family as the crucial element in achievement, mobility, and success.

In Mark Whiting's case, his gross distrust of authority figures was apparent. His problems with authority, stemming from the original authority figure, his father, were never resolved. Because he did not view his father as a helpful, fair, and sincere individual, Whiting was emotionally crippled for his administrative role. It is safe to say that he learned very little from his superiors. Whiting's relationship to his mother, however, was sufficiently positive to enable him to feel comfortable in organizations and to find a useful role. In this respect Whiting exemplifies to some extent the profile of the successful executive pictured by Warner and Abegglen.

ARRIVING IS DEPARTING

The making of an executive occurs within an array of successful separations and attachments. Movement within the ranks of the corporate hierarchy necessarily involves the capacity to become emotionally attached to the authority figures and corporate goals found in the particular work situation. Movement up requires the capacity to detach from previous managerial activities and attach to new conditions. For aspiring junior executives there is a consistent, inward-directing force that guides their upward advance. This inner force allows for the easy separation from present activities and the creation of productive attachments to new assignments. He welcomes these changes because of the intense desire to achieve. For the upwardly mobile, achievement is centered in striving to get closer and closer to the heart of the administrative process. The central values and goals of the firm are represented by the activities of the executive group. This group is charged with the responsibility of charting the overall and long-range direction of the firm and administering these strategies through organization. Success is measured by steady progress toward the central administrative processes symbolized by line and staff people in the executive group.

Because the mobile executive has a need to achieve larger and larger administrative challenges, arrestment of this upward mobility is interpreted as a threat to the opportunity to realize the potentialities of the self. Anxiety, or feelings of inadequacy or incapability, is caused by arrestment of mobility. Evidence gathered from counselling of mobile executives shows that the dynamic basis of anxiety is the threat of becoming separated from the central administrative tasks of the firm. Administrative anxiety is also the fear that one cannot successfully remove the blocks that have been thrown before the upward-striving manager. Administrative anxiety also marks the president who has arrived at the top but who senses a growing threat to his remaining there.

Executives who face separation from the central administrative tasks of the firm, and junior executives who incur arrestment of movement toward those central tasks, feel the essential elements of a career crisis. A career crisis is a crisis of self. Invariably it involves a narrowing of awareness to basically include problems of authority, organizational goals and performance, and self. Administrative anxiety is normal to all those who rise within corporate structures. Whenever there is a separation and a new attachment, there is a degree of anxiety which is most likely to occur at three basic points.

First is the anxiety of entrance into the firm. Entrance anxiety ensues from having to make separation from college life and the unstable commitments of early adulthood. The attachment to the firm is generally made in a technical sense. This entrance phase, lasting about five years, usually places the individual in a formal or informal training program. If he has secured no technical skill in college, he may acquire it in the entrance phase. His attachments are basically those of one who is or becomes technically qualified in accounting, engineering, sales, personnel, or some other functional activity.

The second point is anxiety of movement into the middle ranks, which requires dropping such technical attachments and acquiring managerial ones. Since the middle ranks are essentially managerial, the technical skills remain with subordinates. The manager is required to know how to direct them to accomplish departmental and sectional goals. Accountants, salesmen, engineers, and scientists too often want to keep their technical expertise. They become anxious at making the required separations and attachments.

The third point of anxiety involves meeting the requirements of administration as opposed to management. Activity in the middle and upper-middle ranks is essentially operational. It is concerned with the setting of specific sub-organizational goals within the confines of overall policy directives from above. Activity at the top is concerned with developing overall corporate strategy and designing organized structures to achieve the goals and purposes of the firm. It concerns appraising and evaluating corporate achievement. Here the operating orientation of the manager must be left behind and the strategical, evaluative, long-range concern of administration must be acquired. Separation from the former orientation and attachment to the administrative orientation proves difficult for many.[5]

Different ideas concerning authority, different orientations toward the corporation, and different images of self are involved in all three of these transitions. The capacity to separate and attach without incurring acute feelings of anxiety is crucial to the making of a corporate executive.[6]

OTTO RANK AND ANXIETY

Otto Rank defines anxiety as the apprehension that develops from acts of separation. There are basically two focuses of anxiety: life and death. The fear of life is basically the fear of having to become an individual, autonomous and hence, isolated. The death fear is anxiety about losing individuality. Rank believes that such anxieties occur when the individual feels the emergence of creative capacities within himself which call for the establishment of new relationships to people and things. These creative opportunities bring the threat of separation from previous forms of relationships. While life fear is anxiety at going "forward," death fear is anxiety at going "backward." The individual alternates between these two poles of fear all of his life.

The healthy, creative individual can manage his anxieties by affirming his individual capacities in progressive union with the group. This idea is affirmed in the executive mobility studies of Warner and Henry. Also present in their portraits of unsuccessful executives are the neurotic bearing tendencies ensuing from imbalanced anxiety. Anxiety in the face of autonomy prevents positive affirmation of one's own capacities. Anxiety in the face of dependency renders one incapable of giving self adequately to cooperative effort. Feelings of inadequacy, fear of responsibility, and guilt identify the immobile unsuccessful executive.

Otto Rank believes that the original anxiety out of which subsequent anxieties take form is the trauma of birth. He held that the child experienced his first feelings of fear in the act of birth, which constituted separation from the symbiotic relationship with the mother. Freud took vigorous issue with Rank, believing that awareness is prerequisite to feelings of anxiety and the infant at birth lacks necessary awareness.[7] He saw the origin of anxiety as the threat of being separated from the mother object.

It has become generally accepted that separation anxiety originates in the early phase of psychological development when the infant perceives an increasing number of discrepancies between his needs and their gratification. The infant links the gratification of his needs with the presence of discernible attendants. Then, given the absence of attendants, the infant shows signs of extreme uneasiness, which disappear only in the presence of the returned attendants.[8]

The condition of anxiety that contributes to feelings of helplessness relates back to that period when the infant is aware of being left alone but is not capable of effectively doing something about it. Feelings of helplessness automatically erupt when the child fails to perceive the presence of attendants. He wants his parents around at all times, and when he is able to walk he tries never to let them out of sight or hearing. One motive to walk may be the need to keep his parents in sight.

These parental figures, particularly the mother, become powerful sources of gratification. Protection from helplessness becomes linked to these figures; they assume omnipotent qualities. They can restore the conditions of gratification, overcome helplessness, and assure feelings of attachment. The pangs of separation arouse needs of attachment. The first crisis of the infant, the feelings of being separated, serves as the backdrop to the second crisis.

Upon occasion, the attendants find it necessary to restrict the child's free uninhibited expression of impulse. The objective in mind is to prepare the child for organized living. The basic mechanism in the middle-class family to assure adequate preparation for organized living is the laying down of a series of restrictions and taboos, enforced by the threat of withdrawal of presence and love. The special or personalized skills of parents are many and varied, but the essential objective is to secure conformity. Here the child must separate himself from previous habits of extreme selfishness and attach himself to patterns of belief and behavior that are family-directed rather than individual.

This transition from self to family orientation is assured by the recurrence of anxiety that is rooted in feelings of helplessness and isolation. He exchanges a part of his egoism for membership in the family and the objective that this involves. In exchange for this "giving up" the child is reassured that he is not alone or helpless. This process of exchange reinforces all the more both the need to feel secure and attached and the discomfort and anxiety of separation and individuality.

A third crisis develops when the child learns, through extra-familial associations, through parental statements, and through simple observation, that his attendants may not be forever capable of caring for his wants in exchange for deference and submission. Parents are seen as less omnipotent—they can die, fall sick, or show fears. These fears and anxieties of parents are transmitted directly and unconsciously to the child.

This awareness of the human limitation of parents signals the danger previously experienced as helplessness. The studies of the child psychologist Jean Piaget show that previous to this phase the child believes that it is his parents' world in which he lives, made and constructed by them for their gratification and, therefore, his.[9] It is a severe jolt to learn that the parent inhabits a world that is irregular and unpredictable in nature. Pierre Bovet, for example, refers to the case of the child who was staggered to find his supposedly all-powerful father sobbing over the spectacle of the fruit orchard ravaged by a violent storm.[10]

During periods of economic diversity, unexpected social changes, or cultural ambiguity, the child becomes aware of the possibility that there are stronger forces than parents. Because of his need to fend off his fear of separation, the child seeks to know who has authority over his parents and, thus, himself. He does not yet know that no one can control the universe. It still seems orderly and organized, and the question is how does one propitiate these super-authorities. Depending upon the family belief and faith, these super-authorities may become deities, heroes, presidents, teachers, leaders, and other fathers. Perhaps the continuation of all of these is at some time involved in the child's growing awareness of life outside the family.

The belief that parents control the universe and society is impressed upon the child's awareness and, more or less, introjected to become his own belief system. There are few adults who do not have degrees of awareness about authority and the organization basis of society and the universe.

The Primitive Mind of the Executive

De Grazia's review of parental belief systems is interesting at this point.[11] Studies of political belief systems show that adult subjects through the ages have endowed their kings or tribal chiefs with a special capacity to control those aspects of the environment most important for the continued existence of the political community. Political authority tends to accumulate in the hands of those who are believed to have outstanding skill in the most hazardous and threatening elements of running the community.

De Grazia notes that success in extracting nutriment from the peculiar conditions of land, sea, and air, be it called manna, as in Polynesia, iddhi as in India, or wakan, manitow, or arenda as in Indian North America, is the supernatural quality of kings. "Babylonians looked to their kings for abundance, Fiji looked to their kings for food and prosperity, Polynesians looked to their kings for peace and prosperity. Homeric mythology held kings responsible for food supply. The Burgundians held their king responsible for the fortunes of war."[12]

De Grazia points out that the responsibility for crops and prosperity in the Roman Empire became especially attached to the emperor. The triumphant return of Augustus was celebrated as the return of prosperity. What is important is that the rights of authority are intimately connected with power over the crucial forces that affect orderly life and threaten to disrupt such organization.

Today our leaders are thought to have this power to authorize the dissolution of forces threatening organized living. When disorder develops, with chaos replacing organization, someone usually is called to account. In most cases it is the leader, ruler, or some super-being.

During this third crisis of threatened separation, the child must behave in ways designed to obtain expressions of approval from figures that are heirs to his parental figures. He acquires an elementary awareness of authority figures in religion, government, business, and school. These authority figures carry the attributes of parental figures with much of the omnipotence once attributed to them.

The child is instructed to obey policemen, ministers, judges, and bosses. His previously acquired pattern of conformity to parents is partially transferred to these surrogates. Conformity brings assurance against feelings of helplessness. "By behaving properly and affectionately toward them, the child can become a member of a bigger family, the larger community; he knows that he will always be provided for; he need no longer be anxious."[13]

When parents transmit through their reactions to this larger community and extra-familial authority figures feelings of attachment and confidence, the child acquires a similar disposition. A foundation may be built against dangerous feelings of anxiety in order for the child to proceed to higher forms of separation and attachment. Without the confidence that society is an orderly affair and authority figures a responsible group, the child grows up severely handicapped in making the necessary separations and necessary attachments to organization and authority figures.

Thus, belief in the positive and necessary role of authority and the potential benevolence of organized activity serves as a protection against the anxiety of separation. These primitive or childlike beliefs in the positive values of authority and organization are unconsciously lodged in the mind of the mobile executive. These primitive notions are of decisive importance to the executive's mobility or success pattern. They are emotional anchorages that allow the minimization of separation anxiety as he passes through the mazes of positions, friends, and authorities.

When as a child he failed to receive support and understanding from his parents, the ensuing anxiety stood ready to erupt into a hostile, aggressive style of behavior toward authority figures and organized goals. When the family as an organized unit failed to achieve a stable position in the affairs of the community, the ensuing anxiety may have stood ready to erupt into hostile, aggressive behavior toward all organizations. Or these parental and family-anchored relationships may have bred styles of dependency and passivity which allay the anxieties of separation and attachment in his corporate world.

To the aspiring executive, the business world and specifically the corporation gives him his source of support and gratification, his status and sense of achievement, and his protection against separation anxiety. It receives in return his loyalty, energy, and the devotion prescribed by the authority figures, goals, and values of the corporation.

It is the very organized nature of business corporations and of work that dispels separation anxiety. The commanding sense of authority, its rightful role as a basis of legitimization also dispels separation anxiety. The executive's striving to become a member of the executive group is firmly rooted in the unconscious need to maintain the feelings of attachment and overcome the threat of helplessness that originate in the childhood phases. His drive to achieve is tantamount to affirming the childish notion that rulers are capable of ordering events and forces for the protection and enhancement of corporate life.

The men at the top symbolize this power and wisdom. They are performing the most central acts of human existence: authorizing and controlling. When they do not, they may be replaced and others may rise to these positions. This is what the aspiring executive knows, and this is what he also fears.

It is because authority and control are so central to the administration of corporate existence (family or business) that they become valued by the child and by the executive. Separation from the central administrative process is a threat that signals the same dangerous conditions of helplessness and powerlessness that occurred in infancy and childhood. The need to acquire authority and control begins at the point when the infant first becomes aware of delay discrepancies between his needs and their gratification. As is often said, "The child is father to the man."

THE EMERGENCE OF SELFHOOD

We have thus far accounted for the role of primitive (child-like) notions of authority and organization in the executive personality. Little has been directly said about self. The initial self is forged out of the matrix of family relationships. The struggle for autonomy takes on precise character for the child during the toilet training stage of the development cycle. It is during that phase that discipline and control seem most acute. The child delineates his world as "I" and "you," "me" and "mine." To prepare him for relaxation of ego values and adherence to communal norms, the parent must convey a sense of trust. Erik H. Erickson believes that the infant must come to feel that basic faith in his parents and himself will not be jeopardized by an initiative the child takes that is contrary to family expectation.[14]

As the child becomes aware of the greater power and authority of the parents, he comes to feel ambivalent toward them. He sees the power and authority of the father; sees also how it can be used against him in acts of punishment and control. He sees the great resourcefulness of the mother. The emotional deprivation used to enforce his control may be also threatening. Wanting to be powerful and loved, the child takes into himself parental norms and values as standards of conduct. He gradually becomes regulated from within.

Ideally, he has made the necessary compromises with parents and the requirements of organized family life which enable him to settle down in the years after six or seven to learn the skills and values of school, community, and society. If he has not internalized the parental and familial values sufficiently, he will be uneasy with supra-familial systems of work and play.

The child develops faint but discernible cues from within as to how well he is living up to the mandate provided originally by his parents. That mandate, strongly belonging to middle-class values, is to become somebody in his own right. In the early school years, energy is poured into gaining attention and recognition. Mastery of toys, school skills, and games allow feelings of self-achievement and confidence.

The emerging selfhood carries over into the perilous adolescent period. The child goes through violent internal physiological changes that are disruptive and threatening to his notions of self. Here the parents are once again ambivalently viewed. They may be regarded as old-fashioned squares who intrude in his social affairs. The peer-group becomes an emotional anchorage that oftentimes conflicts with parental wishes and expectations. The adolescent triangle of parents, peer-groups, and self form a conflicting matrix of emotions and sentiments.

The emotional value of the adolescent triangle is qualitatively similar to that of the conflict in early childhood. These two periods of extreme conflict and difficulty, with a transitional period of dormancy in between, allow the child to leave home psychologically. The transportation equipment becomes in turn the peer-group, school, college, and, eventually, career and work.

IDENTITY AND ANXIETY

R. J. Havighurst describes this period of adolescence as becoming an identity in one's own mind.[15] (We have used the term *self* in a fashion similar to identity.) The adolescent boy or girl becomes a young man or woman in the biological sense and learns the appropriate sex role. He learns to get along with age mates and with adults in a manner that is no longer childish. He begins to seek a social philosophy and affiliate with political and social ideologies. He chooses his own friends, clothing, and habits of social intercourse.

Toward the end of the teens, when asked, "What kind of a person would you like to become when you grow up?" he generally desires to be like his parent of the same sex. "He ends this period of adolescence by wishing to be like an imaginary person composed of qualities which are his own choice among desirable human values."

Following the achievement of an identity, Havighurst perceives the next period, age twenty to thirty, as a period in which the young man makes conscious choices in order to become a social identity. "Out of a variety of possibilities, he selects a particular combination which marks him as a unique person." In this period he will emerge from college prepared to take on a job filling the identity he wishes to become. He accepts a marriage partner, takes root in a community, and becomes highly concerned with his immediate personal life. Havighurst calls this stage the "focusing of one's life."

During the ages of thirty to forty the individual collects his energies and thrusts himself into the now very serious job of achieving and gaining valued rewards from occupational success. This is the period of least self-awareness. Doubts about one's self have for the most part been put to rest. The situation is generally stable; few anxieties are felt or apparent. How he presents his self-identity to the business system is illustrated by William Henry. "To the thirty-year olds life seems amazingly simple. It simply demands achievement and accomplishment." They believe that following the lead set them by their more advanced counterparts in business will result in success.

They are oriented to the goals and expectations of others of significance in the corporation.

Henry continues, "These are probably some of the other-directed men (in David Riesman's sense) who respond directly to the pressures characteristic of their immediate social environment and whose sense of identity is highly similar to the formal goals of business organization and of middle-class life in general."[16] Individuals in the thirty to forty age group consult expectations, policies, and precedents set by others than themselves. Expressing no conflict over possible sources of action, they neither debate nor procrastinate. They follow authority figures visibly, uniformly, and methodically. "The thirty-year old's nose is to the grindstone, and he thinks it right and proper that it should be."[17] In short, these men solve the problem of social identity by adopting one from the requirements of business life.

We must add that all the while their inner private notions of self are undergoing a slow transformation as they impinge upon and are impinged upon by their evolving work or career identities. They make instrumental use of their acquired self notions and relate easily to others about them who stand ready to appraise them. Long-run aims and an evaluation of the possibility of their attainment are forged from the integration of their previously acquired notions of self and those emanating from their business roles. A style of life, a pattern of behavior, begins to emerge that is colored predominantly by the values and expectations of the business world. (See Chapter VIII for clarification of life style.)

The forty-year olds see the world as far more complicated. They have by now been burned occasionally by their other-directedness. They see that some authority figures are untrustworthy, that some corporate goals are not worthy of their energies. A period of covert and sometimes overt questioning takes place. A reconsideration of their own inner values and personal desires begins to emerge. Their organizational role and their future possibilities with the corporation are put in juxtaposition to their personal values and goals. Conflict between private notions of self and organizational identity develops. Henry writes, "This frequently takes the form of wondering if they should not have chosen some other occupation, one they propose as more attuned to human values, to the rewards of personal relations."[18]

For those who eventually emerge at the top, this period of conflict of values does not cause them to disavow their earlier goals of administrative venture. Rather, they see these goals in broader perspective and their personal objectives take on greater dimensions. Havighurst remarks that in this period the energies are more directed away from the occupational role. "It is a period of growing interests in civic and cultural study and activity."[19]

This period of self-awareness and critical reappraisal allows for the determination of career pursuits with more attention to their future implications. This criticalness prevents automatic conformity or slavish devotion to immediate ends. This spontaneous reconsideration causes efforts to change various roles acquired in corporate assignments, thus making innovation a direct possibility. Without this questioning, the engineering of consent to perform roles in different and unique fashion would not be as likely to occur. This conflict between the role prescribed by others and the role cast by private notions of self allows maximum contribution to both self and organization. Toward the end of the forties the individual has acquired a distinct style of behavior that stamps him as an important, unique, praiseworthy individual. He is no longer the organization man he once was.

ANXIETY OF THE FORTIES AND FIFTIES

In short, the central challenge of the thirties is to identify with the company so as not to lose all contact with the real self. In the forties the hazard is that of unduly rocking the boat in an effort to reestablish highly personalized values of self. The ability to entertain ambiguity is strongly based upon having fairly well-developed notions of self before entry into the thirties and the serious task of engineering a corporate career. Without these clear notions, the conflicting period of adjustment in the forties at the middle-management levels will exact a heavy toll of anxiety. Severe anxiety brought on by weak feelings of self can lead to neurotic forms of adjustment, including sustained rebelliousness, dependence, or isolation.

The development of identity next faces the test of the fifties. Havighurst calls this the period of striving to maintain position. To him this is the most baffling of the decades of adult life. Success does not come as quickly; expenditure of energy does not bring the decisive payoff. The individual is declining in energy, resourcefulness, and mental acuity, but he does not accept this as realistic. He feels he must exert himself in order to avoid losing ground.[20] What seems to be at work is a gradual retardation of the life style. Energy seems to be increasingly turned away from action to contemplation.

Henry pictures the fifties as the age of contemplation. Men's established identities are submitted to the tests of rationalization and justification. Writes Henry, "The problem encountered by the fifties is that of deriving a rationale and a meaning for their precious experiences. The rationale may be sound, based upon an objective analysis of their previous experience, leading to a guideline to future activity." Thus, notions of self become once again affirmed or re-evaluated and the residue is projected into future courses of action. The individual's identity becomes more firmly rooted in values more highly appreciated from the philosophic evaluation of past experiences.

This rationale of past experiences, however, may be merely a nostalgic reconsideration of successes. "In the latter case, their statements tend to have a ring of unreal and inappropriate finality."[21] The self-identity then remains unchanged and rigidly patterned around the past. The self is merely projected into the future or preserved in the encasement of false self-justification. Living with one's self becomes a matter of upholding past identification. Change is avoided by the idealization of self. The executive's mind appears to be about as uncomplicated as that of the thirty-year old.

The ideal pattern is found in the capacity to entertain a complex view of self that is integrated with realistic approval of past successes and expectation of future rewards. When Warner and others speak of the successful executive as having strong notions of self, it is not suggested that they do not have external conflict. It seems clear from the research that the men at the top get through the anxiety ages of forty to fifty and the insecure upper middle-managerial ranks with a more complicated view of self, its limitations and strengths, and of life in general. The lustre of success is gone, but not its essential challenge to the person. Success becomes more integrated with the total life style of the person. His various roles and achievements outside the firm give a more balanced view of what he is and wishes to become. This is essentially a more complicated view of self and is sustained with minimal anxiety in the more successful executive.

The unsuccessful executive, bogged down in the anxieties of the forties and the middle-managerial ranks, tends to develop neurotic defenses. One such defense is denial, which Rosen reports to be the executive's most common defense mechanism against the anxiety of adjustment to his business career. Denial may be attempted in two ways. First, by denial of the evidence of conflict between private notions of self and those entertained and designed as career instrumentalities. Second, by discounting the hazard of such conflict and, thus, its potential threat to the individual's career. Denial in the latter case may lead to an overly aggressive attempt at success, both to narcotize anxiety and to prove the lack of effect of value conflict upon the course of career development.[22]

In administrative counselling we often see that the source of anxiety may attract great amounts of energy. The executive role becomes feared, and thus actually becomes charged with a higher degree of attractiveness. The frenzied efforts of managers in the upper-middle ranks may be partially accounted for by the denial pattern and the attempt to narcotize by excessive activity.

Two basic patterns among middle managers seem related to patterns of denial. One is the excessive concern with the successes of others. It is commonly known that middle managers practice the encouragement of others to succeed. Praise for good work, aggressive humor, and open razzing keep up a constant pattern of encouragement and support for success. Correlative to encouragement is intimidation. The attempt here is to see value conflict in other managers and executives who are neurotically striving for power. Middle managers seem prone to believe in the themes developed in Whyte's *The Organization Man* and Packard's *The Pyramid Climbers,* because these help to account for their problems. The individual himself cannot be held responsible for conflict between self and his corporate role if others, by their actions, have made the conflict possible. This is intimidation: the projection of one's values into others, thus preserving one's own notions of *self* while ruining the self-esteem of all others.

ANXIETY AND AUTONOMY

The men who frankly confront the value conflicts of the forties and those of the upper-middle levels of management are apt to acquire a stable, realistic appraisal of self, which carries over into a set of reasonable expectations about career and life. Such confrontation of self and role in both past and future tenses prepares the individual for a more constructive approach to any eventual career crisis.

The executive's notions of self become characterized by the kind of relationship he has to authority figures and to the goals and purposes of the organization. This interrelationship exists because of the role of authority and organization in the home, which provides the necessary resources for the development of personalized skills and a style of behavior. Notions of self are never separated from notions of authority and organization. The executive identity grows out of the struggle to fulfill expectations of authority, achieve objective results for the organization, and bring to bear some personal notions of self that achieve realization.

When Warner speaks of the executive as being an autonomous person, he means basically that he has internalized the demands and responsibilities of authority, and the goals and purposes of the corporation.[23] This means that he is morally autonomous in the sense that by his own decisions he can apply the rules of authority and organization. With due regard to the realities of the corporate way of life, he can apply freely and voluntarily relevant notions of the kind of person he is and wants to become. Lending support to the rightfulness of authority and the necessity of organization is a matter of inner choice or freedom.

Riesman also proposes that autonomous persons are those who on the whole are capable of conforming to the behavioral norms of the group, organization, and society and remain free to choose whether to conform or not.[24] In executive language, this essentially means that they are not entirely creatures of corporate circumstances. More precisely, it means that they apply a personalized style to problems of authority and organization and, thus, create the necessary conditions of self-realization and acceptance.

Men of the autonomous type have the capacity to make changes that become legitimatized by authority figures and benefit the corporation as a whole. Instead of feeling separated they feel attached. Rather than feeling helpless they feel a commanding sense of effectiveness and power. They both accept the necessities of authority and organization and effect extension of the latter.

The autonomous executive feels most acutely the advantages of being involved in the central administrative processes of the firm. Naturally, the threat of abrupt, premature separation from these highly valued activities brings conscious self-concern. A career crisis may develop.

A career crisis is basically a crisis of self. The identity of the executive appears to become blocked from further development. Anxiety may be constructive in that it makes the person extremely aware of the contributing conditions. A realistic confrontation of the causes of anxiety is possible if notions of self have not in the past become distorted by the mechanisms of denial or idealization. Idealized or impoverished notions of self may not allow adequate assessment of the causes of the danger. The individual may apply solutions that are aimed directly at allaying the anxiety within rather than attacking the outside causes.

In the case of impoverished, deflated notions of self, the individual may simply accept failure as fate. The threat of separation is in direct proportion to the individual's capacity to appraise reality and find within himself the necessary courage and confidence to alter his administrative behavior.

If in his developing career the executive has played a role that has achieved little validation or little personal commitment, the crisis will be severe and distressing. The individual between the ages of fifty and sixty, with declining energy and awareness, cannot be expected to suddenly learn the difficult feat of engineering validation and commitment from members of the executive group about a role that is foreign to established procedures and expectations. In such a difficulty the temptation is to fall upon the mercy and sympathy of the group. In other words, having no substantial self to fall back upon, the executive falls upon the executive group. Whatever notions of self may have been preserved, they are submerged in the expectations of the group, and become totally lost. The goals of the corporation, as interpreted by the executive group, become completely his, and the rights and privileges of the authority system become the sole basis of his authority.

By his complete submergence in the executive group he attempts to avoid the anxiety of separation. Otto Rank would refer to this pattern as the fear of life, the fear of having to live as an isolated individual. Such a defense against separation anxiety has many of its roots in the failure of self to confront prior anxieties, develop personalized skills, negotiate the crisis, and receive support from significant others on one's own terms.

The forties and the middle-managerial ranks offer the aspiring executive this opportunity. Out of these phases emerge the men referred to by Warner as autonomous persons. They know who they are, where they are going, and how to get there. Warner gives no details on the number of people who get to the top without adequate confrontation with the conflict and complexity of the forties and the middle-management ranks. This fact is not yet known. But we do know a little about the man who does not have the autonomy of which Warner and others speak.

MOBILITY SUCCESS

For many the movement up into the executive group amounts to an emotional transition. Devising corporate strategy, and designing organizational structures and processes to achieve long-range goals calls for distinctly different kinds of emotions than those required in operating a division of the corporation within the constraints determined by top administration. Practically all executives experience some kind of entrance anxiety when they are formally given the more exclusive rights and higher privileges of membership in the executive group. This is the culmination of many years of sacrifice and hope.

In the analysis of executive career crisis patterns, it is this executive group at the top, rather than the presidency, that is more likely to be the most real and tangible object of middle-managerial ambitions. Membership in this exclusive group constitutes one of the most powerful symbols of achievement, status, power, and money. The overriding motive for belonging, however, is found in the opportunity to become intimately involved in the central administrative process of the firm. This is the symbolic value of the executive group.

The activities of the executive group are associated with the total character and direction of the corporation. One can get no closer to the heart of the corporation and to the central challenges of administrative achievement. It is notable in the case history of Mark Whiting how actively he strove to become a member of this exclusive group, and how separation from it was more painful than the loss of the presidency. The power that membership in this group exercises over people both in and out of it cannot be minimized.

The majority of executives have a high need to achieve. The set of drives to acquire money, power, security, and status is secondary. The high achievers at the lower levels show in their career patterns a constant struggle to get closer and closer to the central administrative processes of the firm. At middle-managerial levels this drive to become intimately attached to the central administrative process acquires added energy and direction. Success has been tasted, confidence won, and the dream of triumphant entry into the executive group is no longer distant. For many it has become a reality. Arrestment of upward mobility is tantamount to separation from the central administrative process of the firm. Success and mobility are clearly perceived to be related to achievement.

THE "PULL" OF THE EXECUTIVE GROUP

The executive group holds out great symbolic value for the minority, who are primarily motivated by a drive for power and affiliation. When the executive with a high need for either achievement or power is finally admitted to the executive group, his orientation gradually changes. The opportunity of greater achievement inherent in the presidency may then become the object for many, and the power and status of the presidency the object for some. Whereas failure to be admitted eventually into the executive group is a great source of anxiety for the ambitious middle manager, failure to become president may produce equal anxiety for an established member of the executive group. But the overriding anxiety in both groups is the apprehension of having their movement toward the central administrative process thwarted or blocked. Getting into the executive group and staying attached to the administrative process is the dominant value of both the high achiever and high power driver. In each case, the executive group holds the key to success.

The executive group is composed of a small number of individuals who come together in face to face groupings to determine and fulfill the task of administering the overall long-range activities of the corporation. Frequent interaction within the executive group produces a feeling of sharing and cohesion. The executive identifies with the corporation and the authority system via this group. It becomes an emotional object, charged with values that lie central to the self.

The executive may attempt to guide his conduct in a deliberate effort to maintain membership in the executive group and, at the same time, an acceptable view of himself. This executive is no automaton. The typical executive has strong notions of self that are forged out of the difficult and intimate associations in the middle-management levels. He carries these notions of self, by which he expects to fulfill their promises, into the executive group.

Here he finds two basic problems. He must take a place among others in the executive group. The group has certain expectations about what is appropriate or valid for him in his position. If he develops behavior patterns which the group regards as invalid for him, he is perceived as marginal or alien. The executive tends to adopt initially a role that the group is most likely to validate.

Role validation is only one problem encountered upon entrance into the executive group. A second problem is role commitment. The two roles are complementary. In the latter, the executive adopts certain styles of behavior that more or less reflect the kind of person he is and wishes to become. He commits himself to a role that will preserve his notions of self and give them productive expression.

The executive enters a transactional process of engineering a role in the executive group which will become validated by them, and to which he may become committed. The group validates roles that fit its functional needs of administration; the executive presents himself in ways that express his personal sense of identity and continuity. The engineering is concluded when the executive arrives at a satisfactory definition of himself validated by the groups' acceptance of his role and style. This process, whereby the negotiation produces role validation by the group and commitment by the person, is sometimes lengthy and exhaustive of emotional resources. Individuals with strong notions of self and clearly developed capacities for group activity make the adjustment.

The ideal result is that the executive has a secure position in the executive group with an identity that he finds acceptable and worthy. Not only does he function close to the administrative activity of the corporation, he also feels close. His notions of self are allowed to become fused with the central processes of the firm. Acceptance by the executive group brings closeness to the firm.

Likewise, rejection brings alienation from the firm. Not everyone can achieve this ideal adjustment. Some always feel a little detached and anxious. This psychological detachment from the firm, created by low acceptance in the executive group, need not be related to an individual's position in the hierarchy. A president may feel that his executive group has not really accepted him. When this is the case, clinical experience suggests that this president may not feel intimately attached to the corporation as a whole.

Today the executive group is a powerful psychological entity, capable of making people inside and out of it feel important, marginal, or separated. This includes the president. In the case of Mark Whiting, the former president fought Whiting for a number of reasons, not the least of which was his desire to have a clear and unmediated relationship to his executive group. Whiting attempted to come between him and his team. The president made up his mind that Whiting would never again be on the executive team.

Mark Whiting: A Recapitulation

What Whiting lacked was autonomy. Although he wanted it desperately, he did not know how to get it. His childhood had ill equipped him with the capacity to apply freely and voluntarily the rules of authority and organization. He rebelled at the rightful function of authority. When he deferred to superior authority he did so with the idea of capturing it. If he captured all of the superior authority there could be none left about which to feel apprehensive and fearful. As it turned out, he had to succumb to the dictates of superior authority or be washed into oblivion.

In the middle-management phase of his career cycle, he developed deferential attitudes out of anxiety rather than from a rational appreciation of the legitimate role of authority. He was compelled by the force of painful anxiety to subordinate self to superior figures. In the process he secretly concluded that he was much better than they. Thus started his tendency to idealize his notions of self-importance.

He did not affirm the corporation's goals and values out of choice, but out of a compulsion to get the better of his superiors. Later, he began to innovate changes in the goals and values of the corporation. He performed these maneuvers grandly, in the sense that his changes were validated by the superiors in charge. Because he worked so aggressively for the corporation's goals and values and their improvement, he was promoted over the heads of those superiors who had encouraged him. All the while, he was secretly destroying them by succeeding them. There is certainly little of the autonomy of which Warner speaks in the emotional makeup of Mark Whiting.

By the time he was in his early fifties and in the arrival stage, Mark Whiting believed that he could become president by this same mechanism. He would aggressively work to plan the reordering of the basic posture of the corporation and then seek the approval of the authority set to make him the president.

Mark Whiting revealed, in his counseling situation, that he had planned to then remove the old board of directors and eventually have an entirely new one. Then he was going to get authorization to offer substantial amounts of new stock. The purpose was to broaden the stockholders' base and to make him autonomous from them. Of course, this would be done behind the smoke screen of some logical corporate objective. Ultimately, he would have no one to defer to simply because he had all the authority. He said, "Then I would become free finally to make of my life what I pleased." In this statement we can see a man who believed that he could not be free unless he was without the restraints of superior authority. Obviously, if every executive felt this way the corporative world would be filled with an unending series of revolutions. No semblance of corporateness would exist.

The corporate organization is perpetuated because there is a sufficient number of executives who conform to the requirements of authority and organization. They have resolved the problems of conformity in their earlier years. Because they believe in the moral rightness of authority and the imperatives of organized effort, they can make choices that bring a strong sense of self-realization and satisfaction.

Whiting never confronted the conflicts that occurred in his early thirties as an ineffective sales manager. Rather, he denied that these conflicts ever existed. When asked to explain why he moved around a lot, he replied that he was trying to better himself. After many counseling hours, he finally admitted the number of times he had been fired, including instances in his high school years. Once the denial pattern was broken, Whiting revealed how he would aggressively thrust himself into his work as a way to forget about his problems with authority. In short, to allay his anxiety, Whiting practiced both denial and idealization.

The Whiting case illustrates how anxiety may lurk behind the administrative scenes to influence the way corporations are run and changed. In several of the cases to be presented later, we shall see what happens when a man with administrative anxiety becomes the president, as Mark Whiting almost did. The anxiety-producing forces within the corporation are not to be minimized. The number of men like Mark Whiting, who arrive with bandaged, unhealed wounds incurred in the tense war between self-discovery and realization, and corporation acceptance and validation, is not known.

However, if the executive arrives at the top without having adequately resolved these crucial problems, he may be forced by extreme circumstances to address himself to their resolution. In a way, the arrival stage is the last opportunity in his career cycle to resolve such fundamental issues. He must decide who he is and wants to become, and the role that authority figures and positions and corporation goals and achievements will play in helping him to achieve the success that affirms his self-identity.

In this sense, a career crisis may be viewed as therapeutic. It is a kind of shakedown cruise that enables the executive to safely continue his journey toward self-realization. Having successfully mastered a career crisis, few executives wish to undergo another. It has been the experience of the author to note that most are left with a mild fear of a career crisis. Whiting still gets occasional pangs of anxiety about how to perform his various administrative roles. However, his insight into his particular vulnerabilities allows him to overrule these pangs and to avoid the mistakes that caused his career crisis.

V

Anxiety and Career Crisis

A career crisis is basically a crisis of self. The executive may be a president threatened with overnight expulsion from the corporation, as was the case of William Newberg of Chrysler. Or he may be in an intensive, protracted battle to achieve full control of the firm, as was the case of the late Robert Young of New York Central. Whatever the case, a career crisis is to be distinguished from the kinds of crises an executive faces from time to time that are directly related to corporate achievement. These crises may not, at first, directly relate to the career of the executive, but they may eventually affect it.

A career crisis is a situation in which the executive is faced with a decision to act largely and primarily on behalf of self. It may involve staying in the firm and plotting a strategy to alleviate the crisis, or it may involve leaving and starting a career with another firm. Regardless of the alternatives, a decision is necessary. What differentiates a career decision from other kinds of executive decisions is that the executive has foremost in mind the alleviation of his personal difficulty. If he stays with the firm, his decision may appear outwardly very rational and organizationally relevant. In fact, it must be to be effective. It may not differ in objective content from that of any other decision. It must be situationally relevant and administratively proper. Yet, it does not basically ensue from the requirements of the objective situation, but rather the decision emanates from an inner struggle to alleviate pain and discomfort.

For example, a vice-president of marketing in a large electrical manufacturing firm was faced with the distinct possibility of forced early retirement. To counter this move on the part of the chairman of the board, he devised a new strategy for marketing accessory appliance products. He worked vigorously on the plan, mustered scarce and costly personnel to help in the formulation, and carefully laid a ground work for the plan's eventual adoption. The scheme was basically sound, as its final adoption so testified. However, the executive devised the whole matter as an attempt to ward off an offensive maneuver by the board chairman. Interestingly enough, his career was prolonged by the exact amount of time it took him to see the strategy successfully implemented, which was five years, after which he was better prepared psychologically for retirement.

The distinction between a career decision and a situationally or administratively based decision is indeed tenuous and fine. For the upwardly mobile executive there may not be a distinction. Some believe their decisions are always career oriented. But what if the upwardly mobile executive is faced with expulsion, separation, or rejection? In this case, what makes a career decision different is that a crisis in one's career is subjectively felt and this "felt situation" becomes the major basis of the decision.

The case of Mark Whiting is instructive at this point. He manufactured a long-range program that outlined the future growth and expansion of the Universal Chemical Corporation. He submitted this plan to the board of directors in an attempt to rebut the president's view that he was incompetent, disloyal, and immature. Whiting attempted to reorder the affairs of a vast corporation to allay his apprehension of immediate and total failure.

The number of corporations that are changed or reorganized by executives to accommodate their inner needs to avoid insecurity and anxiety is indeed difficult to determine. The important point is that the sterotyped image of the rational executive, sitting at the center of an impersonal communication network, is not always accurate. He may be deploying units of personnel and scarce resources to relieve a subjectively felt, impending career crisis.

After ten years of counseling big business executives through career crises, it has become apparent that their problems seem to involve a personalized definition of what constitutes the task of administration. Men who have had their upward mobility arrested at a very high level in the corporation evolve a mode of thinking that may not have occurred to them during their prior successful stages. When the chips are down, and the future appears bleak and foreboding, the executive needs to perform what would seemingly be an elementary exercise to any administrator. It is not, however. It is difficult for a troubled executive to ask simple questions as to what is the administrative task, and what he is doing wrong. To be sure, he has entertained such questions, perhaps often in the past, as an academic exercise in seminars, or in ad hoc debate with his colleagues, or as problems brought on by the misconduct of others about him. In fact, it has become quite stylish, today, for executives to raise sophisticated questions about the process of administration and the duties and responsibilities of execution.

In this regard, Mark Whiting often lectured to university schools of business about the skills and capacities of an effective administrator. He had acquired quite a following among university faculty and students in various parts of the country. He often started to lecture with a question about what constitutes the real "guts" of managing today. Like Mark Whiting, many business executives are interested in this question as an exercise in academic theorizing.

However, few executives invoke this question as seriously as when undergoing a career crisis. The thought has often occurred to the author, that perhaps executives who do not seriously ask these questions prepare themselves, unknowingly, for a career crisis. Or perhaps executives who continue their upward mobility do not have to ask these questions. In any case, an executive who is faced with the imminent possibility of being removed or shelved, and who regards this possibility with much distress and anxiety, eventually and invariably questions the very activity in which he has been engaged for the better part of his adult life. But he goes through a song and dance aimed at preserving the notion that other people are his problems, not himself.

The executive in a career crisis does not approach a counselor with naked statements of his emotional distress. He may come out with the fact that the president is trying to get him fired, or a colleague with whom he has had an untold number of clashes and disputes is about to become the boss, or that he cannot really make a big decision when the pressure is on. More often, he comes to an administrative counselor to get help with problems centered in people other than himself, who, however, may have made things very difficult for him. A person earning thirty thousand dollars a year or more is not expected to have many problems more "personal" than these. His administrative difficulties are supposed to be anchored in other people, and their problems are only his by definition of his role as boss, subordinate, or colleague.

However, people who come to an administrative counselor seldom come simply because of other people's problems. Deep-seated internal difficulties propel them unconsciously to gain help. But guilt or shame forces them to disguise the true source and nature of their difficulties. As the counselor achieves rapport with the client, the inner world gradually emerges, and with it the gnawing, vexing disturbances heretofore hidden behind the mask of sophistication and maturity.

THE CAUSES OF CAREER CRISIS

The executive who experiences an active career crisis tends to identify causes in the immediate administrative situation. He points the finger at specific objects and events, seemingly unaware of their relationship to his general career experience. If the reader recalls, the first thing Mark Whiting said when he came to the author for counseling was that the new president, Mr. Gray, should be on the psychologist's couch. He was convinced that the causes of his trouble were largely external to himself. This "externalizing" one's anxiety is very common at the onset of a career crisis. Apparently the threat of a career crisis is too painful to be absorbed by the executive. It must be projected back out into elements in the administrative scene.

The Freudian idea of a trauma or wound is widely accepted today, both by therapists and patients. The trauma concept pictures man as a machine which would continue to operate efficiently unless hit by a sharp blow. No account is given to the cumulative strain placed upon the machine through years of hard wear. In World War I, the term "shell shocked" was attributed to brain damage caused by nearby explosions.

The trauma concept would suggest that the executive who received a lethal blow to his career potential was a fit subject for a career crisis. Using this concept, upwardly mobile men and women with basically positive orientation to their chances of success would be pictured in mid-life as potentially depressed when they took stock and realized that their youth had slipped away, their physical and mental capacities had been taxed to the limit in the struggle to get ahead, and that holding their own was becoming a firm value. However, some people in the middle years of life react less anxiously to their perceived limitations than others. Obviously, what is felt as trauma to some, is not to others.

Langner and Michael's study of midtown Manhattan suggests that the factors associated with mental disturbance are purely additive in their effects. The more negative experiences people have, the greater their mental health risk. Because no specific failures were directly associated with neuroses, the concept of a single "traumatic experience" must necessarily be questioned. "Events in the life history seem to 'pile up' increasing impairment, but there is not one event which by itself automatically spells mental disaster for all who experience it."[1]

It was also noticed in the study that stressful events do not accumulate to a certain breaking point at which all persons are bound to collapse; the notion of the "straw that broke the camel's back" is not explanatory either of the incidence of mental disturbance. "There is no 'breaking point' in the number of factors beyond which there is a sudden marked increase in mental health risk."[2] The data acquired from counseling men in career crisis seem to affirm this linear principle of the relationship of environmental stress factors to mental difficulty. The concept of "the more, the unmerrier" seems to suggest that executives who show a sustained pattern of increasing administrative difficulty are more apt to be candidates for career crisis. They will feel their arrestment as more of a crisis than those who do not have this linear pattern. They have had several or many events in the past that have contributed to the felt crisis of today. These events will be different for each executive, and they may be initially perceived as unique and separate. The difficulty of predicting who might undergo a felt crisis upon arrestment of upward mobility is related to the capacity of the human to attach highly personal meanings to objects, events, and people. One human can acquire an idea of stress where another does not. All can continue to react to the idea of stress even when the stressful situation is no longer objectively real or present.

The mere anticipation of stress can be impairing for some. Some executives may react to the anticipation of arrestment in crisis-like terms, while others may require objective conditions of arrestment to be forcibly present. Administrative anxiety stems basically from anticipation of some future arrestment of achievements and mobility opportunity. The crisis may be the most extreme condition, possessing real clues to the impending arrestment. To say that a career crisis produces administrative anxiety is no more valid than to say that administrative anxiety produces a career crisis. Depending on the person, his history, and the interpretation of that history, any degree of administrative anxiety may be felt as a crisis in his career development. And it is also proper to note that administrative anxiety may bring on the very career crisis which the anxiety is set to avoid.

What seems clear from the case studies of men in career crisis is the presence of a rather extended period of previous experiences associated with administrative difficulties that have not been successfully resolved, and which tend to bring about the ordeal of a consciously-felt career crisis. The objective notions that one will never be better or more advanced than one is at present may actually serve to partially alleviate anxiety. Or they may cause the anxiety to become pervasive and spill over in allied activities.

The causes of a career crisis do not lie entirely in the childhood years. The executive career crisis is a product of a pattern of experiences acquired mostly in the adult years. The midtown Manhattan study seems to show that childhood experiences only slightly relate to the risk of mental disturbances. "His adult life situation is his mental health."[3] Of course, there is no doubt that childhood experiences certainly lay the groundwork for the development of mental health or disorder, but "the life situation of the adult as he functions in the here and the now seems most clearly related to his present mental health."[4] This means that the administrative counselor must analyze the present adult life situation for efficient screening and categorizing of psychological disturbances. To properly get at the underlying structure of the personality, he must understand the child-hood experiences of his clients.

SHAME AND GUILT ANXIETY

Counseling of executives in career crisis must take into account their feelings of *shame* and *guilt*. The dynamic basis of shame is the failure to live up to the requirements of administrative success. To the executive, success involves having little difficulty in performing the administrative role, or in successfully overcoming great adversity. In either case, a career crisis represents failure and hence incurs shame.

Guilt is the feeling of having violated some codified norm or rule.[5] The dynamic basis of guilt stems from the internalization of values of parents and other authority figures, the laws, regulations, and moral practices of society. Guilt is a response to highly codified and commonly accepted standards and practices. Feelings of guilt may be created by deviation from or violation of these standards and practices. These feelings are sustained by the censorship of the conscience, which is these standards internalized in the personality.

While guilt is the feeling of wrong doing and is internal to the executive, shame is the feeling of being weak or inadequate and does not exist apart from the expressed scorn or disapproval of others. Guilt may be triggered by strictly internal cues about violations of highly codified standards and practices; shame may be triggered by disapproval and scorn by others about deviation from uncodified standards and practices. There are really no legal or codified standards of success, especially executive success. Whatever standards exist are part and parcel of the requirements inherent in the executive role. Failure to live up to those requirements and expectations brings feelings of inadequacy and shame. The most important requirement is to maintain adequate functioning as an executive. Coming to a counselor for help is an acknowledgement of not functioning adequately. The counseling situation essentially evokes feelings of shame, and their understanding and removal may help to bring out the more central underlying reasons for failure to perform the executive role adequately.

Shame is largely a surface symptom of the underlying anxiety of becoming separated from the executive role. As these feelings of shame are peeled off during the counseling relationship, the audiences which serve to heap scorn and disapproval begin to emerge. The major audience is the collective or commonly shared opinions of the executive group of which the executive is a member and in which he actively seeks maintenance of membership character. Two basic sets of expectations belong to this audience. One becomes a diffuse but discerned evaluation of whether the executive is pulling his weight in giving vital support to the goals of the corporation and their efficient achievement. The executive group has a capacity to sense who is really helping them perform the administrative functions of giving overall direction and character to the corporation. They tend to exchange eulogisms of the kind that reflect their esteem and satisfaction with each other. Feelings of pride are acquired from such positive affirmations. They also tend to evolve dyslogisms (opposite of eulogisms of praise and appreciation) of the kind that suggest dissatisfaction and disapproval. A dyslogism may be a minimization of what the executive has done, a tendency to negate his arguments, a pattern of interrupting his statements or not acknowledging their having been made, and so forth. Feelings of shame may be acquired from these negative regarding feelings of members of the executive group.

A second significant sub-audience in the executive group is the authority figure or set constantly appraising and evaluating performance and fitness. The authority figure is concerned with whether to legitimatize or validate the role performance of the executive. He may give him the support of his superior authority while the remainder of the group members withhold affirmation. It is not uncommon for the executive to be viewed positively by the authority figure and negatively by the executive group as a whole. In such a case, he may feel pride mitigated by shame.

THE CASE OF STAN

In one particular case an executive, called Stan, produced a very restricted budget for his division that received immediate approval of the president and the chairman of the board. At the next meeting of the executive group, Stan was very coolly treated by members other than the president. Afterward, one colleague approached him with the suggestion that after this, he not embarrass them by failure to work out his budget concepts with them before submission to the boss.

In this case, authority-centered pride and group-centered shame provided a source of diffuse anxiety. Stan wanted to identify more with the group by conforming to their demands. To do so might bring loss of support from the boss. The boss was very much a part of the executive group also. He had to maintain membership character in it due to the complexity of the administrative task in the large corporation. Separation from the group was as potentially threatening to him as to the subordinate executive. Upon noticing severe disapproval of his legitimization of the subordinate executive, the president tried to reestablish his relationship by withdrawing some of his support from Stan. The latter conceived of this possibility too. Consequently, Stan felt an impending sense of danger from both boss and executive group. It is clear that Stan violated no highly codified, internalized law. His conscience did not tell him that he was a bad person. Rather, Stan had fallen short of a role-anchored expectation, which was felt as shame.

To illustrate guilt, we shall have to move to a standard or practice that is highly valued by all members of our society, and which is usually internalized by the child under the influence of parental control and guidance. One such codified norm is obedience to father and mother. In adult life, it is obedience to authority. Failure to obey may bring feelings of guilt. An executive who feels guilt has been mostly censored from within by his conscience.

THE CASE OF GEORGE

Guilt comes from a transgression that is not unique to the executive role, but may occur in any role or any institution in our society. The institution or the role merely serves as a vehicle for transgression and the inception of guilt reactions. In one case, a client, called George, became intensely unhappy with the behavior of the president of the corporation. In anger, George actively but secretly took upon himself the task of slicing the boss's throat by courting negative feelings in important members of the executive group. He and these several other group members began to gather data to support their doubts about the boss's competency, and eventually went to a small group of outside board members. Convinced of the validity of their cause, they finally got a board rejection of the president. George was asked to assume the presidency, and did so with apparent ease.

In a short while, he developed extreme feelings of inadequacy. George became indecisive, aloof, inaccessible, and hostile to the executive group. This hostility was followed by acts of extreme deference to and acceptance of the executive group. Movement back and forth between aggression and submission caused anxiety among the members of the group. They finally took overt action to have him ejected. In the career crisis that ensued, George evidenced considerable unconscious guilt for his acts of rebellion toward the former president. It was apparent that this guilt had been repressed by means of justifying the incompetency of the president and the danger to the corporation. The repressed guilt, however, showed itself in the intense fear that the executive group would do to him what he had done to the predecessor. George became frozen in an unstable pattern of aggression-submission to the executive group.

The dictum, obey your father and mother, is a strong force making for prudent obedience to all authority figures. Those who have successfully internalized this moral directive are seldom without guilt anxiety when they take up arms against authority. Executives may feel guilt when they violate the essential authority of office, role, or superior figure. They may feel shame when they fail to live up to the work expectations of the executive group or the boss.

A very important source of guilt and shame may come from acts of disloyalty to the goals and needs of the corporation. The executive group is the chief interpreter of acts of disloyalty. If the executive fails to show the accepted sense of loyalty to the corporation, he may become the brunt of scorn and disapproval. He may merely be showing acts of loyalty that are not commonly accepted by other members of the executive group. In such a case, shame may be felt because of his deviation. Guilt may not enter in if his conscience gives him support for his intense but unacceptable loyalty to the corporation.

Guilt may ensue if he violates his conscience. The directive of loyalty is deep-seated in the personality of most members of our society. It goes back to loyalty to mother and family, who are perceived and felt by the child to be synonymous. It is the mother's home, not the father's, owing to the frequent absence of the latter and omnipresence of the former. Loyalty to the virtue and values of the mother carries over to provide generalized loyalty to the family, school, community, and nation. It has been shown in research dealing with combat crews in World War II that those most capable of sacrificing life for country were those who had stable and secure attachments to mother and family.[6] The studies of business executives show that when this attachment is not developed, or when it is broken with aggression and hostility, the executive has difficulty identifying with the goals and achievement of the corporation.[7] To be against the corporation is a violation of the emotional directive inhering in the conscience of the typical executive.

In clinical practice, it is not infrequent to find executives who have accepted the advantages and satisfactions of upward mobility and success without the positive emotional attachments to the corporation. They invariably reveal a repressed pattern of guilt based upon their drive for self-centered rewards and satisfactions. A career crisis may ensue because of the capacity of other executives at the top to sense self-centered ambitions and basic corporation indifference and disloyalty. The negative cues provided by the executive group may set off a chain of guilt reactions in the executive that may be every bit as debilitating as those set off by disloyalty to authority. The boss and the corporation are symbolic heirs to the parent and family figures. Violation of their values, directives, and expectations may bring guilt. The guilt may become repressed, giving rise to symptoms of anxiety to allay problems of authority and organization achievement.

In a career crisis, symbolic representations of authority and organization are fused with notions of self. Guilt and shame involve feelings of selfhood. The child's notions of self gradually emerge from the matrix of parental and family relationships. Acts of guilt and shame may lead to violation of notions of self. As in the case of the executive, Stan, who attempted to re-identify with the executive group, the individual may become a submissive conformist in order to allay his anxiety of separation. In so doing he may not like what he sees in himself. His notions of being an autonomous person who can stand on his own feet may press against his picture of a practicing sycophant. Wanting to submit to allay anxiety of separativeness, he may incur the anxiety of lost self-respect. Guilt and shame may be an inner recoil to one's own violation of selfhood. Doubt of oneself is intermeshed with acts of loyalty and disloyalty to authority and organization.

The executive group tends to be the chief interpreter of the acts of loyalty and disloyalty to authority and organization that bring feelings of shame within the executive. The individual himself (his internal directives of conscience) tends to be the chief interpreter of acts of loyalty and disloyalty that bring feelings of guilt. Pure cases of guilt and shame are rare. The executive usually experiences fused mixtures of the two. In this fusion—violation of primitive taboos originating in childhood, and violation of role-anchored taboos emerging from the unique properties of the administrative group—may be found the essential characteristics of the career crisis. Primitive or contrived notions of authority, organization, and self must be separated and analyzed to get at the dynamic basis of the administrative anxiety.

EXECUTIVE ISOLATION

Feelings of guilt and shame involve feelings of isolation. The executive desires to be attached to the central administrative processes of the firm. Charged with the administrative responsibility, the executive group exerts enormous power over the individual who aspires to become and remain a member executive. Guilt represents inner directives that make him feel isolated from this important group. Shame represents external directives that make the executive feel isolated. Feelings of shame imply the acceptance of the validity of the executive group's distinct ways of organizing its activities. Such norms and standards are highly specific to the group and may be different from one firm to another. Feelings of guilt imply the acceptance of the validity of the basic notions of authority and organization that are general to the society of which the firm is a part. A basic quality of the individual is his capacity to feel guilt and shame. Without such capacity, it is difficult to conceive of any lasting element of authority and organization in society.

The big corporation requires a high degree of emotional investment and commitment. Men at the top show a marked capacity to avoid feelings of guilt and shame. Such a capacity is derived from experience in pre-adult institutions, and is maintained and developed by continuous exposure to the requirements of authority and organization within the business firm. The avoidance of guilt and shame most often occurs in the productive expression of the unique powers of the self. The individual learns how and when to conform and to make changes that result in validation of role and self. This is the constructive response to guilt and shame. The self becomes more fully realized.

Self-damage, rather than self-realization, may result from acute feelings of guilt and shame and the incapacity to productively discharge them. The individual may partially though inadequately allay anxiety by developing overly hostile or dependency patterns. Hostility is more easily detected and more morally devalued. Consequently, hostility is less often resorted to, especially by those who move successfully to the top. This means that the aggressive type is less common. The major pattern is conformity and deference.

In a career crisis, a few executives have the overwhelming urge to throw themselves upon the mercies of the executive group. This is essentially a neurotic substitute for constructive resolution of the essential anxiety. It is unproductive because, rather than allaying anxiety, it really breeds more anxiety, owing to the damage to positive notions of self and the arrestment of the powers of self-realization. The executive in a career crisis may be apt to have used the deference pattern somewhat productively in previous states of anxiety. He may overreact to the present danger of separation from the executive group because he has a large residue of anxiety carried over from previous attempts at deference and submissiveness. In some cases, only a few weak notions of self remain, so thoroughly has the identity of the executive been damaged. This man may then become alienated from his real self, separated emotionally from the executive group and from the central administrative activities of the firm. Executive isolation is typically multifaceted and pervasive and may extend beyond the confines of the executive role to include other life areas.

THE CASE OF PAUL

Executive crises may be vast and complex in their impact upon society, but they evolve around problems of authority, goals, and needs of the organization and the self-notions of the executive. Several years ago an executive, whom we shall call Paul, came to the author with a problem that later erupted into a national scandal. Since there were many executives from numerous corporations involved in the electrical manufacturing price collusion conspiracy, this particular case may be partially described. Paul's concern was that he had been given cues to the effect that he should join in this collusion as a basis of job tenure and promotion. Yet these messages were only indirect and could not be easily substantiated. The thought of engaging in this affair was not permissible to his concept of the kind of a person he was and wanted to become. Paul asked for professional help in evolving an extrication strategy that would enhance his notions of self without violating his superior's cues and without grossly jeopardizing his chances for advancement.

However, it was a very difficult strategy to devise because his superior could easily ascertain whether prices in his division were being rigged or not. If they were not, Paul would be held responsible. Because he had not the formal authority, nor the conscience, the case was tricky. The client grew despondent and depressed, fighting alternating fits of aggression and submission, only to face another attempt at adjustment. One day, in a state of anxiety, he sought to confront his superior and determine just exactly what was expected. At this point Paul was told by his superior, "Whatever you do, you do on your own, but please get it done."

Against professional counsel and his conscience, he went to a meeting of representatives of other firms and joined in price rigging. Several days later, he returned for guidance in a state of acute anxiety. Paul was utterly disturbed by the thought that he would get caught and no one would back him up. It became evident that his notions of self were now involved mostly in the fear of getting caught and not in the ethical problem. This being the case, a strategy was devised to minimize the chances of being caught and punished. From then on, he represented the corporation's welfare in these transactions effectively and received the approval of the authority system by increased responsibility. His promotion did not remove him from the collusive activities, but rather made him responsible for more of these types of transactions. However, Paul's anxiety level gradually lowered. He came eventually to believe that the corporation required this kind of effort and that he should encourage subordinates to aid the effort, whenever and wherever justified.

Paul's career crisis, however, was just beginning. Some time later, he and several dozen other executives from the electrical manufacturing industry were found guilty in a Philadelphia court of law and fined, and in some cases sentenced. Paul was sentenced and dismissed from his corporation, which absolved itself of any responsibility for his activities. Judge Ganey remarked:

I am convinced that in the great number of these defendants' cases, they were torn between conscience and an approved corporate policy, with the rewarding objective of promotion, comfortable security and large salaries— in short, the organization or the company man, the conformist, who goes along with his superiors and finds balm for his conscience in additional comforts and the security of his place in the corporate setup.

In these few words, Judge Ganey gave an apt description of anxiety and how it is sometimes dealt with. The expectations of the boss, the requirements of the corporation in an oligopolistic industry, and the conscience of the individual were hung together in a conflicting pattern of psychic tension. Something had to give. Notions of a moral person became partially blurred and gave way to the powerful notions of a successful, dutiful, loyal executive. As the executive stood to hear sentence, he was flooded with his now active notions of what kind of a person he once wanted to become. Shame and guilt drove him into a deep state of withdrawal. His premature death may be largely accounted for by his lost sense of identity and self-worth.

Cue Anxiety

In a career crisis, the question concerning the executive role is always related to the client's perceived position in the corporation in general, and the executive group in particular. Thus a senior vice-president of a large chemical company may define his job much differently than a general manager of a division in an automobile company. Likewise, a staff advisor to the president in charge of corporate planning may tend to see different meanings in his job than a line vice-president in charge of marketing. Also, a career crisis centered around the problem of being fired or retired may call for different meanings than a career crisis centered around thwarted aspirations for the presidency.

An administrative counselor has no particular tricks that will help to dissolve the crisis. The typical tools associated with clinical psychology and psychiatry are useless if the client cannot perform more productively in the managerial role. In the final analysis, the administrative counselor must be able to help the executive formulate a more productive solution of the administrative job than what he brought to the task originally. Some executives may have unproductive notions of authority that block either their handling of their own authority or their relating properly to authority figures. Other executives may have notions of organization that prohibit adaptive and productive responses. Still others have notions of self, inflated or deflated beyond realistic proportions, that restrict their managerial effectiveness. Whatever these notions are, they must be systematically examined in the light of what is generally known about the managerial task.

The corporation is not a hospital. For this reason therapy cannot directly involve enlisting the support of other people in the corporation to dissolve the executive's anxieties. An executive's career crisis can be resolved largely by helping him to become a better administrator. Becoming a better administrator necessarily involves insight into what kinds of tools are being used or abused. One tool is the utilization of cues, rather than spoken words, to show direction, intention, support, indifference, disapproval, and scorn. In the executive group much of what is expected is not directly stated. The use of cues is based upon the reluctance to confront a colleague directly because of the potential damage to self-esteem. At the executive level, notions of self are usually quite strong, and the satisfaction of their maintenance prohibits aggressive confrontation of another person. Also, there is the growing practice to minimize overt authority and emphasize solidarity and cohesion as ways to achieve compliance. This is a general pattern in our society and a highly prevalent one in the big corporation where the executive group, of which the president is a member, is the chief unifying agency between the corporation as a whole and the subdivisions. Combat, then, is a more subtle affair. One way to remove undesirable people from the central administrative process of the firm is to disenfranchise them.

THE CASE OF BILL

One executive, called Bill, faced the possibility of being disenfranchised by the executive committee. This meant that he would not be allowed an opportunity to effect the outcome of certain crucial matters. This would not have constituted a danger had it not been that he was the manager of a high-priority division. If Bill could not help determine the direction and character of the total corporation, he could not substantially control this major division. He saw his future at stake. Yet, no one really told him that he was disenfranchised. Bill gradually perceived that decisions were being made that were more responsive to other division heads' requirements and expectations. At first, he cautiously checked to see if his suspicions were correct. They were.

In counseling, it became apparent that Bill had been here before, so to speak. He recalled that at least twice before he had been gradually excluded from the decision-making apparatus at lower managerial levels. One time Bill panicked and concentrated his energy on leaving the corporation and finding employment elsewhere. Another time he rode out the crisis by a process of associating with those who could restore his prestige and influence. On these two previous occasions, Bill was younger and had time to start over again or to slowly disarm the skeptics. Now Bill was fifty-two and committed to the corporation. He could not take five or ten years to recover lost prestige because he was in a high-priority division, and men do not last long if they cannot help control the affairs of the corporation in general. He had to act fast, but how? What could Bill do that would be responsive to the rapidly developing situation? He knew that in his corporation a man could be in one day and out the next. His was a swift, emerging corporate world in which men could be quickly made and broken. Besides, he was so near to being the next corporation president that he could not give up. The tailspin, at first, was only a faint spiral whose turns grew more acute with the growing evidence of disenfranchisement.

No doubt it was the authority system that made the decisions, but who actually started the cycle? Bill had a powerful position in the organization as the marketing vice-president, but how could this help him now? What did he really want to do to alleviate the situation? What kind of constraints would his notion of the kind of person he was exert at this time?

In his career crisis, the immediate danger was in some way related to his role in the corporation and the impressions and expectations of the authority set, including the president. The danger was perceived as threatening to his notions of the kind of person he was and wished to become. He felt the danger, felt somewhat helpless, and faintly recalled having been in this box before. He turned to a friend, who encouraged him to get administrative counsel.

Anxiety is almost always associated with the inner danger of unacceptable thoughts, feelings, wishes, or drives which elicit the expectations of some kind of harm, loss, disapproval, or punishment. Harm to self, loss of status and prestige, loss of useful employment of his resources, peer disapproval, and corporate disenfranchisement in the form of demotion, shelving, or early forced retirement were perceived as possible.

It was apparent that the prevalent use of cues should force the executive to utilize cues to alleviate his condition. But Bill did not see it this way. He brought his presumed disenfranchisement out into the open, much to the embarrassment of the other members of the executive group. The reaction was lethal. It was much as though this executive group believed that return thrusts should be based upon the manner in which the original offensive action was delivered. The executive group further did not believe such things should be brought up in a group atmosphere. They vigorously denied Bill's accusations and harshly admonished him for harboring ill thoughts about them. Some had made up their minds that because of his indiscretion, he was obviously not suitable for the performance of the executive role. In private, one suggested to Bill that he might want to take an extended vacation. He had obviously overworked himself. The president thought of this solution also. This suggestion, although coming from independent sources, was interpreted as evidence of the ganging up on him that produced his disenfranchisement. Bill had direct confirmation now and resolved that the last thing he was going to do was to leave the scene and have his job completely emasculated.

A career crisis may be aggravated by petite paranoia, a response quite common among disturbed executives who cannot hold up under the anxiety of the cue system. For Bill, therapy constituted breaking through this wall of paranoiac isolation and gaining realistic estimates of the intent of the authority set, the potential or silent opportunities to show usefulness to the corporate goals, and restoration of lost self-confidence.

CAREER DEFENSE

The career crisis invariably marks the first step in the process leading to neuroses. The executive becomes inhibited and restrained in his capacity to be aware of reality. Turning away from reality, failing to allow it to register meaningfully is a decisive step toward distortion or inhibition of the creative processes. The individual's choices of behavior are diminished by the degree to which reality is distorted. Awareness of externalities becomes transferred to the drives to restore lost attachments. This restoration becomes the over-riding value. Lost is the notion that the reality of corporate life prohibits action outside the context of the administrative role. Stan failed to understand the relative uselessness of sentiment. It is not possible to go to the aggressor and plead for forgiveness. However, sentiment often caused Stan to appraise unrealistically the executive role.

Separation from the executive group may be stemmed by understanding what is essentially valued by the group. The crucial value is maintenance of their established patterns and practices, their essential integrity of function. This is highly related to corporate goals and the authority set. Attachment can only be made within the confines of the executive group and the role perceived as valid for the executive. Therapy constitutes splitting of the ego, whereby the awareness-of-reality part is discovered by the client and used in cooperation with the objectivity of the counselor. Unless there is a realistic awareness, therapy can not be achieved. However, in administrative anxiety, realistic awareness is still highly present in contrast to cases of acute neuroses. The reality that is adequately perceived and the capacity to perceive reality are enlisted in defense of the distorted perceptions of the career crisis.

When the executive feels threatened by the impending danger of separation from the central administrative processes, attention narrows and he may confine his interest to the immediate situation. This is called "tunnel vision" and is represented by repression of thoughts unacceptable to self. The result is a highly simplified version of what has happened. The executive seems to maintain this simplified version as though it were a source of security. Such tendency shows up in impatience with the investigating aspects of the preliminary diagnostic interviews, an urgent demand for prompt confirmation by the counselor, and an incessant requesting for easy solutions. A simplified version calls out for a comprehensive solution—a solution that will work now and forever. Such a tendency serves to place a high expectation upon the counselor, which if not immediately fulfilled will develop disappointment.

Positive notions of self are highly prized by the executive, particularly those notions of what kind of an executive he is and how well others think of him. A career crisis essentially means that the notions of self anchored in the executive role are threatened. When this signal of danger to self is felt, defenses may be brought into play that have as their main purpose maintaining the integrity of the self. A common method of maintaining notions of self is aggression. Attacking the aggressor conflicts with the reality of the executive role. This must not be done. Rather, utilizing the energies of anger by sublimating them in the form of constructive administrative activity must be encouraged.

Defense of the self may be performed by projecting hostility and anxiety into others. The executive may defend himself against attack by believing that others are under attack as well. His picture of what has happened may be partially softened by picturing others as facing a similar threat. Or he may defend self by incorporating the aggressor.[8] The executive may unconsciously attempt to allay anxiety by taking on the attributes of the threatening figure. He may identify with the values and beliefs of the executive group, or authority figure, or a significant other. The strength and power of the threatening object becomes the basis of his strength and power.

Just as he may attempt to defend self, he may attempt to enhance self as a basis of maintaining positive notions of self. He may overly strengthen his self notions to a point of idealization. He may come to feel highly inflated and superior. Such idealization of self may cause disastrous consequences. One very common result is to engage in a withdrawal pattern. Believing himself superior and too good for the kind of treatment he is receiving, he may simply discount the danger. Instead of releasing energy in a constructive form, he may withdraw it. The signs may be indifference, aloofness, and condescension. All of these forms of withdrawal send out lethal cues that are negatively evaluated by members of the executive group. Condescension not only causes others to react even more aggressively, but brings a grossly underestimated definition to events in the situation that unfolds during the career crisis.

In either self-defensive or self-enhancing mechanisms, the symbolic object may be the authority figure or set, or the corporate goals and traditions, or both. In some self-enhancement defenses, notions of self may become idealized at the diminution of the value of the corporate goals and traditions. The corporation symbolizes what the executive feels is inferior to what he believes in. Competition, profits, good public relations, and cost-mindedness may become devalued. In their place may be valued such activities as those that are characterized by the career crisis.

THE CASE OF HARRY

Harry consistently failed to run his division in a profitable way. His return on capital invested in his division by the corporation was far too low to be considered satisfactory. His career crisis was largely caused by this continued pattern. He wanted to be more efficient, but could not. His crisis became acutely aggravated by his direct insistence that profitability was not really everything. He prided himself on his permissive style of administration. He felt the necessity to assert this style when it was presumably under attack. He set up a program to encourage the development of a more cooperative type of manager within his division. The response from on top was firm and negative. In the attempt to avoid this threat to self, Harry lashed out at the values of the corporation. He pled for help by his request for a more considerate, cooperative form of enterprise. He vigorously asserted those values which were covertly aimed at giving him the emotional support he desperately wanted. He placed himself in the position of moral arbiter and statesman. All others who were "profit-oriented" felt the sting of his aggressiveness. His self-enhancement met with severe repercussions.

A defence of self may elicit a self-effacement pattern. Here the executive does not identify with his positive notions of self, but his negative. He turns away from any notion that he is equal to the task. Feelings of superiority and eventual triumph are repressed. He grows smaller and smaller in his own eyes, invites abuse, belittling, and further degradation. The appeal of going to pieces and submitting to the actions of the aggressor becomes inviting. It becomes tempting for him to give credence to even the most sinister implication of danger to his career. His career is all over; he invites the worst of all possibilities, yes, even accepts them.

LOST REALITY

In both defensive enhancing and effacing solutions, the turning away from reality is common. A career crisis is a threat to self and, as such, can be realistically confronted by only the most courageous. The result for many is the feeling of being "bad" or "weak." Guilt and shame may be inextricably fused to make feelings of isolation greater than the actual degree of possibility of separation from the central tasks of the executive group.

Feelings of guilt and shame are difficult to communicate. They are repressed, rather than released, because of their potential threat to positive notions of self. The counselor's willingness to understand, his faith in the client's potentialities, his objectivity and firmness in not becoming absorbed into the client's incipient neuroses, his unflagging concern for reality, all become the vital balance and basis of therapy.

It is also crucial to realize that the executive group does not offer a basis of identification because it is simply a group. The attractiveness of the group transcends the peculiar organization of it, or even the characteristics of its membership. The executive group is a magnet because of its essential concern with the central administrative tasks of the corporation. The executive may identify with the authority system and the superior figure who represents that system, or may identify with the goals and purposes of the corporation. In either case, the executive group serves as the means whereby this identification is made practical. The case of John may serve to illustrate. Remember that the motives to associate with the goals and values of the corporation may be to allay separation anxiety. The specific source of the anxiety may be in the executive's relationship to the authority set or the boss himself.

THE CASE OF JOHN

In this man's case, the boss, and subsequently the executive group, placed formidable barriers to his maintaining proper degrees of power and influence with subordinates in the organization. Subsequently, John acquired an intense concern for the corporation, its future and welfare. His interviews revealed the presence of a secondary identification pattern (with corporation) to remove the original source of anxiety.

John's attempt to resolve his anxiety placed him in a triangle of conflicting emotions. He saw his boss and the authority set as definitely threatening, bringing on a crisis involving his notions of self. A crisis of self is commonly precipitated by the aggressive or dominating action of another person or object in the subject's immediate environment. Further, the individual feels no available sources within for dealing with the crisis as it is represented. Theoretically, John had many alternatives. One was that he could have identified with the aggressive object, the boss in specific, or the authority set of the executive group. But this alternative was not open to him. John had a previous history of dealing with authority problems by associating and identifying with the organization with which the authority figure was primarily concerned. In his childhood, when his father threatened him with punishment, John was seen later to be striving hard in the routine work patterns of the home.

Specifically, he would appear to the father as more conscious of the needs of the family, showing more responsibility than might be expected of a child of his age and size. He would aggressively enter into social activities, and thus find subsequent relief from the father's wrath. In school, and later in the work system, he tended to avoid the wrath of the teacher or boss by his concern for the goals and activities of the situation. Although John was partly conscious of having used this pattern of reaction, he was not conscious of how much he had relied upon it in the past.

Because of his inherent capacity to work and his desire to receive a high payoff, he was always interested in knowing the goals and achieving their implementation. This association with the organization, coupled with strong identification growing out of occasional conflicts with authority figures, provided John with an enduring reputation as a corporation man. Inwardly, however, he used his aggressive achievement as a strategic device to acquire authority. His continuing hope was to become president some day.

Authority to him was the measure of man. The men above were viewed as important, wise, extra-capable people. In the performance of his junior executive roles, he enjoyed the thrill of commanding and receiving obedience, and felt anger when his commands were not eagerly obeyed. With subordinates he learned to pitch his commands within the framework of the objective necessities of the organization. This administrative style paid great dividends, except when he came into conflict with superiors who deemed themselves more capable than he of interpreting the objective necessities of the corporation. His strong desire to be one of them was countered inwardly by a suspicion and distrust of them. Thus he occasionally would be distrusted by them and would have his effectiveness diminished thereby. Not knowing how to directly confront the authority figure to exchange information and achieve adequate clarification, he resorted to a positive onslaught upon the corporate goals and needs. Always in the past this administrative style had worked, although he did not know why he pursued this pattern of identification. Identification means that the subject behaves in a way that is subjectively like that of the object. The corporation stood for certain things at each level of his career rise, and these values became completely, rigidly adhered to.

John's arrestment of increasing authority and power occurred because significant members of the authority set persuaded the boss that great changes had to be made in order to take advantage of certain markets and supplier opportunities. These individuals convinced the boss that certain economy measures coming from John's department accounted for their present market difficulties. The president decided that perhaps new corporate designs must be developed, and that John might not be effective in their devising and implementation. These decisions came to John through the medium of interpersonal communciation with several colleagues.

The signals of possible rejection from the central administrative process aroused anxiety that automatically triggered an enlarged and aggressive pattern of identification with the established goals and values of the corporation. At a time when these were under indictment, John nevertheless affirmed them totally and rigidly. The result was to set John on an unalterable collision course. The boss formally relieved him of all marketing duties and placed him in a job as manager of special operations. Literally, he was given problems that

never needed to be solved. The actual separation from central administrative responsibility was too much. He broke down completely
under the strain and was given competent medical treatment. When
he was sufficiently recovered, he was provided with administrative
counseling.

Under conditions of stress and strain, John's inflated notions of the
importance of authority gave rise to instrumental use of the corporation's goal and values. By the successful implementation of this administrative style, John was able to realistically see himself as being
the boss someday. His instrumental use of corporate goals which had
worked on previous occasions, at the end actually caused his formal
removal from office and precipitated an emotional collapse. John's
case illustrates the problem of restriction of reality awareness under
conditions of acute anxiety. He could not see that he was on a collision course, even though there was considerable objective evidence
to predict his impending disaster.

In conclusion, notions of self are related to notions of authority
and organization. The vehicle for the crystallization of notions of self,
authority, and organization is the executive group. Its fascination and
power lies in its responsibility to administer the overall goals and
purposes of the organization. The executive measures success by how
intimately he is involved in the central administrative processes of the
firm. Separation from the executive group amounts to separation from
these central tasks. The danger of separation signals threats to self.
A career crisis becomes a crisis of self.

In the following chapters, an attempt is made to develop the three
basic patterns of career crisis. In Chapter VII, the authority-centered,
organization-centered, and self-centered career crisis patterns are presented by means of actual cases of executives who sought out administrative counseling. In Chapter VIII, several cases are presented to
show what happens when anxiety anchored in the administrative role
is not resolved and breaks out to affect the whole life of the executive.
Mark Whiting's career crisis certainly would be classified as a crisis
of the total self. In such cases the executive's relationships at home,
in the community, and in his various organizations may take on different characteristics. Now the executive is experiencing a crisis that
covers all areas of his life style. To help with the concluding chapters,

we shall next look carefully within the counseling scene to examine the problems of counseling executives in career crises. In Chapter VI, we shall examine the nature of the corporate triangle which under-girds the executive's experiences in such crises.

VI

The Corporate Triangle

When a career crisis develops, executives may react in much the same way as people in any other occupation. Their defenses may be no less neurotic-bearing, their solutions no less imaginative. They may rely upon normal thinking and activity patterns at a time when something different is required. Or they may resort to radical solutions. They are apt to have unmanageable definitions of their problem and to have exhausted their supply of solutions. Some have severely damaged the most important quality of success and health—notions of self-security rooted in confidence. As the counselor knows, those who doubt themselves tend to doubt the whole world. In panic and desperation the executive comes seeking professional help, but even this he does ambivalently, owing to a reputation for superior grace and wisdom which makes him feel that he has fallen. Guilt and shame prevent easy access to his private inner world. Once penetration of this inner world has been made, his problems are less confusing than the size and complexity of his corporation would suggest. It has always been exciting to notice that the men who manage vast corporations have reduced the workings of the corporate system to a few elementary notions. To be sure, there is more than this suggests to running a business, but in a career crisis, certain boundaries are attached to the administrative process that perhaps do not arise in a normal administrative situation.

Instead of becoming generalized to include other phases of his life style, a career crisis, at least initially, does the very opposite for most. The executive begins to shore up the problem and settle upon a few possibly useful ideas. After all, his main concern is to become or stay meaningfully attached to the administrative process. Separation anxiety haunts the executive who has as his central value the active control of the administrative apparatus of the corporation.

Separation, however, is seldom abrupt and discrete. In the large corporation, the gradual removal of an executive from the central administrative process is seldom perceived at the point of initiation. This is the terror of it all. He feels he is not really pulling his weight, that the tempo is moving against him—but he is not sure.

A number of business practices have developed in recent times to cushion the inhumanity of arbitrary punishment or discharge. The executive may be kicked upstairs, by-passed, gradually frozen out, disenfranchised, or placed on a dusty corporate shelf with problems that never need to be solved. When he has finally confirmed the tragic proportions of the situation, it is almost too late to institute strategic changes. All he knows is that he has done something wrong and somebody in a position of authority has directly or indirectly sanctioned his gradual removal for reasons which may be unknown to him, or which are too threatening to be consciously entertained for long periods of time. Let us proceed to enter the inner world of the executive in a career crisis.

AUTHORITY, ORGANIZATION, AND SELF

In the process of counseling executives in career crisis, some uniformities have evolved that characterize those who come to a psychologist for career guidance. The content of a career crisis involves at least three areas of concern: There is always a problem of *authority*, a problem having to do with *organization*, and a problem related to notions of *self*.

By self, we mean conscious and subconscious orientation to himself as an individual with specific qualities, needs, goals, and values. The answers to the questions, "Who am I? Where do I want to go?

What do I want to become?" are difficult to get from the client. But these answers denote a particular kind of person, what he stands for, what he wants out of his life, career, or role.

The self-image of the executive is his psychic center of gravity. In coordination with this psychic center, the two other problem areas come to the fore in a career crisis. Authority involves his orientation toward the initiation of action and the seeking of a superior's consent for that action. The problem of authority may include his activities and that of his superiors and subordinates. The problem area of organization concerns performing roles that relate to the goals and values of the corporation, the construction of goals and values that enhance its purposes and policies.

The executive in a career crisis eventually centers his difficulty upon any one or more of these problem areas. He may feel despondent, inadequate, and insecure because he feels incapable of doing what the superior wants or expects of him. He may feel humiliated, resentful, and lonely because he can or will not make the sacrifices his corporation expects of executives: superiors and subordinates alike. He may feel aggressive, destructive, and rebellious because he places a higher value upon his abilities and skills than others about him.

These three problem areas are interrelated. They swim around together in the client's stream of consciousness and unconsciousness. For example, executives who suffer from an enlarged view of themselves may reveal some kind of emotional reaction to superiors and to some corporate goal or value. Those who initially reveal a strong distrust of their superiors may reveal images of themselves and their corporation that affect and give form to their suspicions. Executives who find the corporation life impossible may reveal orientations toward self and superiors that bear upon their cynicism or apathy.

Anxiety seems to cause a restriction of the executive's span of awareness. He tends to repress or write off many of the other problem areas in his role and life. He then concentrates on those three to the exclusion of most others. Yet the three are not equally represented in the crisis scene.

Mark Whiting had acquired early in life a problem with the acquisition and exercise of authority and with figures who held superior authority over him. He had acquired the capacity to relate positively to the goals and needs of organized activity. Other executives reported upon in this book have problems that pivot around organization or self. Because these three problem areas are highly interrelated, we are justified in referring to them as forming the shape of a triangle. It is a triangle in which each part depends upon the other two. It is whole or corporate in nature. This means that no one part is relative or useful without the other two. However, in each person one part may outpull the other two in its relevancy to the executive's career crisis. But this predominance of one part is never so complete as to render the other two unimportant.

The key factor to understanding the executive in career crisis is that the *corporate triangle* exists within the mind. Apparently the triangle emerges out of a need to make sense of the career difficulties that stimulate the executive to feel anxious. It helps to define the executive's condition of crisis.

To the individual, reality is what he perceives it to be. He does not act upon what the superior is really like, or his organization, or even his self. Rather, his behavior is based upon what he thinks his boss is like, what he thinks the corporation life demands of him, what he thinks he experiences when he is "being himself." The corporate triangle is subjective and wholly individual.

The outside events and happenings that press forward in a crisis situation stimulate their counterparts in the inner world of the executive. These inner events and happenings may be initially called into operation by the crisis situation, but their specific character and form emerge from the many experiences of the executive throughout his whole life. In this sense, a crisis situation may stimulate the executive to feel that his whole life is at stake. This is an acute career crisis.

In such cases, events and happenings relating to childhood experiences may emerge to vitally affect the way in which the crisis is handled. The aggression brought to bear upon the president who opposed Whiting's selection of a subordinate was greatly increased by the many times in his life when he had been rejected or threatened by authority figures. Few career crises can be understood without ascertaining the relative positions of these notions of authority, organization, and self.

NOTIONS OF AUTHORITY

In the managerial mind these notions carry several levels of meaning. One set of meanings may be called conventional. Conventional notions of authority, organization, and self spring essentially from the society at large. Each society evolves certain generalized attitudes and beliefs about authority and what an authority figure should or should not do. Our culture defines certain roles as authority-bearing, and persons filling these positions are viewed as authorities. There are authority roles designated in all of our basic institutions. The role of a superior in any one of these institutions carries certain conventional or well-accepted meanings. Although there are only a few studies on this subject, they generally demonstrate that authority embodies the right to order the behavior of others.[1] In a study of school children's perceptions of labor and management, the boss was perceived as one who gave orders and the worker as one who did what he was told to do.[2] Superiors are generally considered to have the right to expect obedience and loyalty from subordinates.

It is commonly assumed that notions of authority are acquired from birth onward. The main agents for transmitting them are parents and parental figures. These notions become internalized early in the growth process to become basic instruments for making one's way through the world. From one standpoint, life is a maze of authority figures who must be perceived properly and accommondated sufficiently in order to achieve a productive life. By the time the individual arrives at the door of the employment office of the business firm, he has already acquired vast experiences with authority. These experiences have become condensed into brief, simple, often unconscious meanings that allow proper identification with the authority system. To be sure, some have inadequate notions of authority that prohibit their assimilating the authority system of the corporation. However, the vast majority have notions of authority that allow satisfactory relationships to superior individuals.

William Henry's study of thirty, forty, and fifty-year olds in management echelons in business shows that the younger group has an amazingly simple orientation to their immediate world. They see the business world as demanding accomplishment and achievement. They are convinced that assertively following the leads provided them will result in success. "Their interest in their own inner feelings—their emotions, personal desires, and wishes—is negligible. They consult the expectations, the policy, the precedent, not themselves."[3] Here it is apparent that they come prepared to do what is required of them and to look to their superiors for guidance and help.

In another study, the top executive is pictured as being able to inhibit his aggressive feelings toward authority figures because of his high opinion of their function and character.[4] This notion of authority as positive and necessary appears in some studies to be related to executive mobility. Burleigh Gardner's study of 473 executives from fourteen firms shows that the successful executive's idea of authority is that it does not hamper, inhibit, or constrain him; he accepts it without resentment. "He looks to his superiors as persons of greater training and experience whom he can consult on problems and who issue guiding directives to him which he accepts without prejudice." This is a most necessary attitude since it controls the executive's relations to superiors. Gardner goes on to say, however, that "Executives who view their superiors as prohibiting forces have trouble working within an organization. Unconsciously, they resent superiors, or do things to obstruct the work of their bosses, or, finally they may assert their independence unnecessarily."[5]

Two examples of such unproductive notions of authority are provided by Gardner. A young man was accepted for a junior executive training position. He had fine qualifications: good college training, excellent appearance and poise, and agile mental abilities. The psychological analysis detected only one potential source of real difficulty— his concept of authority. He saw his associates as competitive persons whom he must outwit. He had no clear-cut image of superiors as guiding or directing figures. Hence it was predicted that he would soon get into difficulty with his associates and superiors. For about two weeks none of these symptoms appeared. Then his associates began to complain to their department head that this man was being overly critical and cutting in on their work. Soon after, the young man began to be increasingly difficult to direct; he became more resistant to suggestions about his work. The company was finally forced to release him.

The second example concerns a middle-aged man who had been with one company for about two years and requested a transfer to another department. He had been placed in several positions in various departments of the company. In each of these he had done reasonably good work, and there had been no outstanding complaints about him. His name had come up for promotion several times, but somehow he was never promoted. He was tested when he requested another transfer, and the test analyses—made before any of the above history was known—showed him to be a man of good, though not outstanding abilities, and able intellectually to cope with most intermediate-level positions. In his concept of authority, however, he placed himself at the top; unconsciously he felt himself to be better than most of his superiors. When this finding was presented to the man's superiors, they were able to substantiate it completely. They cited instance after instance in which the man acted as if he were "doing the company a favor" by working there. Gardner concludes that the subordinate's idea of authority made it difficult for him to take orders and operate successfully within the organization.

It is apparent from these two cases by Gardner that the notion of authority as inhering in the self of the executive is unproductive. The dominant notion of authority among successful executives involves activities and people in the milieu outside the self. The successful executive feels a part of a wider, more final authority system from which he gains a large measure of his opportunity to act. In contrast, the self-made man has the notion that authority originates with himself, which precludes assimilating with the larger authority structure. William Henry, who has done extensive research on executive personality, remarks, "It is of interest that the dominant crystalization of attitudes about authority is toward superior and subordinate, rather than towards self."[6]

In a study of over 8,000 executives, W. Lloyd Warner and James Abegglen found that "Perhaps one of the most significant personality characteristics of the successful corporation executive is his conception of authority; that is of crucial importance to interpret properly the actions of an executive at a top level position."[7] What happens when youth enters the business world with notions that authority and authority figures are threatening and prohibiting? One possible answer is provided by the Collins-Moore study of 100 businessmen who started their own firms after World War II.[8] Their notions of authority are that it is essentially restrictive, relentless, and rejecting. Their pattern of activity is to run into authority figures, clash and leave, find another job, only to become once again rebelliously involved in another authority system. Obviously, their notions of authority as restrictive largely account for the establishing of their own enterprises where they are their "own boss." In managing their firms they are explicit, overt autocrats in contrast to executives who live within established structures, and who are essentially multicratic or flexible in their administrative styles.[9]

In the corporation world, bosses are the prime givers. Much of the process of the distribution of satisfaction, power, and achievement opportunities is governed by authority figures. It rests largely with them whether the expectations of each member of the corporation are destined to have reasonable fulfillment. In the modern corporation, the key to probably the most potent of all executive needs—the improvement and defense of one's self-image—lies with the authority set. It is these relationships with the authority set that occupy the center of the stage of much psychological difficulty.

An executive, whether president or manager, never completely separates his self from authority influence. The promising young executive's identity is always being influenced by passage through layers of authority. He not only emulates his superiors at times, but adopts their view and opinions as his own. This is aided by certain superiors who identify themselves with the subordinate to an extent, and try to make themselves more assimilable by taking over some of the subordinate's values, beliefs, and standards. In reverse, there are subordinates who are authority resistant. They view superiors as a class that is necessary, but basically useless, reactionary, depriving, or perhaps threatening.

To summarize, the typical executive views authority figures as controlling and helpful, rather than destructive and prohibiting. He has the ability to attract the attention of these older, better trained men, and to learn rapidly from them for considerable advantage. This notion of authority seems to be common to our society, particularly to the middle classes. While this trust pattern seems certainly true for many people, particularly executives, others have a distinct mistrust pattern toward superior authorities. Forthcoming evidence will show that many in the lower classes do not have this positive but reserved attitude toward authority. The entire careers of some executives show the difficulty of effectively maintaining their upward relationships. This mistrust is oftentimes translated into a desire to manipulate and take advantage of their superior. In some cases they learn readily from their superiors and readily terminate detrimental relationships with superiors.

NOTIONS OF ORGANIZATION

The process of becoming an effective executive involves bringing notions of self and superiors into a meaningful, unified relationship within the goal-achieving activities of the corporation.[10] This suggests that notions of authority are closely tied to notions of organization. The notion of authority held by the successful executive involves belonging to a larger order or system of power and prerogative. Obviously, an elementary notion of authority includes the right to order certain kinds of behavior, not just any or all varieties. There are bounds to authority, and a major boundary is supplied by the explicit and implicit purposes for which the authority system is established. Thus, a boss is expected to authorize behavior that is organizationally directed and relevant. In fact, his main task is to show the relevance of his commands to the goals and purposes of the organization. By definition this task is rational authority. Irrational authority involves commands to be obeyed without showing their clear, convincing relationship to corporate objectives and welfare.

What constitutes the conventional notion of organization in its most elementary form seems to be interconnectedness. Our society is highly equipped today to teach children that the universe is orderly and intricately tied together. In this sense, organization essentially means that everything is or in some way can be interrelated. This notion of organization allows individuals to relate to each other and to place a high value upon the products of interaction.

The research of Jean Piaget with children is particularly instructive here. The infant's point of view is that he is the center of the world. A baby, happily watching the movements of his feet, gives the distinct impression of the joy felt by commanding the world. "When the baby takes delight in movements situated in the outside world, such as the movements of the ribbons of its cradle, he must feel an immediate bond between these movements and his delight in them."[11] At this stage of infancy, everything participates in the nature of, and can influence, everything else. Activity becomes possible because what the baby does has its counterpart in responses from others and things. The infant grows into childhood with the confidence that events cause other events to happen, that the world is not without sequence, and that there is an essential amenability to human and physical manipulation. Because of this sequential aspect of events, the child can become an event himself and thereby participate in the affairs of the world. Because every act is seen to have a potential consequence, the child can order his behavior around anticipated consequences. Goal-directed behavior gradually replaces random behavior. He increasingly organizes his behavior by setting goals and determining their efficient achievement. Others are later seen as capable of entering into this organizational process, and the child's activities become expanded to include the goals and activities of others. He achieves the capacity and skill to play the games of others and, later in life, to work for their goals as though they were his own. From early infancy the child becomes gradually organization-prone. All of which is predicated on this primitive belief that all things are in a way connected, or may be connected by the insertion of a human act of will.

In short, through the agency of the home, the child learns the elementary process of transaction, which involves giving and receiving, making demands upon others, and submitting to others' demands. The notion of taking a role and assuming a position within a group serves to provide the youth with a capacity to perform highly specialized jobs and tasks as well as to become properly equipped for them in adulthood. When the young man appears at the employment office, he is prepared to perform limited roles and to seek great satisfaction in their proper achievement.

Essentially, his notion that things must be organized around particular ends allows him to identify with the ends and goals of the enterprise as they are represented to him at his station or position. These more immediate ends or goals become the means whereby the promising young manager learns to bring things together and perform elementary administrative tasks. The notion of an essential interconnectedness among events and things and the affirmative desire to organize makes practical an identification with the corporation as a goal-achieving activity. Through sustained work performance and upward advancement, the goals of the firm take on more precise meaning. Continually adjusting one's behavior to the demands of efficient organization, as measured by the achievement of corporate goals, produces a positive affirmation of the corporation itself. The executive and the corporation eventually come to be emotional counterparts.

Referring to Henry's study of thirty, forty, and fifty-year olds, the man in his thirties seeks to associate himself with the formal goals of the organization as they are defined at his level.[12] In the studies of successful executives, the dominant crystallization of the attitude toward organization is the need to take seemingly isolated events or features and see relationships that may tie them together. Reports Gardner, "The ability to bring order out of chaos is another characteristic of successful executives. . . . In short, they can organize efficiently."[13] What is not said is the obvious. To look for relationships between things and events calls for an underlying notion that there is an essentially possible interconnectedness. This notion of an essential interconnectedness allows operating within vast, complicated systems without losing faith that who one is—one's identity—is important, and does count. It allows, at the executive level, a capacity to hold together the parts of a highly changing organization, and with confidence restructure the parts when necessitated by the goal-achieving requirements.

This notion of organization as an essential quality of human and physical events allows for the direction of vast amounts of energy in narrow purposeful channels that otherwise might be dissipated. Warner and Abegglen show that the successful executive works with facts, is direct in his approach to problems, does not get involved in irrelevant details, organizes his thinking, is markedly crisp and decisive, makes up his mind, and follows through to a solid and definite conclusion.[14] Furthermore, the successful executive is so oriented toward the idea of an essentially possible interconnectedness among things and events that he often over-organizes his environment and himself. Reports Henry:

This ability to organize often results in a forced organization, however. Even though some situation arises with which they feel unfamiliar and are unable to cope, they still force an organization upon it. Thus, they bring it into the sphere of familiarity. This tendency operates partially as a mold, as a pattern into which new or unfamiliar experiences are fit.[15]

Henry concludes that the executive has a strong tendency to rely upon techniques that will work and to resist situations which do not really fit this mold. All of which shows how strongly the executive is prepared to identify emotionally with the organization and goals of the corporation.

The intricate interconnectedness of the big industrial corporation requires vast amounts of faith in the basic benevolence of organization. In 1935, Theodore K. Quinn, vice-president of the huge General Electric Company, and Gerard Swope's self-chosen successor, resigned while still in his early forties. His explanation, "I began to realize that I was serving no socially worthwhile purpose in helping a giant become even bigger."[16] In his book, *Giant Business,* he levels his charge against the monster corporations that have the unilateral power to let others live by tolerance only. He paints a gloomy picture of thousands of small subcontractors and distributors existing in a state of peonage to big business, fearful that at any time they may be cut off and annihilated. He indicts the big organization for what it has done to individuals inside. He contrasts the great self-reliance and ambition of the young men of his own generation with the stunted or idealized notions of self of the young men entering the vast bureaucracy of big business today. He describes the warmth of human association found in the small business corporation, wherein corporate goals are felt to be close to performance and achievement. There is, he maintains, utter inhumanity of man toward man when the corporate goals and organization are involved. "The absorption of human lives in industrial centralization, and in the techniques of less responsible mass movements, belittle the individual. The loss of conscience, mutual respect, consideration, and wholesome humanity becomes greater than any possible gain." To Quinn, what large-scale organization leaves out is an essential personal interrelatedness that comes from "living out one's life in the company of people who really know each other, deep down, and who, living in one community, usually face together social discipline, integration, and maturity."

Many successful corporation executives will take issue with Quinn's notions of the pathology of the big business organization. They will see that they can act within the huge interstices that mark such organizations. Unlike Quinn, the typical executive feels that he can become a significant element in a complex of forces anchored around goal achievement and organization. Several studies show that the tendency to feel inadequate and to throw oneself upon the mercy of the organization is found as much or more in the small company as in the large one. L. W. Porter made a study of the comparative behavior of executives in small and large firms and reported that large companies produce more favorable management attitudes, greater challenges, and less conforming behavior than do smaller companies.[17] What seems clear from this study is that an individual without the capacity to seek out the silent opportunities existing about him, whether he is in a large or small grouping, will become threatened by the demands of the organization. This capacity to seek seemingly hinges upon the internalization of the belief that the organization is basically helpful to the purposes of self-realization. Without this conventional faith, organizations large or small may become threatening.

NOTIONS OF SELF

The Warner and Abbeglen study shows that successful executives "know what they are and what they want and have developed techniques for getting what they want." Of course, how each gets what he wants may be different, but this strength and firmness is a common and necessary characteristic. Henry remarks that too great firmness of self-identity leads to rigidity and inflexibility. "And while some of these executives could genuinely be accused of this, in general they maintain considerable flexibility and adaptability within the framework of their desires and within the often rather narrow possibilities of ther own organization."[18]

These notions of self greatly facilitate organized life. Because the individual feels able to exert some control over his destiny, he is capable of entering voluntarily into organized life and making responsible decisions for others. Our society provides some generally-accepted notions of the kind of person one should become. Once again research is not clear nor adequate. But it is largely believed that conventional notions of self refer to individuals who can act upon cues derived largely from within. The American stereotype of the individual is particularly relevant. He is one who has his feet solidly placed on the ground, knows what he wants, and looks forward to achieving it. It is of interest to note that almost all concepts of mental health regard as important the notion that an individual should be able to stand on his own feet without making undue demands and impositions on others.[19] However, the notion of independence suggests an inner freedom that allows the possibility of choice and decision. Basic to this well-accepted American stereotype is the prior idea that each human being is a unique and separate self. Maintenance and advancement of this uniqueness is the process of self-realization.

The conventional notion of self is simply that of a person who is capable of achieving and maintaining his essential uniqueness or individuality. Registering this essential individuality through activities of work and play becomes the implementation of this conventional notion. From this viewpoint, life is a continual process of developing and realizing notions of individuality. Self-realization implies the capacity to register in activities the resources that stem from one's basic individuality.

Men at the top are firm and well-defined in their sense of self-identity. For example, the executive may view himself as basically a judge. Clarence Francis, former chairman of General Foods Corporation, has said, "Today, most managements, in fact, operate as trustees in recognition of the claims of employees, investors, consumers, and government. The task is to keep those forces in balance and to see that each gets a fair share of industry's rewards." In contrast, Robert S. McNamara, Secretary of Defense, has said, "I see my position here as being that of a leader, not a judge. I'm here to originate and stimulate new ideas and programs, not just to referee arguments and harmonize interests." Both of these executives used divergent views as career guidelines. Both notions of self center around problems of authority and goal organizing.

The executive's view of himself is his most crucial tool of developing and maintaining a productive and satisfying administrative career. When threatened, his career may suffer a partial or complete setback. The search for an adequate executive identity is a central value, and when this search is restricted, such as under conditions of acute threat, the executive's upward mobility is hindered, if not jeopardized. To regain feelings of upward mobility, the executive must once again conduct this search with the resources available to him. He must tap openly and productively the broad range of personality resources at a time when these very resources are being severely restricted. Few people are equipped to draw back from a conflicting situation and gain distance at such a time. Yet it must be done somehow and to some degree if one is not to be continually overwhelmed at each point of crisis.

Few human beings welcome career crises. We may speculate that few arrive at the top without several crises that shake their emotional foundations. A very important event occurs at such times. Essentially, a threat to the executive's feeling of who he is and how capably he can perform requires stepping out of his own identity and scrutinizing it. In counseling situations the executive is encouraged to do more formally and objectively what he might otherwise have to do by himself. He is asked to examine whether what he thinks he is and what he believes he is capable of becoming is at all realistic or desirable. He takes himself as an object. This act does two things. It forces through a clearer, more precise identity or picture of himself in his capacity or role of executive. It allows him to evaluate this portrait. Interestingly enough, he will partially evaluate this identity in terms of what his authority and corporate demands and wishes suggest, and his self-evaluation in light of his own personal needs and expectations. Eventually, all three must become realistically represented and a career strategy devised to lead to an eventual accommodation or balance. The end process provides a better, more reliable definition of what constitutes, for that particular person, the executive role. In short, although a career crisis is not openly received, it turns out to be inevitable for many at some time, and the extent to which it is resolved provides insight into how better to behave as an executive.

THE AOS FRAME

The highly interrelated notions of *authority-organization-self* comprise the *AOS frame*. The successful executive posits authority as controlling and helpful. He identifies with the authority system and gains from this association his own notions of what constitutes proper and improper authority. Porter and Gheselli's study shows that middle-management members identify themselves by the qualities they ascribe to their superiors.[20] These qualities serve as guides for the development of increasingly sophisticated administrative skills.

The self-identity of the executive emerges also as a product of a positive association and affirmation of the organization. The Rosen study shows that "He reacts sharply and at once to its gains or losses, not primarily because he sees in the company's gain a potential advantage for himself, but rather because its gains are his gains."[21]

The author has clinical experience to offer in support of this point. When the corporation achieves success, the executive enjoys satisfaction. Failure causes genuine worry regardless of how his own position is affected.

On top of all of this, the successful executive is also an autonomous person. To be autonomous, first, means having the capacity to find a productive role. This necessitates fitting into a network of human organization. It also necessarily means submitting to the requirements of the authority system. The notion of freedom is forged within this matrix of notions of self, organization, and authority. The autonomous person has the capacity to conform to certain essentials of organization and of authority out of self-choice. Thus, David Riesman defines the autonomous person as one who is capable of conforming to the behavioral norms of his society.[22] Warner refers to the autonomous executive as one who can apply the rules of society to himself, by his own decisions, who knows and can act on what is right and wrong, and who is intellectually capable of making the discriminations that are necessary to a fluid society to operate in positions that are often ambiguous. The autonomous individual is capable of making decisions from within rather than being completely dependent upon the influence of forces coming from without.[23]

The need for autonomy, however, is no guarantee of mobility and success. Warner and Abegglen cite a case of an executive, Evans, who moved to the near top of his corporation. Evans is a man who must, to accomplish his administrative goals, feel that he is free of other phases. He requires a specific goal and will work most effectively when he feels he can concentrate absolutely all his attention, thought, and efforts on that goal. Rules and people, morals and affection, are constricting and dangerous. "They are both tempting and weakening, and serve to prevent the independence and freedom for his situation that Evans requires." Evans has a good deal of difficulty in maintaining the high degree of autonomy he needs to feel comfortable. "His approach to other men is hesitant, and he feels uncertain of himself in relation to them. He mistrusts other men, feels they are thinking ahead of him and using him rather than his being in a dominant position. This causes him considerable dis-ease, and in defense he seeks to establish his own individuality distinct from them."[24] All of which makes his relations with others unpleasant, overbearing, and aggressive, and this seemingly tough, able, independent executive becomes increasingly isolated. Eventually, he is given a position which allows him autonomy, but which is peripheral to the central administrative process of the firm.

Evans' case illustrates that the search and need for autonomy may create administrative isolation. We also notice how Evans' notions of self have become idealized to prevent easy relationships with others of significance in the executive group. Few in this group escape the contempt and superiority stemming from Evans' idealized notions of self. Warner concludes that his kind of executive is seldom seen at the top.

Notions of self also spring from within the executive as an active bearer of skills and potentials of achievement. All executives have private notions of what they are and would like to become which are brought to bear upon their performance of administrative tasks. The successful executive has the capacity to express his self-defined needs and desires within the framework granted by the authority system and the corporate ends of the firm. In a way, he utilizes the goals of the firm and the resources made available by the authority system to achieve self-realization. This capacity to achieve self-realization within the corporate framework provides the necessary changes that assure survival and growth. Men who are only what the corporate system requires, and who take their cues solely from without, are not capable of making the necessary changes that ensure corporate growth and success. In contrast, successful executives have typically strong self-identities.

IMBALANCES IN THE AOS FRAME

We have seen preliminary evidence that the successful executive positively affirms the roles incorporated in the AOS frame as active bearers of productive powers. The AOS frame, or corporate triangle, is essentially a set of basic notions that evolve from active participation in the administrative role. Other ingredients undoubtedly exist to enhance administrative effectiveness. But the notions represented by the AOS frame of mind are irreducible minimums of corporate life. Leave out any one of them and the psychological world of the executive becomes unintelligible. This trilogy of notions may be evoked by the simplest act of interrogation. Merely ask an anxious executive about his administrative responsibility and his remarks will throw up impressions of himself, boss, and corporation.

The key factor to understanding the business executive is that the corporate triangle exists within the executive mind. It is a convenient way of referring to the events and happenings that occur within his inner world. To the individual, reality is what he perceives it to be. He does not act upon what the boss, or his organization, or even he himself is really like. Rather, his behavior is based upon what he thinks his boss is like, what he thinks his corporation demands of members, what he thinks he expects of himself. The corporate triangle is not objective, of course, but subjective and wholly individual. However, the executive may not be cognizant of this difference.

Difficulties in performing effectively are often associated with unproductive and unreal definitions of what the boss is really like, or the executive's understanding of what is required to be a good corporation man may be out of proportion to actual requirements. His self-image may be out of touch with his basic skills and abilities. It is interesting that these images of self, boss, and organization, that may not entirely correspond with reality, may allow for productive adjustments in the executive's behavior. Many times in clinical situations the executive may have impressions that are not completely realistic, but allow him to achieve an inner harmony or to maintain harmony with his boss and organization. Generally, however, the ingredients of the corporate triangle are not simply figments of the imagination. They must largely correspond with actual features and characteristics of the objects represented. Executives constantly search out evidence of what they, their superiors, and their organizational goals are like. This is called reality testing. When they approach a new superior and new position in the corporation, they sample aspects of each. It is much like approaching a strange food by tasting a very little of it to ascertain whether to eat it in larger quantities. Prior experience with a variety of foods helps the individual to determine the qualities of the experience and to make statements of like and dislike.

As the young manager progresses up the corporate ladder, he constantly tests his views of his new superior, or corporation position with reference to prior experiences. He then locates these objects in his own inner world. They take on meaning and value to provide a basis for operating effectively in the new function. By the time he becomes an executive at the higher levels of his organization, he has a well-developed ability to detect what the powers-that-be and the successful achievement of corporate goals require of him. If the images evoked by these requirements of self, superiors, and the organization's goals and policies are unbearable or unmanageable, the executive experiences emotional discomfort. Thus the notion of the corporate triangle serves to provide us with a basis for pinpointing the emotional problems of executives.

It is the view of this book that the executive achieves administrative proficiency by learning to master the strong pressures exerted upon him by the components of the AOS frame. We will show that although these pressures are complex and often inconsistent, they can be resolved. The promising, developing manager who adjusts well to them stands a good chance of moving higher up the ladder of power and responsibility. Those who do not adjust, face the prospect of stagnating in their jobs, or falling back, or even of exhausting their emotional reserves to the point of complete breakdown.

Most executives have a well-defined picture of themselves in their administrative roles. Those who do not, lack a psychic center of gravity and become prey to the conflicting expectations and requirements of corporation life. The consequences of a bad self-image may be disastrous both to the executive and his corporation. An illustration is the recent near-tragedy of General Dynamics, the world's biggest manufacturer of weaponry. Shortly after the Convair Division started an ill-advised venture into jet transports, the board of directors voted to displace Jay Hopkins, the dying founder of General Dynamics, with Frank Pace, an Arkansas lawyer who had held such important posts as President of West Virginia University, Director of the Budget, and Secretary of the Army. He had never run a business before, yet as chief executive officer he was confronted with a highly decentralized empire, operated by strong-minded divisional heads. One of the divisions, Convair, hastily developed a jet transport that was erroneously priced below cost and styled without adequate market potential. The consequence of this development was a $425 million loss. Clearly Pace, at the chief executive level, had not controlled the activities of Convair as a business executive would have done. Pace attributed his difficulty to not having been trained in business. In fact, he never really viewed himself as a business executive. The question, then, is if he had this picture of himself, why did he allow himself to be placed in a position that uniquely required a business executive's point of view and training? Was it because his spectacular career allowed him to believe that he could handle almost any situation?

It is hard to say at a distance what may have been the reason for Pace's misplaced trust in himself and others at General Dynamics. We can suspect that erroneous views of one's self, or failure to act upon proper self-images are important factors in failure. Was political naivete the reason why Roger Blough, chairman of the board of United States Steel, failed to see the possible political repercussions of his across-the-board price rise? During a press conference set up to explain his actions, he confessed that he knew little about politics. If he was as politically naive as he believes he was, why did he not approach an obviously political decision with more caution and advice? Was it because he did not know he was as politically inept as he appeared to himself after his unfortunate decision? No doubt he now has a different or more complete image of himself as an executive. The acquisition of a useful self-image is oftentimes painful.

Clinical experience suggests that changes in self-image are based upon a need. One acquires self-insight because there is some basic reason to be more aware of what one is. The executive's self-image is the distillation of past experiences acquired in the performance of administrative responsibilities. His personal image is linked to and differentiated from the image of his authority figures. An adult person, such as a top executive, is generally assumed to know his own identity. Nevertheless, his reply to, "Who are you?" is often hedged and qualified by his image of his present boss, or his bosses in the past. The reason for this is that the executive who emerges at the top has moved up through a maze of bosses. Each is different, but all have in common the power to give and withhold. The acts of bosses often force through different notions of self.

THE CONCEPT OF PATTERN

The presence of all three components of the AOS frame does not mean that each is *equally* represented in the executive mind. Some executives are preoccupied with what they are and who likes or dislikes them. They may be self-centered, standing in contrast to those authority-centered executives who are moored to the problem of handling superiors or subordinates. The corporation-centered executive may be overly sensitive to the requirements of organizational life, or view with alarm the growing problems of adjusting to bureaucratic tyranny. Whether the executive is self-, authority-, or organization-centered, his disturbance results from a protracted set of experiences. The pattern he reveals goes sometimes as far back as his early entrance into the business world involving difficulties with himself, superiors, or organization.

To be sure, not all executives show a pattern. Some seemingly experience no difficulty until they reach a particular station. If studied at that time, their cases could not be justifiably labelled "centered." But suppose at that point in his career, an executive meets for the first time an impossible boss who scares the wits out of him? Perhaps he handles the situation badly and finds himself on the outside looking in. He may move to another corporation or get a transfer within, only to discover another difficult boss. After two or three extremely difficult superiors, the executive might begin to feel emotionally involved in problems of power, authority, and prerogative. He may even detect at times a dreadful fear of superiors. When his history takes this direction over a period of time, one can legitimately call his case authority-centered. The same history of difficulty would be equally necessary to label the next case self-, or organization-centered.

It is not known how many executives are self-, authority-, or organization-centered. In fact, these categories were not constructed for purposes of scientific research. They came from clinical or therapeutic situations and are somewhat arbitrary in that their identification seldom leads to successful solutions of executive problems. To say that an executive is authority-centered does little to help him. But by starting with his history of authority difficulty, a basis is provided for bringing other aspects of the executive problem into view. It is at this point that the other components of the triangle show up. One can not become self-centered by living in a vacuum. People and activities become the basis for idealized images of one's self. Furthermore, people and activities become the agents of therapy. The only way to help an executive who has grandiose notions of self as an administrator is to help him construct a different picture of those around him and to engage in different administrative activities. The authority system and organizational goals and purposes are inextricably involved in this therapy. This is not to say that other factors are not important. If the executive's anxiety is anchored in his administrative role, however, the components of the AOS frame are always present and serve as the basic factors of his therapy.

HISTORY OF THE AOS FRAME

The requirements of the corporate triangle are historically verifiable. In the early entrepreneurial stage of business activity, the problems of organization, unity, and integrity were minimal. The emotional difficulties of aspirants to the top positions were largely authority-centered. The boss was more crucial to the subordinate than the operationally directed goals of the corporation. These were totally the boss's concern. Authority was directly and overtly exercised by the boss, who set himself up as a model. He tended to believe in a sharp separation between work and pleasure, and to feel personally threatened by idleness and apathy. The subordinate had to love to work, which meant to show great respect and regard for the dictates of the boss. There was considerable use of punishment or coercion in enforcing this strict relationship of submission and deference to his authority.

In this authority-centered period of American business, the trusted subordinate often adjusted by internalizing the norms, values, and beliefs of his boss. He became an extension of his chief in his own conception of himself, while at the same time he performed at an emotional distance from him. The development of a substantially broadened base of corporate activity forced the need for a more cooperative form of executive behavior. Instead of a single authority center, groups and committees—formal and informal—sprang up to give overall direction to the massive concern. Participation brought on an enlarged consciousness of the total base of corporate activity. An increased use of indulgence and casualness in dealing with superiors and subordinates proceeded to shrink the emotional distance between them. Communication, reasonableness, human relations, became crucial qualities. The effect was to allow the aspiring executive to become more attached to the on-going purposes and goals of the corporation. The corporation became emotionally alive in the mind of the subordinate executive as an identity which, as such, was a useful instrument of administration. Executives on the move toward the top learned to feel an obligation to the goals and purposes of the firm that transcended the personal interests of themselves and their bosses.

The executive today must be as organization-minded as his predecessor was authority-centered.[25] This means that the executive does not think separately of the interests of the stockholders, the employees, and the customers. On the contrary, this new executive thinks of the interests of his corporation without regard to the special interests of stockholders, workers, or customers. The corporation exists as a total psychologized reality which is basically the essential interconnectedness of the many interest groups that press claims upon the executive. It is this organization or interrelatedness of these claimant interests that give him his concept of the corporation. To this concept he attaches his notions of self. The result is that he thinks and acts as if it were his corporation, even if he has no ownership share in it. As George Katona shows, when the corporation achieves success, the executive enjoys satisfaction. Deterioration of the firm causes genuine worry, regardless of how his own position is affected.[26] It is interesting to speculate that executives today enjoy more autonomy because of emergence of meaningful identification with corporate goals alongside authority expectations. Executive authority is more rational because it is justified more on the basis of the objective necessities of efficient corporate goal achievements and less on the rights of command.

The development of organization-minded executives does not occur in a vacuum. Some one or group must initiate and reinforce this form of identification. This is where the superior comes in. The executive is not simply a corporation or organization-centered man. He must also be very cognizant of the role of personal, unmediated authorities. He must today be every bit as cognizant of authority figures as was the executive at the turn of the century. Unlike the latter, the present executive must also assume a high identification with the corporation as an entity. In short, the executive's psychic center of gravity pivots around two forms of awareness: authority and organizational. But there is still one more base upon which executive identity develops. It is the expectations that the executive levies upon himself, in addition to those placed upon him by the requirements of authority and corporate goal achievement.

MARK WHITING: A RECAPITULATION

Mark Whiting had been able to make the necessary attachments and separations from jobs and men during his rise to the position of vice-president of marketing for the Universal Chemical Company. As vice-president he became closely attached to the values and goals of the corporation. Some of these he had been instrumental in initiating and executing. The bond between his personal identity and his corporate achievements became strong and complete. Whiting conceived of himself as Mr. Universal Chemical Company. This strong attachment between self and corporation eventually prevented him from deferring to the judgment of his superiors.

He had experienced difficulties with authority figures in the past. Anyone who made him feel puny and weak became a threat to his feelings of self-esteem and confidence. As a young man he was aggressive and cocky to compensate for his feelings of inadequacy and inferiority. In his early business career he continued to lash out at those superiors who tended to make him feel weak and small. In order to move up the corporate ladder, Whiting had learned to quash these aggressive feelings under the mask of a deferential attitude toward superiors.

As he moved up the corporate ladder his self-confidence became disproportionately buoyed up. As vice-president of marketing, he allowed his rapid ascent and his many achievements in the executive group to go to his head. He acquired inflated ideas of who he was, what he could do, and where he was going. In other words, he acquired an idealized notion of self. When he was severely reprimanded by the president for his selection of an incompetent subordinate, his enlarged and exaggerated idea of self responded automatically.

His previous pattern of lashing out at superiors who threatened his self-esteem and respect returned in full force. In the period that followed, Whiting nullified all of the accomplishments that he had so carefully achieved for his career's success. He mobilized his forces to prove that he was a bigger, better man than the president who had made him out to be a fool.

The president, however, brought in a successor who inherited all of Whiting's aggressions. Because he had become untrustworthy, unstable, and vindictive, Mr. Gray found it necessary to immobilize

Whiting's power and support. His collapse was made complete when the new team finally took away "his" corporation by making it into something entirely different. He was now without an emotional attachment to the corporation and without administrative support from the authority set. His loss of self-respect and confidence made his career crisis complete.

He struggled intensely with all three components of the AOS frame. He tried to recover authority, to become reattached to the corporation's goals and achievements, to again become a highly respected and appreciated person. This he did without success. Under professional guidance, however, he transferred his energy and attention to outside organizations. He worked hard for their aims and purposes, gradually acquiring the necessary authority to innovate new and different goals, or ways of more efficiently achieving the old ones. Whiting's understanding of himself grew with each success. He gradually realized what had made him fail in his bid for the presidency.

He now understands more clearly that he has a built-in vulnerability to authority figures. Brilliant programs calling for vigorous action aimed at corporate success do not necessarily overcome bad relationships with superiors who are vested with authority and the power of determining their successors. Perhaps we could argue that superiors should be big enough to overlook difficult human relationships with their subordinates. The facts of life oftentimes do not square with these ideal prescriptions for human character. Big men may become as small as the men who attempt to destroy them.

The case of Mark Whiting is not completely resolved. It may seem fantastic to the reader that Whiting has not given up his aim and ambition to become once again an important person in the Universal Chemical Company. In spite of his rebuffs and humiliations, Mark Whiting refuses to believe that his career there is finished.

To understand the indefatigable stamina and determination that often emerge from executives who are in a career crisis, we must go back to some of the basic values of our society. We shall next see that executives like Mark Whiting are driven by the need to be successful. Success, when achieved, creates the anxiety of possible failure.

VII

Three Basic Crisis Patterns

Successful executives are predominantly *high achievers*. They typically have the capacity to master the administrative situation sufficiently to make real their notions of who they are and what they wish to become. Their self notions become validated through achievements, which, in turn, bring forth new, positive notions of self as goals. Thus they are relatively independent of the opinions of others for their cues to self-identity. For their development and continual growth they depend on their own potentialities and talent resources. This autonomy means relative stability in the face of hard knocks, deprivation, frustration, and the like. It means being independent of the good opinion or affection of other people. The honor, status, reward, prestige, and love they may bestow or receive are less important than self-development and inner growth.[1] These secondary satisfactions serve as benchmarks showing degrees of achievement. They are indicators and not goals: important to, but not dominating of, the self.

In contrast is the *pseudo-achiever* for whom the secondary products are mainly stressed. For him it is not the doing, but the arriving that is all-important. Henry writes, "The person with this latter drive, looks to the future in terms of glory it provides him and the projects he will have completed—as opposed to the achievement drive of the successful executive, who looks more to the sheer accomplishment of the work itself."[2] The high-achiever type is by far the more predominant.

The high-achiever seems to have many things going for him. Why then does a career crisis develop in such a person who presumably is emotionally prepared to take almost everything? The belief that a strong self will necessarily and automatically achieve itself is, of course, naive. This idea is a remnant of the tradition of the Franklinian great man, and the titan's success ethic. No person is perfectly protected from the stresses and strains of corporate living. Any one executive may have built-in deficiencies that may become active and dysfunctional under certain crisis-like situations.

A. H. Maslow has attempted to identify the imperfections of the high achievers. They are occasionally capable of an extraordinary and unexpected ruthlessness. They are strong people who are capable of deploying a "surgical coldness," when this is called for, beyond the power of the average man. "The man who found that a long trusted acquaintance was dishonest, cut himself off from this friendship sharply and abruptly and without any pangs whatsoever. . . . Some of them recover so quickly from the death of people close to them as to seem heartless."[3] In addition to being strong, they are independent of the opinions of others. They live in a more or less impersonal world in which acts of kindness, humor, and careless chatting are not as common as for other people. They are not free from guilt, anxiety, sadness, loneliness, and conflict.

Henry has noted the "self propelled" nature of the dynamics of the achievement-oriented executive who needs to keep moving and to see another goal always ahead. "In spite of their firmness of character and their drive to activity, they also harbor a rather pervasive feeling that they may not really succeed and be able to do the things they want."[4] This sense of the "perpetually unattained" means that there is always some place to go, but no defined point at which to stop.

A characteristic of the corporate top is the limitation placed upon its numbers. There is just so much room at the top. There are many more high achievers than positions. What happens when a high achiever's upward mobility becomes arrested? Henry believes that the executive whose mobility is blocked either by his own limitations or by those of the social system, finds his energy diverted into other channels. This redirection may be manifest in psychosomatic symptoms, interpersonal difficulties, and neurotic solutions. Uncertainty, constant activity, continued fear of losing ground, and the ever-present fear of failure exact a high toll of the personality.

His enthusiasm for organization may become a liability. The Cohens' study shows that the executive derives a sense of well-being and security from knowing how to get others to do things that he decides are worthwhile goals for the department or corporation.[5] However, he may actually set the goals too high, or too low, or organize too efficiently. The dangers in organization are manifold and real. As Gardner suggests, the executive may have an inability to make room for other people—for the right people.[6] This weakness is emphatically borne out by clinical experience with high achieving executives. Rosen shows that a frustrated mobility drive may cause repressed guilt and eruptive fears of failure. Strong negative motivations may result in the form of obsessive-compulsive traits, negativism, irritability, suspiciousness, and feelings of persecution. "Oppositionalism becomes outright obstruction of company policy, hysteroid reactions develop into inability to make realistic decisions, disorganized behavior increases to the point where the executive cannot be trusted."[7] In short, the high achieving personality is not without anxiety potential. The corporation is fraught with anxiety-creating situations. We shall next see that some of the highest achievers break under the strain and become unanticipated casualties.

We shall see that some executives have *authority-centered* career crises, others have *organization-centered,* still others have *self-centered* career crises. This centering on one part is largely a function of the other two. Executives who come to a counselor for resolution of a career crisis are not without difficulties in all three areas in some degree of intensity. We shall call these areas authority-centered anxiety (ACA), organization-centered anxiety (OCA), self-centered anxiety (SCA).

THE AUTHORITY-CENTERED PATTERN

Analysis of clinical cases of executives in career crises suggests that most of their difficulties are precipitated by disturbances in the emotional attachments to the authority system and the goal-organizing and achieving activities. Their mobility may become arrested because of difficulties with superiors that are in no way related to goal-setting and achieving activities. Or they may have excellent relationships with superiors, but are deficient in organizing and goal-setting skills. We shall now attempt to reconstruct some of the more anxiety-producing administrative patterns. Keep in mind that we have no evidence that the successful executive who does not become disturbed by a career crisis usually evolves these very narrow or centered patterns. Evidence for these patterns has come from clinical experience with career crises, and the usefulness of these patterns must be limited to the way in which they were acquired.

The authority-centered pattern represents an executive whose career crisis seems anchored around the relationship between notions of self and notions of the wider authority system of which his self is a part. The authority-centered pattern shows linkages back to previous relationships involving authority. The present difficulty cues off the residue of anxiety repressed or denied by the defensive dictates of the self. The present impending danger signals an alarm more threatening than might actually be the case were there not a previous history. The executive over-reacts, and may unknowingly contribute a major share to his own crisis. In Diagram ACA(1) the relative distances of the lines shows this pattern of identification. He feels moderately close to the goals, policies, and procedures of the corporation (S-O), as well as those that are represented in his particular

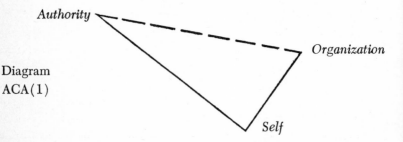

Diagram
ACA(1)

Authority

Organization

Self

administrative situation. The high achievement drive has been productively applied in the service of these organizational forces. However, he feels relatively distant from his authority set. The boss is felt to be threatening and is also perceived as emotionally distant from the organization. Generally, in such a pattern it is found that the executive has always been unconsciously afraid of authority. In childhood he may have viewed parents and parental surrogates with highly negative regarding tendencies for their power and freedom. He may have reacted acutely to the use of their power differentials against him in punishing and corrective efforts. But because hatred of parents is an act against the conscience, the boy may have repressed his negative feelings, and thus may have created a strong desire to be like one of them in his adult life. Lurking behind this positive identification may be the hostility that was never allowed to work itself out. Always he has some feelings of restriction in the presence of superiors. Occasionally, these anxieties break out.

THE CASE OF ARTHUR: ACA(1)

The case of Arthur is especially relevant. He had this inner hostility overlaid by close feelings of identification with authority figures. When Arthur failed them or they turned irrationally against him, he over-reacted as though they were so powerful that he was incapable of handling them. In his developing career, his ambivalence was allayed by directly making stronger identification with the goals, policies, rules, and regulations of the corporation. He learned to allay his authority-centered anxieties by developing an administrative style that was sensitive to realistic and practical goal-setting, and an efficient organization to achieve such goals. He became known as a high achiever. His superiors noted that in his upper-middle management positions he had great organizing ability. He exuded corporate loyalty, and took over assignments courageously and enthusiastically.

Arthur became a member of the executive group at the age of forty. He dug into the job of helping set long-range strategy by acceptance of corporate planning responsibility. Although for the most part the executive group worked closely together on proposing and revising strategical goals, Arthur was often deferred to in matters of reorganization necessary to implement these corporate strategies. Although his behavior showed great corporate loyalty, actually he felt only moderately close to the corporation and to the goals he helped to achieve. This is the usual pattern of the successful executive as Henry, Warner, Rosen, and others see him. He felt that emotional distance from the president and chairman of the board was a decided advantage, since he was extremely cautious in not becoming too intimate. However, Arthur was never sufficiently identified with them to become highly trusted. Trust is not as much of a problem at the lower levels, because the area of administrative freedom is restricted.

It is not uncommon for presidents, especially if they have to assume the role of board chairman, to wish to trust completely any replacement. Some presidents feel difficulty in admitting that this intangible quality is really what they look for in their choice of replacement. The president in Arthur's case was convinced that unless his replacement could be trusted, he should not be allowed to run a large corporation with the vast amount of power available to him.

Arthur was passed up for a man who had less organizational genius. This everybody agreed upon. But the wound had been struck and it now bled profusely. His whole administrative style had been predicated on reaching the top by developing superior organizational acumen. Arthur was not content to be in a staff position the rest of his administrative life. The repressed hostility and fear toward authority figures activated open distrust and hostility toward the new president. His emotional distance grew greater. Soon he found little interest in even chatting with the boss about relevant responsibilities. His preoccupation grew to absurd proportions; he saw all kinds of dangers ahead for the corporation, many of which could not be substantiated. His judgment became compulsively fixed on a few overworked notions. This rigidity cramped his effectiveness.

Although Arthur was removed by the president and given less crucial problems, actually the president hoped that Arthur would work out of his difficulties. Instead, Arthur became worse, openly hostile toward the executive group from which he was disenfranchised. The interpretation of this act of exclusion unlocked a barrage of unreserved anger at the president. A verbal scuffle was terminated by the suggestion that Arthur take some time off to relax and get hold of himself. Later, when he was calm, the president said, "You are too valuable to be lost to us. We need you, but you don't seem to need us." Arthur did not want to leave, fearing what would happen during his absence.

However, he was encouraged by several close colleagues to go away for a month. Arthur set out with his wife and daughter for the Bahamas, only to return three days later in a state of acute anxiety. In the course of his case analysis, it was discovered that he had not really known or enjoyed his college-age daughter before. Her presence made him feel extremely guilty and pressed upon him an even greater need to succeed. Arthur rushed back to throw himself into the task, the success of which alone would justify his failure with his daughter. During the first afternoon back, he had an acute attack of indigestion. This made him extremely concerned about his health. His work pattern showed definite signs of withdrawal and resignation. He spent unusual amounts of time with his daughter, much to the growing displeasure of his wife. He gave unstintingly of his energies and emotions to his concern for his health and his daughter. Finally, the president urged him to seek administrative counsel. Arthur was directed to the author, who, with the aid of a psychiatric colleague, helped him to recover his productive, administrative style.

Arthur's case illustrates a common executive difficulty—how to develop and maintain positive but moderately reserved attachments to authority figures. Arthur's separation from a pattern of steady movement toward increasing administrative responsibility cued off anxiety that eventually became unbearable. He tried, but could not become once again emotionally attached to the remaining administrative opportunities and duties. The anxiety was partially converted into psychosomatic symptoms, and partially discharged in the form of neurotic withdrawal and resignation. (See Chapter VIII for more details of this mechanism.)

Diagram
ACA(2)

THE CASE OF ALBERT: ACA(2)

Albert's case is represented in Diagram ACA(2). This authority-centered pattern reflects a close identification with the authority system and its chief magistrate, the boss (A-S). Like Arthur, Albert was moderately identified with the goals and policies, procedures and rules of the corporation. His corporate loyalty was also moderately positive and reserved, as is commonly found in successful executives. He was known as a good company man, and cheerfully took on new assignments. However, Albert had naive trust in superiors, and unlike most executives, had no emotional reservations about them. He had put his high achievement drive in the complete service of his authority set, particularly the boss himself. He had never really defied authority or stood up to it when reasons were available, and could not even if he were prodded. Albert was completely trusted by every boss during his steady but not spectacular rise through the corporate system. He became the executive vice-president, and as such really acted as a gatekeeper to the president. Through his office Albert allowed to pass only those people and ideas that were relevant and important to the president.

For ten years Albert had carefully modeled himself after the president. He had learned from him how to make decisions, to communicate, to veto, to delegate. Through the president he had learned how to create the necessary myths that represent needed explanations of why things happened that could not be explained by facts. The corporation had come alive in him as the exact duplicate of the president's version. He and the president were as one. (Albert occasionally slipped and referred to this relationship as "we.") Other members of the executive team came to rely upon Albert for decisions, which he could make with the boss's assent. Albert could so well predict the boss's judgment that he would fudge his own decisions as the boss's. It was expected that he would succeed to the presidency.

After the chairman of the board died, the president, at the next meeting of the board of directors, had himself and Albert ratified as chairman and president, respectively. After the annual meeting, which put the formal stamp of approval by a voice vote, the chairman went to Africa on a six-month hunting trip. Three months later, Albert became known as "table it Albert." He could not make a difficult decision. Problems would pile up and when they got so high, Albert would finish them off in one night in rapid fire succession. Many proved to be bad decisions, a fact which made Albert all the more hesitant and anxious. One very bad decision had to do with a pricing policy that placed them out of effective competition with their rival firms. The furor from the board and significant stockholders could not be countered by the now timid, weak Albert. He made the unpardonable administrative sin—he got the board active. The president had what appeared to be a heart attack. Medical authority declared a failure of heart functioning due to extreme fatigue. The chairman came rushing back and assumed the title of chief operating officer. Hearing this while in the hospital, the president made an unexpectedly quick recovery, much to the amazement of his physician and colleagues. Albert assumed his position as gatekeeper and showed his usual presence and judgment. Five years later, both chairman and president retired, "happy together ever after."

Albert's case illustrates the crisis that may ensue when a subordinate becomes merely an extension of the boss. Without firm, personally acquired and authorized notions of self, he had nothing inwardly to rely upon when the boss left. As the image of the boss and how he behaved grew dim, his problems grew big, pushing him into an acute state of anxiety that eventually arrested his administrative style. This style was completely revived upon the return of his beloved boss. The boss's power became his until retirement.

Albert's case also shows how inadequate or improper emotional identification with authority figures eventually became generalized to include inadequate determination of organizational policy. Feeling inwardly weak, without the omnipresence of the power figure, Albert could not trust his own decisions. His acquired notions of self were borrowed and not personal. This constituted his corporate triangle. False notions of self acquired from overly strong attachments to an authority figure resulted in inadequate administration of corporate goal setting and policy formulating.

THE ORGANIZATION-CENTERED PATTERN

Arthur and Albert represent two opposite versions of the authority-centered triangle. We turn next to two opposite versions of the organization-centered triangle. Notice must be given to the relative length of distance between the self and the organization in the OCA(1) pattern. Here the self is felt to be emotionally distant from the goals, policies, rules, regulations, and achievements of the corporation (S-O). The self is felt to be at a medium distance from authority figures and the authority set.

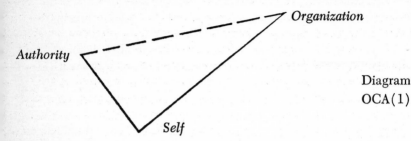

Diagram
OCA(1)

THE CASE OF OSCAR: OCA(1)

Referring to Warner's and Henry's views that the typical executive identifies with the boss but holds a moderate amount of reserve, Oscar's authority relationship seems to be typical or normal for a successful, mobile executive. Because he was not overly attached, he could, if necessary, express clear and meaningful acts of autonomy. However, Oscar failed to internalize the corporate system to make it his own. He successfully held off investment of self in the corporation's goals, policies, and achievements. Consequently, he was free to take them or leave them. Out of the intrinsic rewards of administrative achievement, he accepted them for their instrumental value.

On the surface, Oscar could pass for a professional administrator. Given the goals, he could administer any organization. However, he had a basic weakness. There was nothing really sacred to him. The traditions and precedents built up over a fifty-year period of corporate existence and growth were not respected by him as they were by those who identified more closely with the corporation. This inner freedom to violate easily and unanxiously did not seem to be disadvantageous to him. He was privately proud that he was not an organization man. Valued notions of self were based largely on being a respecter of authority, but not a respecter of man-made institutions such as this corporation. He showed considerable objectivity in a situation where others were partial to the acquired wisdom and achievements of previous corporate officials. To the members of Oscar's executive group, several past presidents were, as Warner illustrates in his Yankee City series, demi-gods. The beliefs and values of these heroes of the past were frequently cited and frequently distorted for winning petty arguments. There were offices named for them, chairs at great universities endowed in their names, a philanthropic foundation established in the name of one of them. Even today, many years later, the corporation is still the length and shadow of the illustrious heroes of the past. Few rise to this executive group who do not incorporate the values and beliefs of these heroes.

In the minds of all members of the executive group, except Oscar, the corporation had become a meaningful, symbolic representation largely through identification with these past giants. The current president is a living shrine to them, his office a museum, his home a replica of a past great. There are many totems erected to the prestige and greatness of this past-regarding corporation. One taboo prohibits smoking in the board of director's room, around the walls of which are hung portraits of the demi-gods. In this room no one is allowed to raise his voice above the sedate serene level of near inaudibility. Dress is always in subdued tones and traditional style is never violated. We could continue to show how the firm today is deeply rooted in the past.

Inwardly Oscar was a totally unadulterated maverick. He used to laugh silently at all of this ritual and ceremony. When he wanted to become president, he did not dare to laugh, even privately to himself. His great ambition was to move the corporation out of the "dark ages" and into the blinding light of the roaring mid-fifties. Oscar could not wait to break the taboos and crush the totems. Carefully he cultivated a repertoire of eulogisms, but they were not really believed. If he was careful, respectful, and patiently loyal, he believed he would become the next president.

In a solemn occasion, marked by no change at all in emotion and expression, the president nominated Oscar for the presidency during the annual board meeting. In this majestic oak paneled, nineteenth-century-style boardroom, he was nominated to the presidency in about the same fashion of forced equanimity that a previous item concerning a minor expenditure was proposed and accepted. The meeting moved on swiftly to the next equally minor affair, approval of the budget that had been in painful preparation since the end of the annual meeting a year ago. Before the meeting was over, Oscar showed his maverick style and it permanently set the tone of his administration.

He dared to get up and express his thanks. This was unheard of, simply because no one becomes president of this great corporation because he feels grateful. However, he did speak quietly to the point and the affair was dismissed as unimportant.

With the passage of time, Oscar showed his disloyalty to the corporate tradition. He proposed a number of new items, most of which were turned down by the board. On one item he invested notions of his whole self: moving the corporation from an essentially manufacturing orientation to a marketing orientation. He began by giving more voice to the marketing people. He identified with their problems, appealed to their itch to become a bigger, better department with more influence. In no time at all, he had a first class fight on his hands, fought, of course, in the emotionless low key of traditional respect and reserve. Oscar had waited ten years for this struggle, had marshalled his inner reserves well, but the accusation of disloyalty was finally and formally made. The corporate gods had been offended; they cried out for vengeance.

The vice-president in charge of production rose up to accept the gauntlet. Oscar was now in a struggle that was to last for two long years, during which time neither side was powerful enough to win or weak enough to lose. Oscar came within one vote of ratification exactly one year after the struggle developed openly. It was a defeat of unexpected proportions. Some had betrayed him, other supporters had not acted prudently. Oscar could not back down, not after almost winning. He changed a few arguments, and reorganized several features of his marketing strategy to gain lost support. Anything could be arranged—the strategical goals, means, organizational design, and implementation policy. Eventually, all became changed, much to his own detriment. One year later, all support waned. Oscar was revealed as having no really sincere commitments.

In the past, he had never replaced his cynicism with a set of highly valued organization goals and strategies. These were worked out in an effort to continue the sequence of movements toward the presidency. The self never actually became identified with his marketing program. (See Chapter VIII on identification.) The fight culminated in his being removed as chief executive officer and kicked upstairs as secretary of the board with a raise in salary.

Oscar's acute anxiety was not due to his removal. It was, rather, based on shame for having been so well stripped of his masquerade. The ignominy was intolerable. Oscar developed a compulsive desire for self-effacement. He sought love, affection, sympathy, and understanding. He minimized self, inflated others, gave vast amounts of time and energy to finding anyone to support who would support him. Always, he took defeat gracefully, since his identification with authority figures was normal and positive. Five years after his solemn nomination to the presidency, Oscar was a confirmed neurotic with a compulsive need for love.

Oscar's case illustrates the need to believe in something other than authority. The administrative style may become severely distorted by the absence of some firm corporate identification and organizational philosophy. Corporate goals cannot be artificially constructed if others are expected to believe in them. Others will test not simply the realistic feasibility of the goals, but the individual's sincerity. Oscar's sincerity was tested in the peculiar tempo of this tradition-directed firm. Other executive groups may have different ways of testing sincerity. Sincerity stems basically from an identification with the firm, believing in its essential character and not wishing to do violence to it without conviction. The firm was eventually moved into a marketing orbit with Oscar an inattentive witness, seated at a lonely distance from the vital center.

An organization needs a philosophy, a reason for existing, and a set of basic beliefs. The chief formulator and articulator is the president and his executive group. A president like Oscar is a dangerous threat to any organization. With no philosophy of what should be the normative position of the firm in society, no commitment to a set of highly valued goals, the Oscars could be sold on some goals and purposes that are basically dangerous. With the presidency occupied by one who will not critically examine each and every proposal in the light of an internalized organizational ethic and philosophy, who is to provide this normative function? Oscar failed to replace his cynicism with a personal philosophy of business organization. This form of moral freedom is anathema to the development of organizational integrity and personal responsibility. This kind of behavior is found often enough in clinical case files to suggest that this is a common pattern when one associates rather than identifies with the organization as a carrier of both a tradition and a future. (See Chapter VIII for meaning of association and identification.)

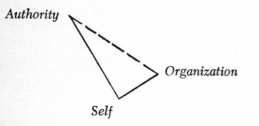

Diagram
OCA(2)

THE CASE OF OLAF: OCA(2)

In the OCA(2) pattern, the executive commits over-identification with the goals and values of the corporation (S-O). He acts very much like the super-ego of the executive group. As the corporate conscience, he seeks to keep the deliberations and activities of the executive group within the framework of the established objectives, policies, procedures, rules, and regulations of the corporation. In the past he has shown strong bureaucratic tendencies. For most executives, the organizational framework anchored around corporate goals and purposes provides a needed guidance and allows them to concentrate upon their achievement and work demands.

Olaf had always shown a strong disposition to over-identify with roles and procedures in his childhood institutions of home, school, and play. He seemed to excel in the ability to recall all the relevant rules operative to the activity situation. Olaf's history shows a strong emotional attachment to the mother figure, the home, and his home town. He had never really left home emotionally, remaining well-attached to the symbols of security and nourishment. He always felt comfortable in well-organized situations and uncomfortable in unstructured ones. His emotional need for order made chess fascinating to him and poker repulsive. In his college courses, his tendency for structure propelled him into the more bureaucratic skills of science as opposed to the humanities. He graduated with degrees in engineering and chemistry with high honors.

In industry he was not an outstanding success as a technician. After several years, he got a job as a management trainee in his present firm. Here he showed a proper identification with the authority system and a sufficiently warm but detached attitude toward colleagues and subordinates. His capacity to work well within the limited confines of lower middle management brought his superiors' attention. They marked him for a thirteen-week, middle-management training program at a leading university where the approach was very traditional, logical, and methodological in the management and organization subjects. He became well-versed in the so-called principles of management and applied them with realistic practicality to the assignments in middle-management positions. He constantly studied the history, precedents, tradition, and rationalization of the corporation at any given level. He showed a strong ability to perfect existing work systems, pouring vast amounts of self into his organizational routines. He became known for his efficiency and precision, impeccable cleanliness, and fantastic memory. He tended to over-organize managerial assignments. But this was not too distracting to his superiors, since most middle managers in this highly technical chemical firm did not excel at organization.

Only once was Olaf given an ambiguous, unstructured assignment. The novel situation was threatening to Olaf, but he was extricated by a wise superior who put sufficient boundaries around his responsibility and suggested several important organizational techniques. Olaf and this superior worked so well together that the superior came to rely upon Olaf for his organizational skill. Olaf's close but reserved identification with his superior placed him in good stead, and soon it became apparent that he was going to get a promotion on the heels of his superior's promotion. These two moved together into the executive group when Olaf was forty-six years old. Promotions had left an indelible imprint upon his administrative style. He increasingly realized the high payoff in identifying closely with the corporation. Unconsciously he was engaged in a subtle process of becoming self-immersed in the bureaucracy, traditions, and policies of the firm. Because many in the executive group relied upon him for his expertise, he came to feel a growing sense of importance, far beyond his relative worth to them. The organization as a whole gradually became substituted for other identifications, including those of superiors and subordinates. It became *his* corporation and pangs of insecurity and discomfort occurred whenever people ignored his thorough, precise understanding of policies, tradition, rules, and regulations. Anyone who defied a rule or treated carelessly a policy received his subtle or overt wrath.

The president came to rely heavily upon him. In the slight economic depression of 1958, the executive group entertained some rather drastic ideas. One of these had to do with a complete reorganization of the firm from a product division system to an industry or family of related products divisional structure. Entertaining this drastic change was too much for Olaf. He liked the present structure, had learned to know it better than anyone else. Of course, others expected him to resist. It was obvious that a man so firmly rooted in the corporation system as Olaf would give them a hard time. Olaf mustered his forces well. Others who felt considerable security in the established system supported him. The president and several "young turks" from marketing and advertising went for the corporate realignment. It was adopted by a majority vote and sent to the whole board for ratification. Olaf saw a last chance to get it stymied. He rounded up several prestigious outside members of the board who placed much faith in his judgment and who liked the system, probably because they were largely ignorant of some of the changes pending in the whole industry. He persuaded four of them to vote against ratification. At the board meeting, the executive group recommendation offered by the president failed by two votes.

To Olaf, the rape of his corporation had been avoided. However, subsequent events proved that he had merely forestalled the attack upon his corporate mother. It became apparent during the board meeting that those who voted against the recommendation had gotten most of their information from Olaf. The president sensed treachery. It seems that a member of the executive group is not supposed to air his complaints to corporate officials outside of the club. Going to an outside board member was a direct attack on the president, his autonomy and control. Knowing of Olaf's support from the outside board members, the president decided to bide his time and remove Olaf at a future date.

A year later the president moved against his enemy with the cunning of a fox. He gradually withdrew Olaf's best subordinate by assigning him to a different position that seemed to be well-fitted for his competence. Meanwhile, he started a deprivation pattern against

Olaf by withholding necessary information and, later, by giving misinformation under the guise of confidence. Next, he promoted Olaf to second vice-president reporting directly to the executive vice-president, a man of strong personality who was one of the last remaining autocratic types. Under Olaf the president placed another very strong, almost rebellious, executive who was ready for reassignment, but who was held on to get into Olaf's hair.

These two executives, a superior and a subordinate, were not sensitive and appreciative of tradition, bureaucracy, and rules and regulations. They had learned to apply them to get the job done and to acquire authority and power. They cramped Olaf in a vise of aloofness and inaccessibility, alternated with authoritarian domination and control. Olaf was constantly at odds with these two who could not be persuaded by Olaf's superior bureaucratic wisdom. To Olaf they were grave threats to the corporation. He set out to crush his subordinate. He was emotionally capable of doing this because, like most mobile executives, he had a typically detached relationship to subordinates in general. Because he had a moderate respect and distrust of superiors that seems very common with executives, he was capable of turning on them, too, when he perceived them to be hostile to his corporation. He turned on both, and out of the struggle his subordinate was removed, but Olaf was transferred to an obviously dead-end position. This movement away from a central position amounted to acute separation from his corporation. Anxiety invaded his whole administrative style, leading to an extreme form of inversion of his affection. Inversion constitutes a withdrawal of the emotional investment, leading to a depersonalization of the object originally identified with.

The corporation gradually grew less and less real and meaningful. He became annoyed at things he once upheld. At times he turned wrathfully upon the very people who had identified with his acts of corporate loyalty. Instability, obstructionism, aggressive humor, and bureaucratic sabotage gradually emerged in his administrative style. He went from bad to worse. His career floundered amidst the corporate rocks where once he had found security and comfort. Emotionally he became mother's bad boy, who, disappointed because he could not protect her, decided to attack her. While attending a meeting of business leaders of the chemical industry, he heard of a case similar to his and responded by seeking out similar professional help.

Olaf's case is clearly over-identification with the corporate figure. His distant, but basically positive, attitude toward authorities allowed him to take them or leave them. What affected his decisions was whether they stood for the same things he did as the active conscience of the corporation. If he had over-identified with authority figures, he could not have rebelled. He would not have gone behind their backs and slit their throats via the garnering of opposition from outside members of the board of directors. The executive group likes to keep the board of directors passive. Olaf activated them and thus reduced the autonomy of the executive group. This is an unpardonable administrative sin. He became a threat to them all. The president and the executive group gradually came together in their opposition to him. Even the several members of the executive group who supported him at first saw the necessity and desirability of supporting the president. Olaf became synonymous with board interference and had to be dispensed with. His career crisis is in many respects unique, as are all executives' crises, but it is one version of organizational over-identification.

The important consideration in all four of these cases of career crisis is that each executive had a high need to achieve. The life style of each had taken shape early around this important value. Each developed positive notions of self as an achiever and believed he could continually grow in his capacity to achieve. Each showed in the early stage of his career the application of this style to his managerial situation. For each, an administrative style, predicated on strong feelings of continued achievement, eventually became arrested at some crucial point, causing anxiety. Each executive had the necessary neurotic potentials to cause the arrestment of his achievement drive. In all four cases, this arrestment became a crisis of self. The deficiencies became active, and mastery of the administrative situation became correspondingly difficult. Thus, high achievers are not perfect, but rather possess imperfections as do low achievers.

Unproductive notions of authority and organization have thus far been accounted for as neurotic potentials. These potentially neurotic notions of authority and organization lead to drastic changes in the self. The whole administrative style becomes out of tune with the reality of the impending danger. We must next account for productive notions of self that in career crises spill over to distort productive and adequate notions of authority and organization.

The Self-Centered Pattern

The self-centered anxiety pattern constitutes basically unrealistic, idealized notions of self. In the SCA(1) diagram, the distance of the self from the authority and organization system and these two systems' perceived proximity constitutes the idealized self. Here the notions of self become so dominating and inward-directed that the executive feels emotionally distant from both authority and organizational objects (S-AO).

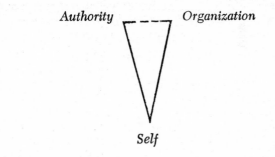

Diagram
SCA(1)

The Case of Sam: SCA(1)

Sam was a supreme egotist, who felt infinitely superior to the administrative task. In Sam there never were any conscious doubts that he could become president. Few reservations were entertained about his ability to perform any assignment, if he wanted to. From early childhood, everything he did was to overcome feelings of inferiority. He became compulsively addicted to proving his prowess, mastery, and potency. In his late adolescent sex life, he became a Don Juan, moving from girl to girl to prove he could handle even the most resistant. In attitudes, he had a flair for the dramatic, as though he was always very conscious of each person in the audience watching him. Defeat, stupidity, failure, or inadequate skill brought him to the edge of intense shame. Always he bounced back to prove that he had merely not tried hard enough. He thrilled at glory and bled at failure. In track he out-ran others, not because he wanted to test his inherent strength, but to prove his superiority. In college he set about continuing his adolescent successes but with greater competition. The drive for glory was not yet too great to require him to take account of reality. He measured his rivals, observed their defects, moved against them with the studied zeal of a chess player. He remembered all successes and repressed all failures as quirks of fate, oddities of situation, and peculiarities of people.

His reputation as a big wheel on campus and his high scholastic average made him an attractive candidate for a large corporate managerial training program. He decided, however, to stay for a master's degree, and during this period he married the daughter of a very prominent upper-class family. His successful marriage added to his already idealized image of self. The case files show that this pattern of marriage could belong to any number of self-centered executives.

We next observe Sam in a middle-management training program several years ahead of most men. In the classes, he was extremely quick to show understanding and very facile in asking profound questions. He still had a boyish trait that made him appear to be bright, hungry, but socially immature. His superiors decided he needed grooming and placed him in a very difficult position in the firm. They wanted him to get in over his head and to call for their help, hoping that he could become more cognizant of the need of help from others. He did much worse than they had anticipated, and got into severe trouble. He could not find enough excuses; he implicated innocent persons, and defended his own competence. He was thoroughly admonished and sent back to a position several grades lower. He used a trick he had learned in college football. He had sufficient alertness to again study his superior and the mobile managers around. He realized that they all tended to look positively to their superior for help, and supported organized goals and procedures that included others. He developed a pseudo-democratic style, much to the internal anguish of his idealized self. He acquired instrumental identification (association, see Chapter VIII) with authority and organizational objects to enable him to avoid any failure again. While he was working hard and actively releasing energy resources, he was not aware of how emotionally isolated he was from the authority system and from the values and goals of the corporation.

Sam developed an administrative style that took him far up the road toward the top. At the age of thirty-eight and in a position commanding a salary of $35,000, Sam had his next crisis. It was extremely unexpected. Basically it stemmed from misreading the cues of authority figures; a mistake that is common to self-centered executives due to a tendency to be concerned only about self. He was asked to become a special assistant to the public relations director: a staff man to another staff man. This was interpreted as arrestment of upward mobility. Actually Sam was being placed on a temporary shelf away from an authority figure who was knifing him behind his back. Sam had never been told of this treachery, or that he was to be reactivated as soon as possible. To say this might reveal a respect for him that his superior felt was not yet completely justified. Yet, they saw great things ahead for Sam and, for this reason, took him out of incipient trouble.

Sam's idealized self prevented reading these cues. He immediately took flight and accepted a position in a competitive corporation that always needed junior executives and evaluated highly those developed by Sam's corporation. He received a substantial promotion as sales manager for the whole corporation, reporting directly to the vice-president of marketing. This spectacular rise enhanced his long-standing conviction that he could do anything and the top was merely waiting to receive him. The members of his corporation extracted valuable ideas from him, which he had obtained from his experience in the previous corporation. He felt big and important and manufactured as much information as he had actually obtained.

Luck entered the picture at this point. The marketing executive sent his key subordinate to the Continent to set up a multi-national market structure for the sale of the corporation's products abroad. The boss and Sam developed workable relationships by which Sam acquired a great deal of corporate visibility. He could still control his self-centered tendencies to gain information, experience, and support. Suddenly, the marketing executive died of a fast-developing malignancy. The executive group picked Sam because they could not bring the other subordinate back from Europe at this time. They told him he was acting manager of marketing, and that the other executive might be given the title of vice-president of marketing upon his return. Determined that no one would dislodge him and that no one could, he pitched into the task of making the opportunity over to fit his career designs. It became increasingly apparent to the executive group that Sam, now forty-three, was immature. They could see what he had in mind and set up blocks when it was strategically desirable. Hemmed in, and without permanent portfolio, Sam took to cultivating a few select members of the executive group. He hauled out his prize possession, his well-to-do, charming, sophisticated wife and used her to penetrate the closed circle of executive wives. She did her job well. Because she was basically a nice person, they took to her, and thereby she and Sam moved into the social world of the corporate system.

All the while, his self-centeredness was beginning to show in his administrative situation, and it began to show now in combination with the social situation. Sam had committed a mistake that egotists, by their very nature, are apt to make. He overexposed himself and, thereby, his idealized self too. The effect was lethal. The president called for the return of the executive in Europe whose assignment was almost completed. For his own sake and that of the corporation, he was apprised of the situation, but not completely informed about Sam. However, one of the prerogatives of a vice-president in the corporation, and in many other institutions, is that he is allowed to select his own crucial subordinates. Believing in this principle, the new vice-president of marketing immediately had Sam's name given to the executive personnel committee for relocation. Sam found the entrance of the returning executive intolerable, his ascendancy to the vice-presidency threatening, and his own transfer unassimilable to his massive self. He immediately resigned and, much to his surprise, he was encouraged to leave.

For the first time in his life, Sam felt the pangs of complete isolation and loneliness. Because he had neither emotional identification with authority figures nor emotional identification with the corporation, he could very easily entertain the thought of resigning. He did, and they called his hand. Now his lack of identification with authority and organization brought extreme feelings of anxiety. He was alone for the first time, separated from the instruments of self-glorification. The tailspin was acute and complete. The thought that he had failed could not be entertained by his grandiose self. The others were completely wrong, stupid, foolish, for letting such a good man as himself go. All of his achievements, extending as far back as his college and high school days, paraded before him in semiconscious review. Of his mistakes, weaknesses, and failings, he was not conscious. By means of this review of his past accomplishments, he could not understand how anyone could fail to realize that he was a "big" man. To add to his troubles, his wife was thoroughly embarrassed, as were her upper-class parents. The story he concocted to keep her on his side was a mixture of rationalizations, untruths, and projections all geared up more to preserve his idealized notions of self than to preserve her pride. By the time he faced her parents, his story had been told so many times that he thoroughly believed it—and so did they.

With the help of her parents, he acquired the vice-presidency of marketing of a small firm in the upper-eastern region. Having by now a low capacity to respond to reality, he failed to see how incapacitated his idealized self had made him. His weak, hostile administrative style was no longer simply compulsive competitiveness. It became a weapon to destroy others. He appealed to aggression. This appeal involved his whole life style, even encompassing his marriage area. (See Chapter VIII for meaning of life style.) He argued with his wife, beat her, and stripped her of dignity and self-respect. She left him, and with the children went to her parents. He did not care, for now he could put his whole life into achieving vindication. He manipulated authority figures and conceived attractive goals for the organization. He charmed, wined and dined, pushed, retreated, and complied, all for one purpose—complete and total success and vindication. He got several stockholders and a banker to put up money for enough stock to gain control of the corporation. At the age of fifty, Sam became the president. However, under his maniacal direction the corporation went steadily downhill. When the capital assets became substantially greater than the value of the stock, a giant corporation bought the majority stock out from under him. He was absorbed into the big corporation as a member of the board of directors because of the large block of stock that he owned and controlled. But because of his record as a poor president, he was given no administrative post.

The case of Sam is one of isolation and loneliness. A real emotional cost is paid for incapacity to relate positively and meaningfully to authority figures and to corporate goals and values. Sam is a rebel whose cause is himself and whose glory is in the complete and total defeat of others. To all ordinary appearances Sam is, today, a man of position. His initial investment of $100,000, partly borrowed and partly acquired from savings, is now worth about two million in stock of the large corporation. He dresses well, drives a fine automobile, makes frequent speeches for the chamber of commerce and trade association groups, and has many acquaintances. He has few close friends, no wife and family, no real identification with society, community, and corporation. Outwardly successful, inwardly he is weak and impoverished. Around the night clubs he is his old Don Juan self. In his church he has now become an elder, and in his political party, a loyal champion. He has addressed himself to all the self-enhancing positions in his society. He seeks always to prove his superiority.

Sam is no respecter of authority or organization. His notions of self make him appear to be bigger and above the laws of human association. It is possible for the self-centered executive to feel strong superiority feelings toward either authority or organization. In Sam, neurotic feelings of superiority were directed toward both the authority figures and the goals and values of organization. When only one becomes the object of superiority feelings, the administrative situation is potentially less anxiety-creating. The executive may feel vastly superior to the requirements of authority, but his rebellious tendencies may be kept partially in check by his organizational identification. Or his tendency to rebel against the values and goals of the organization may be kept in check by positive identification with the authority figures. The completely self-centered person is a rarity in large business corporations. Usually some internalized respect for authority or organization will keep the idealization-of-self process within more productive and realistic proportions. Sam is an example of an exceptional case.

ACA, OCA, SCA

It might seem that self-centeredness runs high throughout the other two basic crisis patterns—ACA and OCA. The executive may show an authority-centered pattern because he is only concerned with self needs. The authority-centered pattern essentially reflects an overly-pronounced concern with the problems of authority and authority figures. This concern may stem either from irrational needs and fears of authority (ACA) or from an enlarged view of self

(SCA) that prohibits easy relationships with authority. Likewise, the organization-centered pattern essentially reflects an overly-pronounced concern with the problem of organization. This preoccupation may stem from irrational needs and fears (OCA), or an idealized self (SCA), that will not allow adequate integration with organizational realities. Then, too, it is possible for there to be self-centeredness that is not accounted for by the emotional possibilities inherent in the other two patterns.

In all three crisis patterns, there is more importance attached to one feature of the AOS frame to the detriment of the executive's career. Authority, or organizing and directing goal-achieving activities, or self may be the constant active concern of the anxious executive. When one factor assumes transcendency, disturbances in administrative relationships usually ensue. We turn next to see what happens to the executive when his anxiety spills over the boundaries of his administrative role to flood all other areas of his life.

VIII

Crisis of the Total Self

Of significance to the study of administrative anxiety is the notion of life style. The formulation of life style is original to Alfred Adler's thinking concerning the developing personality. In all personalities, Adler posits a basic feeling of inferiority and an urge to overcome it by achieving the goal of superiority.[1] Accordingly, the basic fear of feeling inferior sets the child on a course to achieve the necessary feelings of superiority. The more feeling of inferiority, the stronger the drive for superiority. Once a direction is set, the life style emerges. Events and meanings are assimilated that fit the life style, others are rejected.

In describing the outline of a life style of a particular person, Adler gave particular attention to the significant external circumstances with which the person has had to cope, and the attitudes he has adopted toward them. These attitudes are seen particularly in the pattern of his overt behavior, occupation, illnesses, beliefs and moods, relations with his family and business associates, love relationships, and eating and sleeping habits. In other words, the life style manifests itself in all of the characteristic areas of human activity and determines the ways in which the person will handle his life problems. The life style will show certain essential, predictable qualities that mark off the individual from all others.

It is best seen when his efforts to achieve the goal of success are in conflict with the external possibilities. Conflict and anxiety emerge in response to blockages of the life style. Although Adler did not use the term anxiety, it is clear he uses the concept when he describes feelings of inferiority as basically feelings of inadequacy and helplessness.[2] It is the fear of confronting a feeling of worthlessness that drives the neurotic into retreat or establishes unrealistic estimates of self marked by implacable demands for success.[3] The danger of having his worthlessness and inadequacy revealed is worse than the defects or defeats inherent in any attempted solution. The closer he is pushed to recognition of possible failure, the more vigorously he asserts his drive for success. In the neurotic, success striving springs from feelings of inner weakness or, to be more precise, from the attempt to avoid the pain of being inadequate and helpless.

LIFE STYLE

We shall use Adler's term, *life style,* but vary the meaning so as to indicate ways in which an individual copes with his many areas of life. Life areas involve those activities that are more or less valued. Values are structured in a series of concentric circles, with those at the center comprehending and organizing the peripheral values. Values held central to life arise from sustained activity, rather than casual or random activity. They are a product not only of activity, but also of choice. The individual does not value all things he deals with and produces. "Certain things or conditions or experiences are seen as 'better than' certain others. This perception and decision are essential to the emergence of value."[4]

Adler constantly referred to three life areas: social adjustment, work adjustment, and adjustment to love and marriage. The three areas represented the basic problems of life. Although he made no attempt to classify further the social and cultural values, it is necessary for us to see that the whole life style represents relatively permanent ways of handling valued activities, ranging from religious through educational, community, political, economic, familial, and sexual association.

Out of the variety of possible activities, the young adult selects a particular combination which marks him as a unique person. He takes on a job and starts to grow with it, accepts a marriage partner, selects a community and begins to function within it, and forms an internally consistent political-social ideology.[5] As Havighurst suggests, a good many young people take the whole decade of the twenty to thirty age years to accomplish this task of focusing their lives and acquiring a sustained pattern or style of life. They experiment with a variety of occupations, they have several love affairs, try out several religious variants and several political ideologies.[6] What emerges from this decade of focusing on one's life style is a more particularized notion of what one is and wants to become—self identity.

In the next decade of thirty to forty age years, there follows a rather stable period of collecting one's life resources. These resources are channeled into the life areas that mark the dominant concerns of self. Success becomes a matter of acquiring skills and experiences and focusing them upon valued areas of life for which they were devised. In our society, one area of life that is most highly valued is that which concerns making a living. Success is largely found in occupational activity, and this area tends to organize many of the other peripheral areas of life, such as religious, educational, political, and social. The studies of adult patterns of life show this convergence upon the occupational area and that it moves to the center of all other life areas.[7] Achievement in the occupational choice is for many tantamount to becoming successful in life. Failure in this one life activity cannot be easily compensated for by success in any of the other life areas. For this reason, feelings of inadequacy and worthlessness largely derive from perceived failure in the occupational role. Or to put it more precisely, the most painful form of anxiety ensues from impending dangers in the occupational role.

Much of what passes today under the label of mental health or maturity is related to the values inherent in the Protestant success ethic. A man is considered healthy if he can work and achieve, and when he cannot, the presumption is that he must not be well. Studies show that worry, when it interferes with work, increases the risk of mental health impairment.[8] The childhood training of the middle-class child is aimed at tangible success and achievement within an occupational role. The blockage of the drive for occupational achievement brings on a higher risk of mental health impairment. Anxiety that originates in the occupational role often spills over to invade other areas of life. The whole life style may reverberate in sympathy to the stresses and strains of occupational failure. Suppose that one does not value highly a rich assortment of other life activities. The midtown Manhattan study suggests that failure will be all the more perceived and generalized to the whole self.[9]

One possible reason why the lower classes incur a greater risk of psychoses is because they have fewer opportunities to work off their anxieties arising from economic failure or deprivation. The anxieties of the middle classes may become arrested at milder stages of mental disturbances because they more highly value and have more effective access to other life activities, such as entertaining, organized leisure and recreation, status-giving social affairs, and so forth. For most, the relationship of occupational identity to the whole life style is clear and unmeditated. Successful achievement of one's occupational values brings a high estimate of self-worth to all other life areas. No one can sit quite as comfortably in church, on the board of directors of a charity organization, with a political party committee, or on a board of trustees of a school or college as he who has become a success in his occupational role. Likewise, those who have achieved success in highly valued occupations are usually asked to become officers and directors of these organizations. Given the evidence available, it is justifiable to believe that for many, particularly the middle classes, the whole life style of the person pivots or gravitates around his occupational identity.

The salient feature of the big business executive is his administrative style. By this is meant a patterned way of approaching problems of authority and organization that distinctly marks him off from all others. His administrative style may be directly seen in all corporation situations, where problems of authority and organization are primary, and only indirectly seen in other activities, including leisure, community activities, church related celebrations, and services. Wherever the demands of authority and organization lie central to the maintenance and development of the executive's life style, we may observe a specialized section of his life style: his administrative style. For this reason, the administrative style may manifest itself in problems of authority and organization in the home, school, community, and church. There is a strong tendency to maintain consistency of administrative style throughout all life areas involving authority and organization.[10]

The executive is a person who has a unique life style, which he seeks to maintain and enhance. This life style represents the sum total of his notions of self. Further, clinical experience with career crisis of the executive shows that persistent identification with the managerial problems during his lengthy rise through the corporate hierarchy tends to develop an administrative style which is central to his general life style. A part of his sum total notions of self are those that meaningfully relate to his administrative role. These specific notions of self represent his administrative style. In short, his whole life may become gradually nucleated around his administrative style.

What is needed to prove this shrinking of life style to administrative style is evidence that the executive becomes completely wrapped up in his career demands and goals. This evidence would show that over a protracted period of time, administration occupies a major share of his life. It becomes, so to speak, his whole life. Scientific evidence is not yet sufficient to clearly affirm this point.[11] However, clinical evidence suggests that for the vast majority of executives, life and work tend to become overlapping and synonymous. Literally speaking, his work of life is the work of administration. In other words, the major object of emotional attachment for the typical executive is the administrative role. It is not simply, as many people believe, the corporation or the presidency. This is the essential mistake of the popularizers of the organization man thesis.

ADMINISTRATIVE IDENTIFICATION

The big business executive is emotionally committed to the task of becoming an increasingly effective administrator. This bond between self and the administrative role is often what people mean when they use the term "professional administrator." It so happens that the better part of administration has to do with matters of authority and organizational goal achievement. However, the counselor must see that these matters are relevant only insofar as they pertain to the administrative task. It is for this reason that a middle manager may have only fuzzy notions of the long-range goals of the corporation and still be emotionally identified with his managerial role. Being a good manager, he is no doubt identified with the sub-goals of his section, department or division, since these are within his administrative grasp. The same reasoning may be applied to authority and authority figures. In other words, while the middle manager may entertain distant emotional attachments with top authority and long-range corporate goals, his most intense attachments are with figures closer to his managerial task. At the top, of course, he attaches himself to top authority and overall corporate goals, since these symbols are close to his administrative task. Here his personal goals and the goals of the corporation become intimately fused.

An essential ingredient of an administrative style is the kind of attachment involved. In *identification,* the individual may be observed to respond to the behavior of other people or objects by initiating in phantasy or in reality the same behavior in himself. Identification tends to be subjectively identical.[12] That is to say, the individual tends to behave as his interpretation of the other's behavior dictates and allows. It is possible to identify with objects as well as ideas. Administration is foremost a set of notions that an individual possesses about what he wishes to do and what is required of him in a particular occupational setting where matters of authority and organization are inextricably involved. He learns to identify with these ideas by means of seeing how others assume the administrative role. He may distantly identify with superiors and goal-achieving activities, but he is essentially using these identifications to show himself how to achieve personal identification with the authority and goals of his own administrative role.

This pattern seems typical of the high achiever. The studies by Warner,[13] Henry,[14] and Dill[15] seem to concur in this finding. The high achiever seeks to enjoy the acts and results of a job well done and looks only secondarily to someday becoming the boss and engineering long-range corporate goals. All of this pertains only to the individual who emotionally commits himself to the serious job of becoming an administrator. Those who arrive at the top seem to have made this strong identification with the administrative role.

Some have not, of course. For these individuals the term identification may not be properly used. Rather, the term *association* is more useful to designate the kind of attachment, and may be used to convey the idea that an individual draws next to an idea or object but does not become firmly attached to it. Thus the middle manager or executive at the top may associate himself with his work role, but that may be as far as he goes. The test is that when he leaves his firm each evening and goes home, he freely, if not gladly, leaves behind those burdens that beset him at work. In a way, he practices disassociation (non-psychoanalytic sense) because he has not the qualities and ambitions necessary to become firmly attached and absorbed by his work. Disassociation is relative and never complete. Even the worker feels at home to some extent in his role as an employee. However, studies by Dubin show that many workers do not intensely identify with people at the factory or office. Their primary identifications are not with work groups, but self-selected groups at home and in the community. This is largely accounted for by the little opportunity to achieve personally and show tangible evidence of achievement in a highly organized, impersonalized mass-production factory. The worker associates more than identifies with his work, corporation, and boss.

Some executives reveal, in clinical data, only weak identification to the administrative task. They stand emotionally next to their ·jobs, but not firmly attached to them. This is not the majority pattern. Rather, the majority are emotionally anchored in administrative achievement. In a career crisis this may change, however, and the executive may become unduly concerned with particular aspects of administration. These possibilities are described in the previous chapter under authority-, organization-, and self-centered patterns. This centering may occur as a response to acutely felt anxiety. The ideal would seem to be to identify with the administrative role as a balanced, integrated scheme of notions of authority, organization, and self.

AFFINITY OF LIFE AND ADMINISTRATIVE STYLES

The importance of acts of attachment lies in the effects upon the life style. Young men whose emerging styles of life fit them favorably for the lower managerial roles may find through identification a permanent way of life. They come to attach themselves to the managerial, and later, upper administrative roles so that their whole identity becomes directly affected, enriched, or restricted. By the time they are ready for the executive ranks, the administrative style occupies the greater share of their lives.

In numerous instances, the author has noted that executives who identify with the administrative role may practice association with other roles in the community—school, political party, or charity organizations. They may drop their roles and take on others, largely because of how they relate to their administrative identification. Whereas they may be emotionally capable of dropping all of these activities in the other life areas, they cannot long endure the thought of not being an administrator. Clinical experience shows that perceived success and failure in the administrative role helps to predict the kinds of activities valued by the executive in outside organizations and how they will be approached. Often, the executive will interpret his administrative role to include participating in these outside affairs. These external activities may be associated with, not identified with. In such a case, the executive may become a director of a community campaign fund, not because he really believes in it, but because this is what a successful person can do and what a business executive should do. Because all other life areas become nucleated around the administrative role, the executive enjoys internal consistency and self-consistency.[16] We may speculate that he is successful in the administrative role because all other life areas are committed to the primacy of administrative success.

In the case of acts of association (drawing next to but not being firmly attached) the administrative style does not enjoy the full support of the whole pattern of life. There may be intra-psychic compartmentalization and even conflict because of the hesitation of the individual to commit his whole life to the tests and strains of administration. Many times it is found that individuals who have an unconscious fear of failure actually contribute to their failure because of the disassociation of life style and the style of administration.

When the whole living pattern is committed to the successful performance of administration, vast amounts of energy are made available that otherwise would be held back. The life style directs energy into activities which can be assimilated with it.[17] When these activities are held alien, energies are withheld. Failure or precarious marginality may result.

The successful executive is typically a high energy type. He freely expends vast amounts of psychological and physical energy in the administrative task. Inwardly, he is not in conflict because through positive identification with the administrative career, he enjoys the support of the life style. He has first things first and has organized his whole life accordingly. Because of the affinity between his total identity and his administrative self, blockage of the latter is recorded psychologically as blockage of the former. When his style of administration is threatened, his whole self-identity may become threatened.

This executive can no longer sit as comfortably on outside boards and committees owing to his perceived failure in his occupational area. Such a failure may create a career crisis threatening his whole life style. Thus a career crisis may become a crisis of the total self. Likewise, because of the affinity between administrative style and life style, knowledge of the former provides insight into the latter. The counselor can gain information about the whole person by knowledge of his administrative style. In association types, this is not possible and calls for a different handling of the case.

Administrative identification is more or less an unconscious act. This is what differentiates it from administrative association, which is more casually responsive to the immediate objective demands of the job. In administrative identification, the client who comes for career counseling is not aware of how much his whole life pivots around his administrative role. Identification with the administrative role actually involves the absorption of large quantities of the total self.

The threat of separation from the administrative role reveals anxieties that penetrate his whole concept of self. These gross anxieties may be denied their full implication. The client may deny that they mean so much to him as to make him uncomfortable at home, in church, in the community, and so forth. This act of repression may give rise to symptoms of behavioral disturbances in these other life areas. This is a form of displacement. It is not uncommon to find dysfunctioning in the client's parental, social, and community roles, or his role as husband. Through repression, separation anxiety may become generalized to the whole life areas. The complaints may or may not be about these disturbances in human relations in non-business activities. Often complaints are limited to the administrative situation. Seldom does the client initially know how severely his whole life style is being threatened. He expresses a more or less sub-clinical difficulty having to do with a specific administrative problem about which he is gravely concerned. Further information may show how much he has staked his whole life on his administrative career.

It may frighten him when he is confronted with the full implication of his career crisis. Until then, he may maintain great faith that if worse comes to worst, he will not be fired. (At the executive level very few are actually fired. The failures are frequently put on nicely prepared shelves, often with additional pay.) Or he may feel that he can start over again, which, of course, is not possible because of his age. Few corporations that can afford his salary and need his competency will hire him at lower levels because pension rights, stock options, and ancillary privileges become far too expensive. He may feel that he can go to work for another company at his present level or higher, but this idea becomes threatening to him too. The reason is that he becomes fully conscious of how much his present administrative role means to him, and failure in it means failure in life. He must succeed in the present role because his whole life style presses toward final success. Anything less, such as a shelf or movement to another corporation, is a recognition of failure and becomes a source of intense threat. These thoughts are held alien to the self, and unreserved attention is devoted to overcoming the immediate administrative difficulty.

The executive who forms an elementary association with the administrative role faces his crisis situation somewhat differently. Typically, he is motivated to perform well not by the satisfaction of administrative achievement, but by the satisfaction of the secondary rewards of money, power, prestige, and status. These secondary rewards have become primary. When this is the case, separation from the immediate administrative situation may not be intolerable if those secondary rewards are not threatened. Shelving or lateral employment may be positively received, whereas in the identification case, they may be threatening. However, if these secondary rewards that have become primarilized are threatened, he may tailspin just as acutely. In this case, his crisis situation may be extended to invade his whole life. His social, family, and religious life may evidence difficult human relationships.

It must be understood that his tailspin is qualitatively different from that of the identification type. With the latter, his crisis becomes generalized to the whole life style because the administrative style is threatened. He has identified with the administrative role and the primary rewards of achievement. In the former case, the client has identified with the secondary rewards of money, power, status, and prestige and made them the central values of his life style. He, too, cannot sit as comfortably on outside, non-business boards and committees, not because he is a failure in his job, but because he so desperately wants the glory, status, and power that comes with these appointments. Of course, he may actually want to stay on these boards and committees because he genuinely believes in their purposes. In such a case, the above statements have no relevance. We all know, however, the individual who searches for the glory in the high-status job and in the high-status positions in the community. Of course, his career crisis may be felt every bit as intensely as the other, but its genesis is entirely different. It is quantitatively similar, qualitatively different. Hence the necessity to check out the true basis whereby the executive relates to the administrative role.

The executive who merely associates with the administrative role may have repressed the extent to which he is acting only to gain secondary benefits. This repression is likely to occur if he harbors guilt for accepting money, power, and status under "false pretenses." In such a case, the success ethic based on achievement is deeply imbedded in the personality. Speaking anthropomorphically, it says, "put the whole self in the service of your employer." "Seek ways of achievement first, and all other things will be granted unto you."

Guilt and shame may ensue from his loose attachment to his administrative role. Likewise, he may have partially repressed the extent to which he has made secondary gains primary to him. In the clinical situation, this repression will have to be reversed to adequately diagnose the crisis situation. Many times it turns out that he is in a crisis of separation from the secondary satisfactions because others have sensed this lack of commitment to administrative achievement. He may have over-identified with these secondary satisfactions to the point that he fails to give careful attention to the primary responsibility of achievement and performance.

PROBLEMS OF OVER-IDENTIFICATION

The question of *over-identification* is next to be analyzed. It is convenient to say that too strong an identification essentially constitutes going over and beyond the administrative role and directly attaching to the values of authority and corporate goal achievements. These become values in their own right, which is contrary to our picture of the typical mobile executive. In a way, over-identification means over-shooting, going beyond the administrative role per se. The values of authority or corporate goal achieving, or both, become maximized. Instead of identifying with the boss and corporation enough to adequately perform his administrative tasks, he identifies with the administrative task enough to pursue the ends of authority and corporate goal achievement. (These solutions are described in the previous chapter as specific reactions to career crisis. These reactions did not take account of their effects in other life areas, which is the major concern of this chapter.) Gaining authority and determining corporate goals becomes the basis of his drive toward the central task of administration. Others in the executive group become merely instruments for his acquisition of greater authority and greater control over the corporate goals and purposes.

Of course, it is entirely legitimate to use others in the executive group to fulfill one's special duties and responsibilities. This is interpreted as cooperation and teamwork. The executive is applauded for his sincerity and competence. He is essentially non-threatening to them, since his competency is channeled into a prescribed role. The authority he uses is not to get more authority, but to get his administrative job done. The goals he sets and helps others set are not to fit his personality as a glove, but to enhance his administrative responsibilities.

It is well-known that those who help shape the overall goals of the corporation are usually called upon to assume leadership within the executive group. This leadership may be informal or formal. In the latter, the title of president is usually given. When it becomes suspected that an executive is trying to set goals of the corporation to enhance his position, he usually becomes a direct threat to others who have similar aspirations. Over-identification is quickly and often unfairly ascribed, because it is often projected by others similarly inclined or constituted. Consequently, over-identification is hazardous for two reasons, one psychological and the other sociological. In the former, it traps the executive because he invests energy in high payoff activities, leaving little reserve for the necessary menial and routine administrative tasks. He overshoots. In the second case, it is hazardous because it is felt by others (oftentimes invalidly), and they set up countermoves to curtail him. Now he is in a power struggle.

The typical successful mobile executive identifies positively but somewhat reservedly with authority and authority figures, and with goal achieving organization and policies. He may even entertain the ambition of becoming president and occupying the most central position in the organization. But his primary identification that overrides all others is to the challenge found in the administrative task at any given level. Administrative achievements cause him to want more challenge and to look up and to the center of the firm. The position of the president is attractive mostly because of the administrative challenge and not primarily the power and the glory.

The authority-centered executive has his commitment to administration largely distracted because he finds authority too fascinating or threatening to treat as a mere means. (See the cases of Arthur and Albert in the preceding chapter.) The organization-centered executive has his commitment to administration distracted because he finds organization too fascinating or threatening to treat as a mere means. (See the cases of Olaf and Oscar.) The imperatives of structure become the ends, as we have seen in cases where individuals have over-identified with bureaucracy. Norms, rules, policies, and purposes become upheld as sacred.

The case of Sam in the preceding chapter illustrates over-commitment to self to the exclusion of sufficient amounts of respect for authority and organization. Usually, notions of self, organization, and authority are kept in balance by the necessity of doing the administrative task well. This advances corporate purposes and causes the receiving of support from authority figures whose tasks have been aided by such performance. When performance of the immediate administrative task no longer receives the primary loyalty of the self, others are likewise affected. The integrity and viability of the corporation become jeopardized by a mad scramble for the secondary rewards of power, money, and status. In such a turmoil, no one has the security of power or status.

In a way, each would-be administrator enters into an unconscious social contract to make the job at hand more important than the job ahead or behind, and the achieving of it more basic than the extrinsic rewards that might emerge later. Many in the executive set are able to sense and feel, rather than actually describe, the individual who by character and attitude seeks achievement first, and authority and organizational security, or status, second. By the efforts of this type of individual, successful corporations, communities, and nations may be built, but by the efforts of the man motivated by secondary rewards they may be ruined.

It would seem that the executive can over-identify with the administrative task. This may very well mean the shrinking of the life style so as to become totally synonymous with the administrative style. The repercussions upon the individual as a person are well known. He becomes a stunted man with a trained incapacity or occupational deformity. He may injure outside groups and organizations by his tunnel vision. The evidence by Henry, Warner, and Gardner, however, seems to suggest that this form of over-identification does not hurt the individual's chances of success within the corporation as much as it does outside of it.[18] There may be harm done to the individual, and the corporation for that matter, but perhaps not to his career. It is for this reason that over-identification with the administrative role per se is somewhat less dangerous than over-commitment to self. If, however, over-identification develops from a neurotic base, the consequences to self and corporation may be great. (In this regard see the section, "The Search for Comprehensive Solutions.")

Having said this, it is now necessary to make an addition to the above thinking. There is a form of over-identification which relates to maintenance of the *acquired* administrative role and position. Just as over-identification may occur with authority and organizational goals beyond one's administrative sphere and responsibility, so may it occur within the administrative sphere and with regard to *present* levels of authority and goal achievement. An executive may be so anchored in his present status that he cannot entertain notions of separation and movement elsewhere, even upward.[19] Where the executive is firmly attached to his present position and is anxious about movement out, there usually is an underlying dynamic. The force may be an over-identification with the acquired level of authority or the particular established sub-goals of his section or department. There are perhaps many individuals who feel a healthy sense of challenge in the accomplishment of the goals and purposes of their immediate departments. They literally do not want to go higher. Or they may feel a 'comfortable sense of security with the kind and amount of their present authority.

In the latter case, it may seem upon cursory examination that they have overly-identified with the administrative task in general. In all probability, they have actually over-identified with some significant attribute of it and have blown that part up into whole proportions. Usually their case histories reveal an administrative style of unequal proportions. To them authority is far more of an asset, or problem, than it might otherwise be, or organization and administration may become co-dependent. A general tendency to emphasize one or the other pervades their administrative style. They do not want more. If they did, they would actively aspire to higher administrative positions. They merely want what they already have, no more or no less, and feel threatened when their authority is ill-received or diminished. Anxiety for them may be cued off by the threat of separation from their administrative tasks, particularly their authority relationships. This fixation on authority or departmental goals and purposes is not normally found in the more mobile executive. The upward-striving type does not mind becoming separated if it will bring new and more challenging administrative assignments. The defensive type does mind, simply because separation brings new forms of attachments.

Four Basic Patterns of Anxiety

Separation anxiety occurs in these several ways. For the mobile upward-striving type, it occurs when his forward thrust is blocked. This essentially means his administrative style is predicated on higher and higher forms of achievement. If his administrative style dominates his life style, a career crisis becomes a crisis of his whole life. Another way to say it is that his whole identity, who he is and what he wishes to become, is threatened. In such cases of acute arrestment of upward mobility, the anxiety may become generalized to invade all life areas. The executive may incur disturbed human relationships in many of his activities in and outside of business.

For the individual who is happy with what he has and wants no more, separation anxiety may occur precisely because he is being considered for promotion. Demotion will throw either person into a mild-to-serious case of anxiety. This factor is common to both and may now be discarded. In the defensive case, the executive may have evolved an administrative style to maintain his present position. No doubt his whole sense of identity becomes sympathetic to his cause and no internal conflict may arise. Except, however, when he feels a threat to his present position by the possibility of a promotion. It has been noticed in clinical experience that this threat of separation via promotion may become just as debilitating and real to the executive as demotion.

Administrative anxiety basically constitutes a feeling of impending danger due to either wanted or unwanted movement upward. Administrative anxiety breaks down into the following sub-categories:

MA1: Mobility is wanted and is impending.
MA2: Mobility is wanted and is not impending.
SA3: Mobility is not wanted and is impending.
SA4: Mobility is not wanted and is not impending.

In the case of MA1 (mobility anxiety), anxiety may be aroused because of some impending danger to a strong attachment to the present position, but may be kept in check because of the anticipation of future and more challenging attachments in the positions ahead. This anxiety would seem to be typical of those individuals who committed themselves to a style of administration that held out hope for movement closer to the central values of the firm. This being the case, mild anxiety may develop because of the fear of the unknown future, which will involve the necessity of making new attachments in order to achieve role commitment and validation. This anxiety stems from the risk of attachment upward more than separation downward. He may want the promotion but may fear it, and the ambivalence may generate formidable anxiety.

In one case of this type, the executive was elected to office on a Monday, and on Tuesday he was taken to the hospital suffering from a complete emotional breakdown. Several of his personal friends reported that for the six years after he became vice-president, he both feared and wanted the presidency. The psychiatric physician reported that he simply used up all his emotional energy handling the intense, protracted ambivalence. When he became president he had no emotion left and fell into a state of catatonic-like rigidity.

In the case of MA2 (mobility anxiety), anxiety may result when an individual's administrative style is predicated on growing amounts of administrative responsibility. However, he feels anxious because he is given cues about his lack of potential for promotion, or is not given expected positive cues that he is doing well. Additionally, no cues either way may be as anxiety creating. The anxiety here is the danger of remaining attached to his present level. Little anxiety seems to stem from the fear of the unknown difficulties that may be found upstairs. A case that is called to mind here is that of a youthful executive who merely picked up his sticks and joined another corporation. In studying the mobility pattern of successful executives, it becomes apparent that too many executives do not make the break when the institutional blocks are formidable and unamenable to removal.

In the case of SA3 (separation anxiety), anxiety stems from the individual's wanting to remain at the present level, and perceiving signs that he is wanted in a more responsible administrative position. Here the administrative style may be oriented to help attach to present tasks or similar kinds of tasks. The cues from above are threatening because a realistic evaluation of ability, or psychological arrestment due to over-identification with the immediate administrative role, or over-identification with a special aspect of the task, has made the part abnormally important (authority or goal achievement challenges inherent in the department or division). His anxiety may arise from the perceived danger inherent in the higher or more responsible job and the desire to remain attached to present levels of competency and security. His is separation anxiety of the kind that is based on the desire to remain where he is.

A case that is called to mind here is that of a bright scientist who became the first of his kind ever to assume the vice-presidency of his corporation. Heretofore, there had been no Ph.D.'s at such a high level. In his climb up, he had stayed in research or close to it. His whole identity revolved around being a great scientist, and his national prominence was made possible by the scientific discoveries found in his laboratory career. Now he is in charge of all scientific research and feels somewhat alienated from his scientific identity. Movement into the presidency would sever more completely, if not entirely, this professional identification. He chooses not to be too successful as an administrator of research so as to diminish his excellent chances of ever becoming president. In private he longs to return to the laboratories. It is clear that if he continues his present course, he will be back there whether he wants to or not.

SA4 (separation anxiety) is based on an administrative style that is predicated upon the individual's maintaining his present or similar position. No signal is coming from above to challenge such a position. Many who recline on the corporate shelves do not feel anxious. There is a great need for competent people who will do a good job at low, intermediate, and high managerial positions. Some persons belonging to this category do feel undue anxiety. At this point we must reintroduce the life style concept. They may have developed an administrative style rationally geared to stay put. This trick in itself is an engineering feat. How does one stay put when good work is often rewarded by promotion? To turn down a promotion is a corporate sin. The whole corporate system is geared for the man who will work to achieve, and who will seek to achieve still greater tasks. There is little in the way of positive corporate therapy for the man who will not work and strive to go up, or for the man who cracks up because he has worked too hard to go up and now faces signs that he will not. The problem of the contented, defensive type is that he is out of step with the success ethic of the corporation, and of society for that matter. Obviously, he must adjust his life style eventually to accommodate his retrenched administrative style.

An internal conflict may result from the expectations of others and his own limited, arrested ambitions. In some cases, an ambitious wife, family, or parents lurk behind the scenes exerting pressure to go higher. To them, the achievement opportunity and the primary satisfaction that it supplies him may not be important. His secondary gains, which may become directly or vicariously their gains, may place his administratve style under extreme pressure from them. With such powerful love objects as wives and parents pushing and punishing him, it may be hard to develop a whole life style that will accommodate his self-chosen restricted administrative style.

At work he may administer in such a way that he does not become jeopardized by upward mobility and the hazard of declining a promotion. At home he works hard at keeping his other life areas sympathetic and in control. The conflict may reach intolerable proportions. The loss of positive emotional attachments may place him in a position where he must escape the anxiety by either symptomatology (neuroses) or a change in his administrative style. Regarding the latter, he may decide that if it is money and status and prestige that they want, he will get it for them.

Now secondary satisfactions become "primarilized." He begins to reconstruct an administrative style that he hopes will bring an alignment with pressures from the other life areas. He re-energizes inhibited patterns of administration. Changes occur in his handling of authority, in his way of designing or achieving the goals of his section or department. He attempts to engineer validation by identifying with an administrative style that seems to be common to those who move up. He plays a role without commitment. He associates rather than identifies. He may feel the necessity to distort himself and what he believes himself to be. This executive or middle-manager may become a statistic in Whyte's book, *The Organization Man.* What he does not yet feel is the possibility that his mask will be torn off and his real self revealed. This danger increases with each small gain or success. Wanting desperately now to succeed, he may actually fail after all. Life is never quite as complex and anxiety-ridden as for the executive whose administrative style is out of phase with the expectations of significant others.

When the administrative style shares the blessing, respect, and support of all other life areas, the crisis of career is not as intolerable. Vast amounts of free-flowing energy are systematically aimed and directed, and with it the satisfactions of unmitigated achievement. When the administrative style does not receive the enthusiastic support of other life areas, energy becomes blocked, anxiety develops, and neurotic symptoms may be formed to allay the anxiety. These neuroses are basically found in collaboration with the administrative task. In other words, neurotic symptoms may develop to allay anxiety that can not be controlled through positive, constructive, creative adjustments in the administrative situation.

THE SEARCH FOR COMPREHENSIVE SOLUTIONS

Intense conflicts originating from the administrative role may give rise to comprehensive solutions upon which the administrative style begins to pivot and acquire a new dynamic of its own. A comprehensive life solution is one that attempts to force total domination of the executive's administrative style by his total self-identity (life style). In other words, he sets out to preserve his overall self-identity by distorting his administrative style beyond realistic proportions. Commitment is withheld from the present administrative role, and he becomes indifferent or ambivalent toward it, thus preserving his sense of wholeness or integrity by shutting off the conflicting administrative part. He sets out to find in his other areas of life the necessary achievements and satisfactions that will restore wounded pride and placate his idealized notions of self.

Or the reverse, found in the comprehensive administrative solution, may develop. Here the executive may bring all of his energies to bear upon the one thing that emerges as a transcending value in life: administrative success. He sets out to succeed at all costs, regardless of damage to himself as a person, to his colleagues, his corporation, or to his loved ones. He shuts down identification with all other areas of life to over-identify with the one: administration.

If the executive's whole identity and his particular administrative self have become intimately associated during the course of his successful rise in the corporation, shutting off energy in one phase of his life affects his whole life style. To achieve a balance, a previous level of psychological development is unconsciously appealed to. It may be neurotic aggressiveness, effacement, or resignation.[20] Any one or a combination of all are eagerly appealed to as a comprehensive relief of anxiety. In short, administrative anxiety of the neurotic kind may develop strong identification with outside life (comprehensive life solution) that tends to minimize the mundane requirements of administration, or it may develop strong identification with the administrative role (comprehensive administrative solution) that tends to minimize and reject other values and areas of life. The three basic techniques to accomplish either one of these two opposite goals may be the appeal to aggressiveness, effacement, or resignation.[21] All three techniques represent regressions back to attributes of previous life styles, usually associated with adolescence and preadolescence.

In such regressions, previously inflated notions of self break through in the form of idealized or unrealistic images of self.[22] In the administrative solution, the inflated self is manifested in the using of the instruments of authority and the setting of organizational goals and policies with little regard for reality and the shared opinions of others in the corporation. At times it is more than the individual can do to be civil to other members of the executive group. Reality-centered institutions in the corporate system, such as reports, committee deliberations, or scientific studies may be relegated to the wastebasket of imperfection. He alone wishes to decide, can decide, must decide. The corporation is placed in jeopardy by the nincompoops in staff and the technical psychoses of production people. If he is in production, the marketing people appear as grave threats to the corporation. In actuality, all may become puny in his eyes.

In the life solution, the idealized self shows up in the utter disregard for business authority and goal-setting activities. These become unclean, crass, materialistic, selfish, inhuman, or socially irresponsible. He turns to the noble life areas outside the corporation and seeks a haven by identifying with society. Profitability, return on capital investments, liquidity, or even statesmanship appears to the idealized self as beneath dignity and self-respect. It is not that these activities and the people who perform them are puny (shame anxiety) as in the administrative solution, they become grossly immoral. His idealized self incurs feelings of sin, which are projected into others. In the life solution in which the idealized self incurs neurotic guilt, the executive feels guilty for having spent the better part of his life in immoral, materialistic servitude. He feels punitive toward all other business executives, either for their ignorance of the real facts of life or for not facing up to them.

In either case, the executive seldom withdraws physically. Typically, his mission becomes one of vindictiveness and he cannot accomplish it by bearing this guilt or shame alone. *They* should feel guilty or ashamed, and he will help them. He sets his course of administrative action to achieve his ultimate vindication and their ultimate defeat. These inner dictates cry for proof and support. He compulsively works his solutions, varying only their behavioral attributes. These latter he sets forth with sometimes the flair of an actor playing several parts in the same drama.

THE AGGRESSIVE SOLUTION

The *aggressive* technique manifests itself in movement against authority or goal-setting activities, or both.[23] Left far behind is the challenge of achievement—of having an exciting time at a given administrative task and looking forward to advances. In the administrative solution the moving toward may show up in attempted seizure of power and authority. The individual may so wish to earn his authority that he will use fair means or foul. Ultimately he seeks total domination. In goal and policy-setting activities he may be just as aggressive, using the goals and policies of his own department to thwart those of other departments. He may take logical, well-thought-out positions that show the importance of his department. He may work his group hard to show proof of his superior capacity to set high goals and organize for their achievement. The efficiency and superiority of his department may be realized at the expense of the corporate welfare. Nothing matters but that he shame others whose puny statures deserve his condescension.

The life solution uses the aggressive technique by rebelling at life in the complex, massive corporation. This shows up in the individual being careless with his own authority and that of his subordinates in making logical but unnecessary claims on the boss or on the authority set in general. He may rebel against his own departmental goals and those of the corporation. He may twist them, turn them, and reshape them to reduce the sting of immobility. He may plead for such social or human values (as opposed to economic or business) as more social responsibility over profitability, or more stability and permanence rather than growth and opportunism. He may work hard to show his colleagues the wisdom of "public utility" pricing and letting competition live. He may practice fair rather than free competition. Oftentimes he pushes his subordinates to identify with worthy, moral activities in the community. He is first and foremost an extra-organization man. The life outside beckons him, and he may make sure it beckons others in the corporation. He uses his authority to get his subordinates to participate in community affairs. It is often seen that this appeal to life calls him to turn to religious, charitable, and liberal ideologies. He may become a Sunday school teacher, friend of the library, or a grateful and charitable alumnus. Life outside becomes neurotically embraced through corporate and personal activities and goals.

THE EFFACEMENT SOLUTION

The techniques of *effacement* essentially involve moving with or into, rather than against.[24] Here the appeal is to love rather than hate and usually involves rejection of the individual's evolved administrative style. His administrative style is contorted to plead covertly for acceptance and affection from others. He shrinks himself in presence and competency. Anything suggesting superiority or triumph must be avoided. The anxious shunning of pride, triumph, or superiority is revealed in many ways. Privileges turn into liabilities, power differentials into communication bottlenecks, and legitimate requests into taking advantage of friendship. He fears triumph in goal-setting activities and, thus, sets very modest ones for his department and encourages the same for the corporation. He appeals to a more relaxed corporate setting and shows instantaneous affection for those who become ill or maimed in the horrible corporate struggle.

In the attempt to be self-minimizing, he slowly forgets what he knows, what he has accomplished, and what good he has done. He is quick, however, in seeing these qualities in others and offering them incessant eulogies. He foregoes the enjoyment of many pleasures normal for his high position because to enjoy them would be selfish. He seeks to exert little authority, relying mostly upon people's affection and respect to get the job done. All of these things are contrived for the gaining of attention, affection, sympathy, and love. His salvation lies in others. Through them he makes the administrative role bearable. They will give him peace and unity, and the means to become the grandest administrator of them all—his own idealized self. His whole life becomes anchored around this administrative style. All others in his life areas become instruments of his idealized self. They are praised, adorned, and elevated to high positions. Members of the educational, religious, and charitable elites are openly eulogized and praised. Their achievements are blessed by little notes and letters personally addressed. Never an opportunity goes by to show what a wonderful boss he is. But these others are actually being used. He is showering them with plaudits because they really mean nothing personally to him. Actually, they are being sacrificed on the altar of business. He absorbs them into his administrative self by proving to them that he is a socially responsible and sensitive business executive. To prove his point and also to effect absorption of his whole life and his administrative style, he carries to them the gospel of administrative love. He may practice on boards of education, in church councils, and in civic groups the philosophy of administrative love. This may involve specific examples of how business does it, and how they must not fail to benefit from this great technique. His administrative style creeps into all areas of his life. In the life areas he practices association, not identification.

The appeal to love may be found also in the life solution. Here the executive rejects his evolved identity acquired from his administrative role. He struggles to achieve attention and affection principally from the world outside business. This means that he transports little of business life, its successes and values, into his other life areas. Instead he seeks out ways of gaining love, sympathy, and affection by making his primary contacts in church, civic, charitable, and educational affairs. He identifies with these outside organizations. The values basic to the external institutions are eventually carried into the corporation by his socially responsible stride. The business firm may become an educational institution with emphasis on training for all, or it may take on the appearance of a religious institution in which individuals become reattached to the brotherhood of man through love and sympathy. Vast amounts of money may be appropriated to help colleges, widows, and disabled employees. The union may be cheated out of the privilege of bargaining because he is always one step ahead of them in representing the employee's welfare. Labor costs may rise, profits shrink, and liquidity be cancelled out by corporate welfarism. The corporation may eventually act like a charitable, educational, and religious institution all mixed together. Lost in the attempt to accede to the higher values of life is the narrow, efficient, profit-oriented administrative style of the past. It has become blotted out completely. In the process of showing love and affection for external groups, he has been diminished in stature. This, of course, is really what he wants. He wants to be lovable, and the more he appeals to others the more he feels meek and small.

The moving against and the moving with patterns may evoke pseudo-autocratic and democratic styles respectively. Few "normal" executives can be arranged into any one of these two styles completely. Each is a multicrat, adopting a unique mixture of the two.[25] The reason for this amalgam is certain administrative deficiencies in the two. Too much authority brings disadvantages as great as too much democracy. Few pure types exist today because of the reality of the superior effectiveness of the multicrat. The neurotic executive clings to one type almost exclusively. He overworks it to the detriment of his administrative responsibility. He does not become an autocrat or democrat out of choice, but rather out of the dictates of his inner conflicts. He must adopt administrative extremes because he seeks a comprehensive solution. He hates compulsively or compulsively seeks love.

THE RESIGNATION SOLUTION

The third technique to resolve the conflict is found in a moving-away administrative style.[26] It is basically marked by apathy and indifference, leading to psychological *resignation*. Here the executive achieves a pattern of withholding investment of energy. In the administrative solution, energy inhibition may occur in his work pattern. Other areas of his life at first may appear unaffected. In the administrative situation there is a noticeable lack of goal-directed activity and thinking. The goals of the firm have lost their challenge; the corporation ceases to be a meaningful object. He basically becomes an onlooker, peering at people as though they were completely strange, detached from him. Restriction of wishes, inaccessibility to others, and depersonalization of the administrative scene may develop. He becomes super-sensitive to pressure, orders, schedules, changes, and involvements of any kind. At best, he becomes a well-adapted automaton; at worst, a cantankerous old man. Seeing no special gifts in his superiors, he becomes intractable to them. He cannot be moved by airs of prestige, indignation of superiors, or rivalry of colleagues. He slips into oblivion, with one hand remaining in the life areas external to the firm. Here he is still at home, but perhaps not for long. The administrative style may eventually take over all of life. He may appeal to resignation in all his social, community, and family relationships.

In the life solution, energy is not inhibited primarily in the administrative area. The executive may become resigned to the dictates of family life, give in to his children's wishes, completely submit to "momism." He becomes inaccessible to old friends, drops engagements of long standing, forgets and then purposely drops out of poker, bridge, or other kinds of social enterprises. He comes home each evening to sit and do very little. Television consumes him until he falls asleep to be rudely awakened in the wee hours of the night by the termination of broadcasting. His wife becomes sloppy, her age shows, her attractiveness is gone. He resists her suggestions, helpfulness, or submissiveness. Although he reserves himself each night for the battle of the next day, this battle, too, may lose its challenge. His whole life style becomes internally consistent by domination of resigned administrative style.

To the reader, the mechanism of resignation, activated initially in areas outside the administrative role, may seem to be unrelated to administrative anxiety. Therapists are familiar with life problems that seemingly have no bearing upon occupational successes and failures, and many, of course, do not. In such cases, the anxiety or neurotic disturbance is not anchored in the administrative role and cannot be classified as administrative anxiety or neurosis. But it is well known that anxiety may be initially displaced upon innocent objects. This is entirely possible for administrative anxiety. In such a case, disturbances may first appear in areas seemingly alien to business administration. Some executives are so closely tied to the successful performance of the executive role that anxiety in that role will not be allowed to affect performance. Because acute anxiety may not always be successfully repressed or denied, it may pop up in alien contexts.

Of course, an executive may incur a great disappointment in a non-business role with which he has intensely identified. This anxiety may spill over to affect his administrative performance. This is what is meant when personnel men say, "You can't hire a pair of hands, the whole self comes to work." But does it always? Some persons have sufficient ego strength to compartmentalize the emotions, or work creatively to alleviate them in the contexts of their origin. Under these circumstances, they may not bring non-business anchored anxieties into the administrative role performance. Likewise, some executives who incur administrative-anchored anxiety may not displace its effects upon outside innocent activities and objects. This control of anxiety formation appears common to many successful executives. If administrative success is intensely sought after and blockage to this dominant drive occurs and the self is not strong enough to handle the anxiety, anxiety may be either displaced onto innocent objects and alien life areas, or focused on the basic origins or objects, or both. Mild anxiety may be restricted to specific objects or situations, and acute anxiety may pervade the whole life style. We turn to examples of neuroses of this latter kind.

THE NEUROCRAT

Neuroses involve disturbances in the relationship between the self and others.[27] These disturbances may tend to move farther and farther into the protected life areas and infest them too. Eventually, conflict between administration demands and the demands emanating from other life areas may become less consciously intense because of pseudo-realignment. However, these neurotic solutions may be made at the price of self-damage. Highly valued notions of self may become distorted, idealized, and implacable. The pleasure principle tends to displace the reality principle. In many cases the executive career crisis becomes irreversible. His decisions made by these neurotic solutions and techniques have placed unalterable blocks in his way.

On the other hand, neurotic solutions and techniques may actually contribute to success. When held in bounds by the reality of corporation life, neurotic solutions may be an asset. For the sake of brevity, the executive whose administrative effectiveness may be largely attributed to neurotic solutions is referred to as a *neurocrat*. When a neurotic element is attached to cooperation, considerable gain may come from the ensuing teamwork and high morale. When excessive aggressiveness is diminished by a mild case of neurotic indifference and resignation, advantages in the form of stability and consideration may be expected. Not all fail who evolve neurotic components in their administrative styles. In fact, many seem to succeed, and through their successes keep down the neurotic element. They literally work themselves back to more tolerable levels of anxiety and away from the dangerous psychoses. In short, the neurocrat is often successful because of situationally acceptable amounts of aggression, effacement, or resignation.

Today, men at the top of the big business corporation show an active concern for problems of society that lie outside of the immediate administrative role. The executives of oligopolistic concerns have the necessary absence of traditional restraints to theoretically project the corporation into a socially responsible orbit. Clinical experience with executives shows that sometimes this identifying with society comes from neurotic solutions to the administrative anxiety. This act of statesmanship lacks the qualities of sincerity. It stems more from the attempt to allay intrapsychic conflict than from a genuinely enlarged view of corporate citizenship.

It has been seen that the individual who pursues the executive career constantly grapples with problems of authority and organization. His notions of self are contained by these basic parameters, and idealized notions of self are somewhat inhibited by superiors who demand obedience, and organizational goals that require teamwork. But who or what constrains the executive's self-identity when he reaches the top? Imagine for a moment, what dreadful fears and anxieties combat-weary executives may feel when, finally at the top, they find themselves unbounded by the realities of dominating superiors and prescribed, limited organizational goals and policies. At the top, the administration function is today highly ambiguous. The classical forces of the market place, the liquidity and profitability requirements of capital lending formations, the narrow restriction of a small ownership group have been largely transcended by the nature of the large, complex business corporation. The top executive has more choices open to him for the establishing of corporate goals, and more choices open to him for utilizing his authority and power. This ambiguity may attract neurocrats and may also help to produce them.

THE CASE OF NORMAN

The case of Norman, vice-president of a huge corporation, is illustrative. His anxiety in the administrative role gradually grew into a neurotic need for effacement. Over the years, Norman had acquired an attitude very much like Theodore K. Quinn. As executive vice-president, and next in line for the presidency of General Electric, Quinn suddenly quit because he could not see that a life devoted to making a big corporation bigger was worthwhile. In like manner, Norman grew to despise his administrative role.

It was as though he had suddenly seen through appearances to the naked reality of corporate inhumanity, materialism, and self-indignity. Norman reacted with intense hate for the kind of administrative style he had perfected, and unconsciously projected this hate into his corporation colleagues and business associates. He acquired idealized notions of self that exerted moral claims upon himself and others. He sought dignity in other life areas. He took on a vigorous program of community and civic responsibility. For this he received so much personal publicity and praise that the public image of the corporation was considerably enhanced. Because about this time the corporation was ready to move into a more statesmanship-like posture, he was promoted to the presidency. Norman accepted this promotion with ambivalence. He wanted to live a life different from that of a typical business executive. He saw this promotion as an opportunity to show that as a businessman he was a moral person. Yet he wanted to quit business life and get into a "human-centered" occupation. However, Norman was fifty years old and he could not turn around and start over. He felt that he must make the best of a bad situation. He pledged to be the kind of business executive that represented his ideal self.

Norman's corporation is a major oligopolist with considerable freedom from the restraints of classical business enterprise. Within three years, Norman has successfully spun off a foundation to aid scientific research and the education of scientists, got practically all men from division managerial levels and up actively engaged in a wide assortment of social responsibilities, written two books on statesmanship, given slightly more than two-hundred speeches, and established a conference of businessmen and clergy for the study of business ethics and morals. For all practical purposes, Norman is a corporate philanthropist whose money is not his own but that of his stockholders. He has won a highly-sought award, conferred upon him by a high governmental dignitary.

Norman is next seen as searching for new ways to show his statesmanship, but becoming often deeply depressed because he has spent so much of his life in the role of business executive. These depressions are usually followed by intense efforts to articulate still higher meanings of social responsibility. Each time, these new thrusts psychologically shut off the disturbing, depraving elements in his prior and present administrative tasks. He is now chairman of the board and a prominent national figure, championing the social responsibilities of the modern business corporation to provide humanity with the necessary weapons to fight poverty, war, and disease.

The tragic element in all of his obsessive concern for mankind is that his idealized image of himself as a kind of "savior" has become for him a reality. He drives himself to actualize his idealized image without regard to the conditions of realistic feasibility and his own psychic condition. Nothing is or should be impossible to him. On the other hand, everything is wrong with the world, particularly traditional, profit-oriented business. His perfected, idealized image and the evils of the business world only make for greater inner conflict. Coerced from within, he flays randomly at the evils from without. His friends and many supporters are of the ultra-liberal viewpoint and believe that the nemesis of modern civilization is irresponsible business giganticism.

Meanwhile, under his absentee administration, the corporation has become flabby, inefficient, and uncreative. Such dysfunctioning is made possible by oligopolistic practices of administrative pricing, live and let competition live, and carefully contained and unilaterally dominated stockholder's meetings. We repeat, he practices safe enterprise, not free enterprise. Without this power of the corporation to be relatively indifferent to the forces of the market's price mechanism, Norman could not have so vigorously devoted himself to these activities external to the corporation. We may speculate that if more competitive forces were dominant in the industry, Norman would have had to be a working president and a chairman of the board more directly concerned with economic goals. Instead, he is now an international figure, periodically circling the globe, preaching the gospel of business morality.

To many, he is the epitome of business statesmanship. But to his counselor and confidant, he is estranged from what he actually is.

Because he cannot live up to his implacable, idealized self and because he hates his real self, he is at war within. Behind his preachments of world peace through economic prosperity and moral responsibility, there lies an intense war against both idealized and real selves. It has been noted in human affairs that good often comes from evil. Norman's case may not illustrate this observation, however, because his appeals to statesmanship lack the moral seriousness of genuine ideals and regard for their feasibility and the conditions under which these ideals could be fulfilled. Norman's case may be illustrative of that "good" that dies with the man and never leaves behind a lasting monument to change and progress.

THE CASE OF NEAL

The case of Norman does not involve only the appeal to self-effacement. He is not simply trying to become an object of appreciation, love, and virtue. We have seen in his case description vast amounts of aggression indirectly unleashed against the people and the corporation symbolizing his hated administrative identity. The case of Neal is more uniformly illustrative of this neurotic appeal to aggression. Neal is the vice-president in charge of finance of a firm every bit as big as Norman's. He was formally trained in business administration and specialized in accounting and finance. Unlike many of the mobile types who move around, in and out of the several functional areas before arriving at the near top to specialize in one administrative area, Neal moved to the top, staying in accounting and financial administration all the while. By the time he reached the upper middle-management levels, it was too late to turn back or to move over to another function such as production, personnel, marketing, or research. His reputation had been firmly made in accounting and financial administration. However, Neal actively set his sights on becoming a member of the executive group and did not feel too disturbed by this institutional block to his ascending to the presidency.

When he arrived in the executive group as controller, he realized that he was not really a member of the "club." His opinion was asked for strictly in matters of finance, and then he was not allowed the full privilege of throwing his weight toward or against new corporate goals and their strategies. He felt *of* the executive group, not really *in* it. His marginal membership was a substantial blow to his self-esteem and dignity. He thought that matters of finance were crucial to corporate success or failure, and a representative of his competency should be vitally involved in administrative responsibility. As he moved around the periphery of the executive group, his repressed desire to become president emerged into active awareness. This urge transcended all other values. He realized finally what his administrative career really meant to him. It all added up to the presidency, and there was no substitute for this achievement. He vowed that he would not be further humiliated. He was too good a man to be treated so ignominiously. He had come a long way, and no one, "not any one on this green earth," was going to cheat him of what was due him. "Besides," he said, "few people really know the company as well as I do." His growing idealized notions of self reflected the puniness of those around him. He began to organize his resources to serve this implacable aim, shutting down emotional investment in other life areas. At home he became a man obsessed with the idea of becoming president. Few activities such as family vacations and recreation were allowed to continue their relative independence from his corporate career. Everything became subordinate to his career aim.

He learned that one's administrative ability was reflected in the size of the budget one was charged with directing. Since marketing and production were the largest, and finance and personnel the smallest, he conspired to show evidence of his administrative ability by increasing the size of the financial budget. This scheme took two directions. He set up a program to develop a computerized approach to accounting and financial activities and to help sell such an approach to marketing and production. He asked for and received training from a computer producer that gave to him a monopoly of knowledge and skills within the corporation. His program became successful enough to substantiate requesting more expert help. As this department of computer analysis grew, it reached out to help marketing and production. Soon his team of computer experts were informally directing many computer strategies and techniques in the departments of marketing, production, and eventually, research and personnel.

Because he studiously acquired and maintained this monopoly of expertise, a corporate reorganization plan placed him in charge of a new department, administrative analysis and control. Here he had access that few other executives had to information that virtually affected appraisal and evaluation of all corporate activities and goal achievements. Now, he was a force to be reckoned with. The executive group, resistant at first, gradually acquiesced to his ascendency. Two members held out to fight against his leadership. He became executive vice-president of the corporation, a position especially created in the new plan of organization. Here his appeal to aggression took on clear-cut proportions. He began moving members of the executive group around into less threatening and crucial positions. He caused the premature retirement of one executive who had been a powerful figure in the past. He created the necessary conditions whereby another powerful figure was revealed as basically incompetent in this new technical world of the computer. He moved against people and ideas of the "old school" with a vengeance that was made possible only by his neurotic need for power and vindication. He did this at a time when the corporation was entering a rather shaky market picture and cutbacks in overhead were objectively necessary. In this vogue, he moved against many employees in the lower-management ranks, causing over two-hundred personnel to leave. However, the president, chairman of the board, and other members of the inside board were extremely pleased with the positive financial picture that emerged.

Three years after he had set out to become president at all costs, he was formally elevated to this post by a grateful board. In this position, he proceeded to make the whole corporation over to fit his neurotic need for power and authority. Financial men who had served him loyally began appearing in substantial numbers in top executive positions in production, marketing, and even personnel. This acute change in mobility channels to the top caused vast numbers of middle managers to feel frustration and career anxiety. He exploited these anxieties by rewarding those who were scared enough to defer to him completely. Now he had many members either actively dependent upon him or withdrawing their identification with the corporation and practicing simple covert association. Although neurotic, Neal had enough alertness to pick subordinates who had both abundant deference and sufficient competency. Six years after becoming president, he retired to become chairman of the board; he hand picked his successor, a toady in both appearance and manner.

Today there are many who speak of Neal as ruthless, heartless, authoritarian, at best, amoral and at worst, immoral. But few will deny that he gave the corporation what it needed, a complete shake-down. He is today a nationally prominent business executive who enjoys a fantastic reputation as an administrator. In his few speeches, there is little of Norman's social responsibility and corporate states-manship. He believes in classical notions of competition—the survival of the fittest, the law of letting the devil take the hindmost. He is aggressively against government, liberalism, socialized medicine, civil rights, and human and political equality. He does little work in any of the life areas surrounding his business career. He helps with no civic, political, social, or charitable organization. He practices association with his family, club, church, and "friends." He has no hobbies, disrespects his son's judgment and occupation (social worker), lives with his wife much as though she were valued only for her instrumental qualities of making a home, preparing food, and being an occasional companion to prominent affairs.

One does not have to be his counselor to understand the intensity of his intra-psychic conflict. He over-indulges in food, liquor, and cigarettes. He has frequent attacks of constipation, which he treats with voluminous quantities of a well-known laxative. He came to the administrative counselor because a vice-president was acting strangely and was in need of career counseling. During this session he monop-olized the situation with his Nietzschean philosophy of ruthless ad-ministration. It did not take much professional expertise to uncover the whole situation that gave rise to his ascendency and success. He was very proud of his successful pattern of self-vindication.

Neal's neurosis actively aided the success which others have at-tributed to his administration. Not all neurocrats become as success-ful as Norman and Neal. Many have unspectacular careers. The executive's neurosis must be highly attuned to the situational possi-bilities in order to actually contribute to administrative success. In fact, his neurosis often exploits an emerging situation, as the cases of Norman and Neal illustrate. In this sense there may be a weird relationship between a successful neurosis and a certain degree of situational realism.[28] When the executive's neurosis is out of phase with the requirements of administrative success, or when the administrative situation is not conducive to neurosis, an executive may be cheated of a spectacular career.

What all of this suggests is that while the executive may be administratively free from the confining restrictions of the market's price mechanism, capital lending institutions, active profit-minded ownership groups, he may not be free to make choices that stem from realistic notions of self. If autonomy means the capacity to order and make choices freely, based upon the principle of reality, Norman and Neal are not autonomous types. Each has actively contrived a style of administration and life that is born of intense feelings of inner weakness and unworthiness. Norman came to despise his administrative self and appealed to active involvement in the life areas and values outside the firm. Neal came to despise all life areas except administration. Into this one category he threw his whole self. He fused business authority and organization into a symbol of power and put all of his resources into the struggle to become that symbol. Norman rejected the traditional power of business authority and organization as immoral and attempted to find justification and salvation in the moral haven of statesmanship. Into this category he, too, threw his whole self.

Norman illustrates the neurotic drive for love that identifies some, but certainly not all, executives; Neal, the neurotic drive for power. Eventually, all phases of their life styles were affected by the anxiety cued off by impending dangers to their evolving self-identities.

Their crises involved their total selves. Their dangers were perceived as anchored in their administrative situations, and their neurotic solutions were addressed to these severe stresses and strains. It is important to note that both practiced over-identification. Neal elevated corporate authority to arbitrarily set corporate goals to the level of ultimate values. In the initial stage of his career crisis, he did not seek authority, and he set goals as a consequence of his achievement drive. Later, he administered his computer program to serve his growing obsession with power. The studies by Henry and Warner show that the typical successful executive seeks first the joys of achievement and second the satisfaction of power, money, and status.[29] Neal has primarilized the secondary satisfactions and practices association with the other remaining life areas.

Norman over-identified with business authority and organization too, which became to him ultimate values. The effects of his anxiety became displaced upon institutions outside of business. He practiced association with his administrative role as evidenced in his absentee administrative style (traveling, circling the globe). Not satisfied with dispensing authority and directing the goals of a single corporation, he set about to authorize and establish goals for society and, eventually, all of mankind. For that matter, Neal in his own way attempted to reset the course for mankind. Neal appealed to social Darwinism, and Norman to social responsibility. The one wanted to make the world into a jungle, the other wanted to make it into a hospital.

Neither philosophy of administration was grounded in the conditions of realistic feasibility. What bothered Norman so terribly was that the business corporation was still a profit-oriented organization and, in spite of his railing against it, he could not, and basically did not want to make it into a social organization. His huge corporation had enough stability and power to afford the utilization of a wide selection of corporate purposes and policies beyond the traditional economic goals. In this sense, his social responsibility theme was in part grounded in factual achievements of the corporation. However, the corporation essentially was used to feed Norman's neurotic needs for love and affection.

Neal's corporation, likewise, could order goals and policies affecting the aim of corporate citizenship. However, his neurosis drove him into a pattern of compulsive power seeking. It is interesting that after he became president, Neal tampered very little with the overall corporate goals and strategies. He became little goal-directed. He sought power and, to avoid guilt, he attempted to legitimatize his power by appeals to the conventional notions of business authority. His board meetings always resounded with airs of respect for the property rights of stockholders, who were the legitimate authority and for whom he made his arbitrary decisions. This appeal was made in transparent mockery because some twenty thousand well-dispersed, unorganized, passive stockholders could not effectively levy claims upon his corporate administration. He ruthlessly replaced directors and was once heard to say, "If you don't like my board, find another."

Owning very little of the corporation himself, he had what Berle would call power without property.[30]

Neal's administrative style had all the semblance of the domineering titans of the past, but without the blessings of a compatible institutional and social framework. In spite of his efforts to justify his power by appealing to obsolete nineteenth-century capitalism, he felt guilty for his frequent violations of conscience. Yet his guilt could not be effectively assuaged, owing to the fact that there was no effective ownership group, no genuine competition with other oligopolies, and no capital lending institutions to go to for money, since his firm largely created the necessary capital. Without these sources of justification, Neal could not effectively handle his feelings of guilt. Although the board members who remained or were allowed to remain, praised him and gave him vast amounts of credit, he was not foolish enough to be taken in by them. He knew they were scared, or incompetent, or weak. Consequently, they could not provide the necessary means of his justification and legitimization.

No doubt a neurotic potential existed in corporate life when the traditional laws of competition prevailed. We may speculate that at that time the choices available were fewer, and traditional restraints of the market's price mechanism prescribed boundaries that made neurocrats less effective, or caused their liabilities or weaknesses to become more quickly identified. The same effect was provided by the liquidity and profitability requirements of capital lending institutions and a small, active, control-minded ownership group. When these restraints were withdrawn, what was to control the neurotic potential in the administrative role? Mistakes by the entrepreneur under classical competition were cancelled out. Today, acts of anxiety that are not subject to cancellation by the forces of competition become absorbed by society. The acts of neurocrats in large, economic concentrates may result both in the benefit and liability of all society, so powerful is the big business corporation today. Much more needs to be known about the big business executive, for much more of society depends upon the forces inherent in his personality.

In conclusion, given these freedoms *from* traditional restraints, the question is whether the big business executive is free *to* fulfill his historically novel role and devise corporate strategy that realizes the essential national character of his firm. This freedom *to* involves inner qualities of character in contrast to the external freedoms granted to him by the changed character of the business corporation. The real problems that beset the executive are less technical and strictly economic, and more moral and psychological. The big business executive could very well be entering a crisis of personality. His problem is to maintain and use the positive, constructive inner resources that are subject to distortion by the neurotic potentials of executive life and of our era of chronic anxiety. Failure to handle this psychological problem will perhaps determine whether the executive today will give way to still another type as did the titan of our heroic past.

IX

The Incompleted Man

The big business executive is mastered by a single force. It is something deep inside of him that is a product of his childhood experiences. It is the drive to achieve. To *achieve* means to perform increasingly challenging tasks. Early in his career he sees that the more challenging jobs are arranged hierarchically upward. He sets his sights upward, using each responsibility to show proficiency for a higher position. At any given level he experiences impatience. He dare not enjoy the assignment too much or relax too much. He must prepare to depart shortly after he arrives at any point in his emerging career.

The big business executive does not enjoy the plateaus between achievements. He is never satisfied with himself, his successes and opportunities; for each new success he posts higher goals for himself. The achievement drive increases geometrically to eventually become insatiable. For this reason he can never relax and enjoy internal rest.

Men who arrive at the top have reputations. They are known for having done things differently. Achievement, in order to be meaningful to them, means making things happen their way. Their efforts must largely ensue from their own choices if they are to count. This eminently qualifies such men to be innovators or change agents. But to be an innovator the potential executive must have more than a high need to achieve. He must know how to achieve within the boundaries established by the corporate environment. Men at the top have learned to channel their achievement drives by a process of simplifying their highly complex environments. From a myriad of forces and situations, only a few emerge upon which they base their career patterns.

In the mind of the big business executive, the authority system and its crucial members are identified apart from other features of the corporate environment. The reason the executive learns to single out the authority group is because effective performance does not identify itself. Performance is judged as effective by someone who is in a position to know and has the necessary resources to evaluate and approve. The executive looks to authority figures for their approval of his achievements. Evaluation and legitimatization emanate from authority figures. To win their blessings, the executive must know how to relate to them, to learn from them, and, by access to them, gain the necessary resources to fulfill the achievement drive. In this way the achievement drive becomes oriented toward the values and expectations of the authority system.

The mobile executive has the necessary facilities to relate properly to the authority system. He believes that authority figures are necessary and useful, but at the same time distrusts them enough to rely upon his own resources.

While his achievement drive compels him to do things his way, his notions of authority compel him to receive his superior's blessing. He resolves this conflict by working hard to make his boss look good and then engineering support for his unique orientations and views. A superior and subordinate who work in close harmony in this way will together provide a package of skills and achievements that are highly prized by the corporation. The impact upon the organization of two such men who together are crucially effective is far greater than any two individuals working less coordinately; for this reason, superiors and subordinates who are crucial to each other's effectiveness tend to move up together. Mobility is based upon mutual achievement. The capacity to enhance the effectiveness of another is a basic prerequisite of garnering trust. Few men get to the top of the big business corporation who are not trusted by someone already there. Achievement plus trust spells high upward mobility.

The mobile executive singles out another part of the corporate environment. This is the corporation's goals, policies, and values as they are found in each of his positions in his emerging career; to these factors he lends his achievement drive. Achievement becomes effective when executing these requirements and demands. In any position, conflict may develop between what the corporation expects of him and what he wants to do. He must live up to the norms and expectations that follow from the objectives and policies of the corporation. His innovative thrust is given form and direction within boundaries established by the corporation's goals and policies that are found in his station.

As he gains effectiveness and support, he may be asked to help define the objectives and policies under which he and others must achieve. Now his innovative potential is released in terms which more fully realize his drive to make things happen his way. As he nears the top of the corporate ladder, he is given still wider freedom to release his need to achieve. At the top, he experiences the thrill of attempting to change the direction and character of the corporate enterprise. What makes life at the top exciting is the feeling of mastery and sense of identity that the opportunities afford.

The rocky road to the top is a journey into self-insight and development. Executing within the demands and expectations of the authority set and corporate objectives and policies calls for strong internal controls. An individual with a high need to achieve, to get things done his way, needs these internal controls that keep a check on impulsive performance. In the course of his career, these internal controls are usually strengthened adequately to fulfill the achievement drive. *When they are not sufficiently strengthened, difficulty will eventually ensue.*

The case of Mark Whiting is instructive at this point. Whiting had difficulty gearing his high achievement drive to the norms and expectations of authority figures. When he finally acquired the necessary discipline, he moved ahead rapidly. At the near top, these internal controls on his achievement drive became weakened. He moved disasterously against his president and lost forever the presidency. The cases of Olaf and Oscar illustrate the lack of internal controls that prohibits proper adjustment to the demands of organizational life. The case of Sam illustrates the lack of both authority- and organization-oriented internal controls.

When any one of these three anchorages becomes too set or too weak, the other two are adversely affected. In a way, the executive becomes out of balance. He leans too much toward one angle of the triangle. He may become authority-centered, organization-centered, or self-centered. The unbalanced executive allows his achievement drive to be too much or too little directed by any one component of this triangle. Career difficulty may develop eventually. The probability of career arrestment is high but not sufficient to guarantee it. The unbalancing of the corporate triangle is a necessary but not a sufficient cause of career arrestment. The necessary causes inhere in the situation. Perhaps if another person has been president or if another person besides Mr. Gray had succeeded to the presidency, Mark Whiting would be more alive career-wise than he is today.

The cases of Neal and Norman illustrate how a career crisis may not restore the balanced posture of the executive. Under the right circumstances, an unbalanced executive may actually be promoted to the top position. Also, Neal and Norman had sufficient internal controls to disguise their distorted orientations. Mark Whiting apparently did not. His distrust of authority became too apparent, whereas Neal and Norman were able to hide their neurotic tendencies by latching onto favorable situational circumstances. Their neuroses actually exploited an emerging situation. More typically, however, an unbalanced orientation will prevent mobility to the top. The unbalancing of the corporate triangle and the presence of individuals who may react negatively to the distortions spell career arrestment in a vast majority of the cases.

But career arrestment may not throw every executive into a state of acute anxiety. Some executives gradually adjust to "topping out" at levels lower than the presidency. The cases in this book represent men who were not able to make this adjustment smoothly. In fact, their career arrestment greatly affected their whole style of life.

From these case histories it is apparent that the achievement drive will become frustrated without proper notions of authority and organization. But the mobile executive has a third anchorage upon which he builds his career pattern. He simplifies his environment by supplying specific notions of who he is and what he wants to do and become. The executive's notions of self constantly exert pressure upon him. He must achieve in terms of these inner expectations before performance becomes achievement to him; from his specific achievements he derives his sense of identity. Men at the top know who they are and what they want to do. They typically have strong, clear images of self.

At any point along this path to the top, the executive's notions of self may get out of line with the requirements of authority and organization. Sam acquired an idealized notion of self that prohibited serving authorities and corporate objectives effectively. Impoverished notions of self may prohibit innovative behavior too. The individual may become merely an extension of a boss, who uses him as a yes man. Just as there are few Sams at the top, so are there few with weak, impoverished notions of self.

The executive learns to master his complex environment by the development of three orientations, each of which is related to the other two. He must achieve within the boundaries set forth by the expectations and demands of the authority, organization, and self system. In turn, he must learn to levy expectations and demands upon the corporate triangle. Without the latter, achievement does not occur. If he does not fulfill the expectations of the former, the latter will not be possible. Achievement is made possible by living up to and changing these systems of expectations and demands of his corporate environment.

What prohibits adequate adjustment to career arrestment may be the gradual distortion of the achievement drive. This drive is geared to success at all costs. In the early and middle management phases, the potential executive dares not allow himself to set his goals on the presidency. He looks upward and to the center of the corporation. The object in focus is a small group of men who, with the president, run the corporation. It is almost as if the young manager is saying to himself, "If I set my goal for the presidency, I may be sadly disappointed. I shall be happy to become a member of his executive group." The executive group becomes the best opportunity to realize his achievement drive. Because there may be six to twenty members of this group, the chances are greater to achieve at this level. He sets his sights and begins to work his way through the many mazes. At some point he decides to go all the way. It seems that this total commitment is a function of the frequency of interaction with the president. If this is true, it occurs upon or after entrance into the executive group. Once this commitment has been made and has been reinforced by a few successes, there is seemingly no turning back; the executive's whole self becomes engaged in the move for the presidency. If he makes it, his fondest notions of who he is and can become are affirmed. He becomes a big person in the eyes of others and particularly himself.

But suppose he does not make it. Suppose his career becomes arrested enough to greatly jeopardize his chance of ever making it. Then this commitment becomes hazardous and filled with terror. This is the story of Mark Whiting. The last step happened to be the biggest. It was the final act needed to complete his development as a person. Without this final step, he does not feel fully developed, his identity is only partial. To this day Mark Whiting feels incomplete, only part of a man.

When career arrestment comes to an executive whose achievement drive is directly tied to the presidency, a career crisis follows. A career crisis is a crisis of self. It is a painful, humiliating, and degrading experience. Some men destroy themselves. Directly or indirectly they may decide to do away with this "half of a man" that they have become, or they may decide to stay alive and ruin those who are responsible. Their clever skills and managerial brightness may be used to reduce the efficiency and profitability of the corporation. (We may note parenthetically that the emotional cost of having only one president for each corporation must be enormous. It is an expense that does not show on a profit and loss statement.)

Where does all of this misery start? Ours is a society that places a high value upon success. It hands out big identities, so to speak, to those who have gone all the way. Great wisdom and competence are ascribed, status and dignity are granted to presidents of our great institutions, including big business corporations. It is understandable that the achievement drive becomes eventually affixed to the presidency. At this point the individual enters a phase in his life that holds out the possibility of both triumph and terror. Mark Whiting has been terrorized. He has experienced a penetrating fright every bit as intense and real as that encountered under combat conditions.

From the outside he appears to have made his adjustment. Inwardly, he cries out for relief. Just one more step and he would no longer be in pain. He would be a master of his corporation rather than a prisoner; a boss of bosses rather than an appendage to a board of directors. Mark Whiting, chairman and executive officer of an educational consortium, secretary to the board of Universal Chemical Company, senior advisor, community and national figure, and friend of many, said in confidence to the author, "You know, I have almost made the adjustment. I know I won't be president. I can almost live with myself. Almost!"

Footnotes

CHAPTER II

1. E. S. Mason, *The Corporation in Modern Society* (Cambridge: The Harvard University Press, 1961), p. 101.
2. S. Chase, *American Credos* (New York: Harper & Brothers, 1962), p. 78.
3. *Ibid.*
4. *Ibid.*, p. 80.
5. *Ibid.*, p. 104.
6. M. Weber, *The Protestant Ethic* (New York: Scribners & Sons, 1930), p. 54.
7. *Ibid.*
8. D. Wecter, *The Hero in America* (Ann Arbor: Ann Arbor Paperbacks, 1963).
9. R. W. Wohl, "The 'Rags to Riches Story': An Episode of Secular Idealism," in R. Bendix and S. M. Lipset, *Class Status and Power* (Glencoe, Illinois: The Free Press, 1953), pp. 388-95.
10. *Ibid.*, p. 390.
11. S. Diamond, *The Reputation of the American Businessman* (Cambridge: The Harvard University Press, 1955).
12. R. Bendix, *Work and Authority in Industry* (New York: John Wiley & Sons, Inc., 1956), p. 251.
13. *Ibid.*, p. 257.
14. *Ibid.*
15. *Ibid.*, p. 256.

16. M. Lerner, *America As a Civilization* (New York: Simon and Schuster, Inc., 1957), p. 277.
17. *Ibid.*
18. Wohl, *op. cit.*, p. 390.
19. *Ibid.*
20. H. S. Commager, *The American Mind* (New Haven: Yale University Press, 1950), pp. 34, 231.
21. Lerner, *op. cit.*, p. 279.
22. Diamond, *op. cit.*, p. 179.
23. *Ibid.*, p. 181.
24. *Ibid.*, p. 179.
25. R. S. and H. M. Lynd, *Middletown in Transition* (New York: Harcourt, Brace & Company, 1937), pp. 404-406.
26. M. Rosenberg, *Occupations and Value* (Glencoe, Illinois: The Free Press, 1957), p. 34.
27. M. Mead, *And Keep Your Powder Dry* (New York: William Morrow and Company, Inc., 1942).
28. R. Cohen, *Delinquent Boys* (Glencoe, Illinois: The Free Press, 1955), pp. 88-93.
29. S. A. Leavy and L. Z. Freedman, "Psychoneurosis and Economic Life," *Social Problems*, IV, 1 (July, 1956), 59.
30. L. Reissman, *Class in American Society* (Glencoe, Illinois: The Free Press, 1959), p. 362.
31. T. S. Langner and S. T. Michael, *Life Stress and Mental Health* (Glencoe, Illinois: The Free Press, 1963), p. 305.
32. R. Lynes, *A Surfeit of Honey* (New York: Harper & Brothers, 1953).
33. Reissman, *op. cit.*, p. 302.
34. *Ibid.*, p. 362.
35. W. L. Warner and J. Abegglen, *Big Business Leaders in America* (New York: Harper & Brothers, 1955).
36. Reissman, *op. cit.*, p. 363.
37. Rosenberg, *op. cit.*, p. 57.
38. Langner and Michael, *op. cit.*, p. 460.
39. Reissman, *op. cit.*, pp. 315, 318.
40. Mason, *op. cit.*, p. 107.
41. See M. Newcomer, *The Big Business Executive* (New York: Columbia University Press, 1955).
42. Bendix and Lipset, *op. cit.*, p. 462.
43. W. E. Henry, "The Business Executive," *American Journal of Sociology*, January, 1949, pp. 286-91.
44. Warner and Abegglen, *op. cit.*
45. B. B. Gardner, "What Makes Successful and Unsuccessful Executives," *Advanced Management*, XIII, 3 (September, 1948), 116-22.
46. E. Rosen, "The Executive Personality," *Personnel*, January-February, 1959, pp. 10-20.

CHAPTER III

1. G. H. Haugen, *A Therapy for Anxiety Tension Reactions* (New York: The Macmillan Company, 1963), p. 12.
2. T. S. Langner and S. T. Michael, *Life Stress and Mental Health* (Glencoe, Illinois: The Free Press, 1963), p. 487.
3. R. L. Munroe, *Schools of Psychoanalytic Thought* (New York: Holt, Rinehart and Winston, Inc., 1955), p. 28.
4. A. B. Hollingshead and F. R. Redlich, *Social Class and Mental Illness* (New York: John Wiley & Sons, Inc., 1958), p. 226.
5. T. A. C. Rennie and L. Srole, "Social Class in an Urban Population," *Psychosomatic Medicine,* XVIII (November-December, 1956), 449-56.
6. A. Gurin, J. Veroff and S. Field, *Americans View Their Mental Health* (New York: Basic Books, 1960), p. 28.
7. S. Arieti, *American Handbook of Psychiatry,* Vol. 1 (New York: Basic Books, 1963), p. 308.
8. S. Hiltner and S. Menninger, *Constructive Aspects of Anxiety* (New York: Abingdon Press, 1963), p. 38.
9. *Ibid.*
10. S. Freud, *The Problem of Anxiety* (New York: W. W. Norton, 1936).
11. K. Horney, *The Neurotic Personality of Our Time* (New York: W. W. Norton, 1937).
12. E. Fromm, *The Sane Society* (New York: Holt, Rinehart and Winston, Inc., 1955).
13. D. Riesman, N. Glazer and R. Denny, *The Lonely Crowd* (New York: Doubleday & Company, Inc., 1955).
14. A. Kardiner, *The Psychological Frontiers of Society* (New York: Columbia University Press, 1945).
15. R. S. and H. M. Lynd, *Middletown,* 1929; and *Middletown in Transition* (New York: Harcourt, Brace & Company, 1937).
16. R. May, *The Meaning of Anxiety* (New York: The Ronald Press Company, 1950), p. 345.
17. R. R. Willoughby, "Magic and Cognate Phenomena," in Carl Murchinson (ed.), *Handbook of Social Psychology* (Worcester, Massachusetts: The Ronald Press Company, 1955).
18. R. E. L. Faris and H. W. Dunham, *Mental Disorders in Urban Areas* (Chicago: The University of Chicago Press, 1939).
19. R. E. Clark, "The Relationship of Schizophrenia to Occupational Income and Occupation Prestige," *American Sociological Review,* June, 1948, pp. 325-30.
20. Hollingshead and Redlich, *op. cit.,* pp. 366-80.
21. Langner and Michael, *op. cit.,* p. 314.
22. S. A. Leavy and L. Z. Freedman, "Psychoneurosis and Economic Life," *Social Problems,* July, 1956, pp. 55-67.
23. A. W. Green, "The Middle Class Male Child and Neurosis," *American Sociological Review,* February, 1946, pp. 31-41.

24. L. Reissman, *Class in American Society* (Glencoe, Illinois: The Free Press, 1959), p. 269.
25. Hollingshead and Redlich, *op. cit.*, pp. 357-81.
26. Reissman, *op. cit.*, pp. 371-72.
27. Langner and Michael, *op. cit.*, p. 427.
28. In E. S. Mason, *The Corporation in Modern Society* (Cambridge: The Harvard University Press, 1961), p. 115.
29. E. Rosen, "The Executive Personality," *Personnel*, January-February, 1959, pp. 10-20.
30. L. Huttner, S. Levy, E. Rosen and M. Stopol, "Further Light on the Executive Personality," *Personnel*, March-April, 1959, pp. 43-50.
31. Rosen, "The Executive Personality," *op. cit.*, p. 17.
32. *Ibid.*, p. 18.
33. *Ibid.*
34. B. B. Gardner, "What Makes Successful and Unsuccessful Executives," *Advanced Management*, XIII, 3 (September, 1948), 117-25.
35. *Ibid.*, p. 124.
36. W. L. Warner and J. Abegglen, *Big Business Leaders in America* (New York: Harper & Brothers, 1955), p. 73.
37. W. E. Henry, "Identifying the Potentially Successful Executive," *American Management Personnel Reports*, 14, pp. 12-21.
38. Langner and Michael, *op. cit.*, p. 438.
39. Hollingshead and Redlich, *op. cit.*, p. 130.
40. O. F. Collins, D. G. Moore with D. Unwalla, *The Enterprising Man* (East Lansing: Bureau of Business and Economic Research, Michigan State University, 1964).

CHAPTER IV

1. O. Rank, *Will Therapy and Truth and Reality* (New York: Alfred A. Knopf, Inc., 1945).
2. W. L. Warner and J. Abegglen, *Big Business Leaders in America* (New York: Harper & Brothers, 1955), p. 63.
3. *Ibid.*, p. 51.
4. W. E. Henry, "The Business Executive," *American Journal of Sociology*, January, 1949, pp. 286-91.
5. A. D. Chandler, Jr., *Strategy and Structure* (Cambridge: Massachusetts Institute of Technology, 1962).
6. Warner and Abegglen, *op. cit.*, p. 100.
7. S. Freud, *The Problem of Anxiety* (New York: W. W. Norton, 1936).
8. S. deGrazia, *The Political Community* (Chicago: The University of Chicago Press, 1948), p. 11.
9. J. Piaget, *The Language and Thought of the Child* (New York: Meridian Books, 1955).
10. P. Bovet, *The Child's Religion* (London: Dent, 1928).
11. DeGrazia, *op. cit.*, p. 18.
12. *Ibid.*, p. 19.

13. *Ibid.*, p. 21.
14. E. H. Erikson, *Childhood and Society* (New York: W. W. Norton, 1950).
15. R. J. Havighurst, "Dominant Concern in the Life Cycles" (Unpublished document, The University of Chicago, 1963).
16. W. E. Henry, "Conflict, Age, and the Executive," *Business Topics*, IX, 2 (Spring, 1961), 17-25.
17. *Ibid.*, p. 9.
18. *Ibid.*
19. Havighurst, *op. cit.*, p. 9.
20. *Ibid.*, p. 12.
21. Henry, *op. cit.*, pp. 24-25.
22. E. Rosen, "The Executive Personality," *Personnel*, January-February, 1959, pp. 10-20.
23. W. L. Warner, *The Corporation and the Emergent American Society* (New York: Harper & Brothers, 1962).
24. D. Riesman, N. Glazer and R. Denny, *The Lonely Crowd* (New York: Doubleday & Company, Inc., 1955).

CHAPTER V

1. T. S. Langner and S. T. Michael, *Life Stress and Mental Health* (Glencoe, Illinois: The Free Press, 1963), p. 15.
2. *Ibid.*
3. *Ibid.*, pp. 267-80.
4. *Ibid.*, p. 270.
5. H. M. Lynd, *On Shame and the Search for Identity* (New York: Harcourt, Brace and Company, 1958), p. 22.
6. R. R. Grinker and J. P. Spiegel, *Men Under Stress* (New York: McGraw-Hill Book Company, Inc., 1963).
7. W. L. Warner and J. Abegglen, *The Big Business Executive* (New York: Harper & Brothers, 1955).
8. A Freud, *The Ego and the Mechanisms of Defense* (New York: International Universities Press, 1961).

CHAPTER VI

1. W. B. Miller, "Two Concepts of Authority," *The American Anthropologist*, April 1955.
2. M. Haire and F. Morrison, "School Children's Perception of Labor and Management," *Journal of Social Psychology*, XLVI (1957), 179-97.
3. W. E. Henry, "Conflict, Age and the Executive," *Business Topics*, IX, 2 (Spring, 1961), 15-24.
4. E. Rosen, "The Executive Personality," *Personnel*, January-February, 1959, pp. 10-20.
5. B. B. Gardner, "What Makes Successful and Unsuccessful Executives," *Advanced Management*, XIII, 3 (September, 1948), 116-25.

216   *Footnotes for pages 122-143*

6. W. E. Henry, "The Business Executive," *American Journal of Sociology*, January, 1949, pp. 286-91.
7. W. L. Warner and J. Abegglen, *Big Business Leaders in America* (New York: Harper & Brothers, 1960).
8. O. F. Collins, D. G. Moore with D. Unwalla, *The Enterprising Man* (East Lansing: Bureau of Business and Economic Research, Michigan State University, 1964).
9. E. E. Jennings, *The Executive* (New York: Harper & Row, Inc., 1962).
10. W. R. Dill, T. L. Hilton and W. R. Reitman, *The New Managers* (Englewood Cliffs, New Jersey: Prentice-Hall, 1962).
11. J. Piaget, *The Child's Conceptions of the World* (Littlefield: Adams & Company, 1960), p. 153.
12. W. E. Henry, "Conflict, Age and the Executive," *op. cit.*, p. 18.
13. B. Gardner, *op. cit.*, p. 117.
14. Warner and Abegglen, *op. cit.*, p. 69.
15. W. E. Henry, "The Business Executive," *op. cit.*, p. 287.
16. T. K. Quinn, *Giant Business* (New York: Citadel, 1950); and *Unconscious Public Enemies* (New York: Citadel, 1956).
17. L. W. Porter, "Where Is the Organization Man," *Harvard Business Review*, November-December, 1963, pp. 53-61.
18. W. E. Henry, "The Business Executive," *op. cit.*, p. 286.
19. M. Jahoda, *Current Concepts of Positive Mental Health* (New York: Basic Books, 1938), p. 80.
20. L. W. Porter and E. E. Gheselli, "The Self Perceptions of Top and Middle Management Personnel," *Personnel Psychology*, X (1960) 397-406.
21. E. Rosen, *op. cit.*, pp. 10-20.
22. D. Riesman, N. Glazer and R. Denney, *The Lonely Crowd* (New York: Doubleday & Company, 1955).
23. W. L. Warner, *The Corporation in the Emergent American Society* (New York: Harper & Brothers, 1962).
24. Warner and Abegglen, *op. cit.*, pp. 94-97.
25. E. Dale, *The Great Organizers* (New York: McGraw-Hill Book Company, Inc., 1960).
26. G. Katona, *Psychological Analysis of Economic Behavior* (New York: McGraw-Hill Book Company, Inc., 1951), p. 197.

CHAPTER VII

1. A. H. Maslow, *Motivation and Personality* (New York: Harper & Brothers, 1954), pp. 199-234.
2. W. E. Henry, "The Business Executive," *American Journal of Sociology*, January, 1949, pp. 286-91.
3. Maslow, *op. cit.*, pp. 228-29.
4. Henry, *op. cit.*, p. 105.
5. M. B. and R. A. Cohen, "Personality as a Factor in Administrative Decisions" (Unpublished manuscript, 1962).

6. B. B. Gardner, "What Makes Successful and Unsuccessful Executives," *Advanced Management*, XIII, 3 (September, 1948), 116-25.
7. E. Rosen, "The Executive Personality," *Personnel*, January-February, 1959.

CHAPTER VIII

1. A. Adler, *Understanding Human Nature* (New York: Greenberg, 1927); and *The Neurotic Constitution* (New York: Greenberg, 1926).
2. R. May, *The Meaning of Anxiety* (New York: The Ronald Press Company, 1950), p. 132.
3. R. L. Munroe, *Schools of Psychoanalytic Thought* (New York: Holt, Rinehart and Winston, 1955), p. 434.
4. A. Wheelis, *The Quest for Identity* (New York: W. W. Norton, 1958), pp. 177-79.
5. M. Rokeach, *The Open and Closed Mind* (New York: Basic Books, 1962).
6. R. J. Havighurst, "Dominant Concerns in the Life Cycle" (Unpublished document, The University of Chicago, 1963).
7. M. Rosenberg, *Occupations and Values* (Glencoe, Illinois: The Free Press, 1957).
8. A. B. Hollingshead and F. Redlich, *Social Class and Mental Illness* (New York: John Wiley & Sons, Inc., 1958); T. S. Langner and S. T. Michael, *Life Stress and Mental Health* (Glencoe, Illinois: The Free Press, 1963).
9. Langner and Michael, *op. cit.*, p. 284; and J. K. Myers and B. H. Roberts, *Family and Class Dynamics in Mental Illness* (New York: John Wiley & Sons, Inc., 1959).
10. P. Lechy, *Self Consistency, A Theory of Personality* (New York: The Shoe String Press, 1961).
11. For evidence, see W. L. Warner and J. Abegglen, *Big Business Leaders in America* (New York: Harper & Brothers, 1955); also B. B. Gardner, "What Makes Successful and Unsuccessful Executives," *Advanced Management*, XIII, 3 (September, 1948), 116-21; W. E. Henry, "The Business Executive," *American Journal of Sociology*, January, 1949, pp. 286-91; E. Rosen, "The Executive Personality," *Personnel*, January-February, 1959, pp. 10-21; and W. R. Dill, T. L. Hilton and W. R. Reitman, *The New Managers* (Englewood Cliffs, New Jersey; Prentice-Hall, 1962).
12. N. Sanford, "The Dynamics of Identification," *The Psychological Review*, LXII (March, 1955), 107-18; and A. Freud, *The Ego and the Mechanisms of Defense* (New York: International Universities Press, 1961).
13. See footnote 11, and W. L. Warner, *The Corporation in the Emergent American Society* (New York: Harper & Brothers, 1962).
14. Henry, *op. cit.*, p. 287.

15. Dill, *op. cit.*, pp. 20-40.
16. Lecky, *op. cit.*, pp. 66-192.
17. Adler, *op. cit.*
18. See footnote 11.
19. See the case of Jeffrey Collins in Warner and Abegglen, *op. cit.*, p. 84.
20. I am indebted to Karen Horney for the elaboration of these neurotic mechanisms and for help in developing their administrative applications. See K. Horney, *The Neurotic Personality of Our Time, Our Inner Conflicts, New Ways in Psychoanalysis, Neurosis and Human Growth* (New York: W. W. Norton, 1933, 1945, 1939, 1950).
21. Horney, *Neurosis and Human Growth, op. cit.*, pp. 187-290.
22. Horney, *Our Inner Conflicts, op. cit.*, pp. 97-114.
23. Horney, *The Neurotic Personality of Our Time, op. cit.*, pp. 162-212.
24. *Ibid.*, pp. 147-61.
25. E. E. Jennings, *The Executive* (New York: Harper & Row, 1962).
26. Horney, *Neurosis and Human Growth, op. cit.*, pp. 259-91.
27. Horney, *Neurosis and Human Growth, op. cit.*
28. This is frequently seen by the therapist in cases of mild paranoia where the individual is often correct in his interpretation of other people's hostilities toward him.
29. See footnote 11.
30. A. A. Berle, Jr., *Power Without Property* (New York: Harcourt, Brace and Company, 1959).